Keeping the Edge

Keeping the Edge
Managing Defense for the Future

EDITED BY ASHTON B. CARTER & JOHN P. WHITE

A Publication of the
PREVENTIVE DEFENSE PROJECT
A research collaboration
of the
Kennedy School of Government
Harvard University
and
Stanford University
ASHTON B. CARTER AND WILLIAM J. PERRY, CO-DIRECTORS
Cambridge, Massachusetts
Stanford, California

2000

WITH CONTRIBUTIONS BY

Denis A. Bovin
Ashton B. Carter
David S.C. Chu
Victor A. DeMarines
John M. Deutch
Jane Harman
Robert J. Hermann
Arnold Kanter
Michael J. Lippitz

Judith A. Miller
Sean O'Keefe
William J. Perry
Brent Scowcroft
John M. Shalikashvili
Elizabeth Sherwood-Randall
John M. Stewart
John P. White
Herbert S. Winokur, Jr.

ISBN 0-9705414-0-6
The Preventive Defense Project
<www.preventivedefenseproject.org>

Harvard University
Belfer Center for Science and International Affairs
Kennedy School of Government
79 John F. Kennedy Street
Cambridge MA 02138
Preventive Defense Project Coordinator
(617) 495-1405

Stanford University
Center for International Security and Cooperation
Encina Hall
Stanford CA 94305-6165
(650) 725-6501

From January 2001, this book will be available from The MIT Press, Cambridge, Massachusetts

September 2000

Edited and designed by Teresa Lawson Editorial Consulting
<tjlawson@ultranet.com>

Cover designed by Graciela Galup
<ggalup@mediaone.net>

Printed by Puritan Press

This book is dedicated to David Packard,
whose vision of quality management in
defense it seeks to continue

Contents

About the Preventive Defense Project viii

Preface and Acknowledgments ix

1 Keeping the Edge: Managing Defense for the Future 1
Ashton B. Carter

2 Keeping the Edge in Joint Operations 27
John M. Shalikashvili with Bruce Rember, Phil Ehr, &
Thomas Longstreth

3 Exploiting the Internet Revolution 61
Victor A. DeMarines with David Lehman & John Quilty

4 Keeping the Edge in Intelligence 103
Robert J. Hermann

5 Countering Asymmetric Threats 119
Ashton B. Carter & William J. Perry with David Aidekman

6 Keeping the Technological Edge 129
Ashton B. Carter with Marcel Lettre & Shane Smith

7 Advancing the Revolution in Business Affairs 165
Michael J. Lippitz, Sean O'Keefe, & John P. White with
John Brown

8 Ensuring Quality People in Defense 203
David S.C. Chu & John P. White with Nurith Berstein &
John Brown

9 Managing the Pentagon's International Relations 235
Elizabeth Sherwood-Randall with Christiana Briggs &
Anja Miller

10 Strengthening the National Security Interagency Process 265
John Deutch, Arnold Kanter, & Brent Scowcroft with
Christopher Hornbarger

11 Implementing Change 285
Judith A. Miller

About the Core Group and the Authors 303

Other Publications of the Preventive Defense Project 316

About the Preventive Defense Project

ASHTON B. CARTER & WILLIAM J. PERRY, CO-DIRECTORS

The Preventive Defense Project is a joint venture between the Kennedy School of Government at Harvard University and Stanford University, co-directed by Ashton B. Carter and William J. Perry. Preventive Defense is a concept for American defense strategy in the post–Cold War era, premised on the belief that the absence of an imminent, major, traditional military threat to American security presents today's leaders with an unaccustomed challenge and opportunity to prevent future Cold War–scale threats to international security from emerging. While the U.S. defense establishment must continue to deter major regional conflicts and provide peacekeeping and humanitarian relief missions when necessary, its highest priority is to contribute to forestalling developments that could directly threaten the survival and vital interests of American citizens.

To this end, the Project focuses on forging productive security partnerships with Russia and its neighbors, engaging an emerging China, addressing the lethal legacy of Cold War weapons of mass destruction (WMD), and countering WMD proliferation and potential acts of catastrophic terrorism. In doing so, PDP seeks to devise creative, new policy approaches that reflect a preventive defense posture and, through intense personal interaction with political and military leaders around the world, nourish a highly informed but non-governmental "track-two" dialogue that explores opportunities for international agreement and cooperation. In addition, PDP has undertaken an intense review of the U.S. government's structures and practices for carrying out foreign and security policies, which have not changed in half a century.

Preface and Acknowledgments

In its three years of existence, the Preventive Defense Project, a research collaboration of Stanford University and the Kennedy School of Government at Harvard University, co-directed by William J. Perry and Ashton B. Carter, has worked to devise and promote policies to advance U.S. national security and international security. The Project's efforts have extended from Russia to China, and from counterproliferation to counter-terrorism. In all our work, we have sought to prescribe specific policies and actions the U.S. government can adopt to prevent new security threats from emerging in the post–Cold War world.

Like most other policy thinkers, we have tended to assume that once Washington got the policy right, implementation of those policies would follow smoothly. This assumption, however, has increasingly seemed to us unwarranted. While the U.S. military capability for joint operations is unquestionably the best in the world, the "back room" of the Department of Defense (DOD) — contracting, personnel policies, and managerial practices — is not up to the standards found elsewhere in our society, nor is it up to the level that the taxpayers have a right to expect of their government. While the United States has defined the key defense missions of the post–Cold War world, the structure and practices of DOD have adapted only incompletely to the job of accomplishing them. In the short run, the potential benefits of wise strategy and policy will not be fully realized, but it is in the long run that shortcomings in management and organization will really come to haunt us, diminishing our presently unmatched military capability.

With this book, the Preventive Defense Project seeks to prescribe remedies for some of the organizational and managerial deficiencies of the national security establishment. Our focus is largely on DOD and the interagency process of policy and program coordination. We believe these problems and proposed solutions warrant high-priority attention from the next U.S. presidential administration and Congress. Both executive and legislative branches will have new beginnings in January 2001, and there is no better time to tackle problems of the underlying functioning of the government. Management and organization problems are not the juiciest of issues for campaigns and high politics, to be sure. However, when newly elected and appointed officials take office, they will find that their ability to translate their policies into results will depend crucially on making the kinds of adaptations described in this volume.

Not all of these issues are new: problems of defense management, particularly reform of DOD's cumbersome acquisition system, were of deep concern to the late David Packard, Deputy Secretary of Defense and co-founder of the Hewlett-Packard Company. As deputy secretary and later as Chairman of President Reagan's Blue Ribbon Commission on Defense Management — which became known as the Packard Commission — David Packard pioneered many of the themes that animate this book. Preventive Defense Project co-director William J. Perry served on the Packard Commission; as Secretary of Defense two decades later he promoted Packard's vision of quality management in government. Our work here is in many ways an attempt to fulfill this vision. We were therefore particularly gratified to receive early support for the preparation of this book from the David and Lucile Packard Foundation; we thank President Richard T. Schlosberg III and Cole Wilbur of the Foundation for giving us this opportunity. In token of our respect and gratitude, we have dedicated this book to the memory of David Packard.

The Project also received critical and generous support from The Simons Foundation, the Herbert S. Winokur, Jr. Public Policy Fund, and the MITRE Corporation. The Preventive Defense Project as a whole was launched and has been nurtured by the Carnegie Corporation of New York and The John D. and Catherine T. MacArthur Foundation. The founders and staff of these supporting organizations not only provided resources vital to the completion of this book, but were collaborators in conceiving and shaping the ideas that appear in these pages. The Project also received key inputs and inspiration from David Baxt, Vance Coffman, Stephen Hadley, John Hamre, and Philip A. Odeen.

It is in the long run — on the watch of the next generation of defense policy leaders — that uncorrected management problems will really make themselves felt if steps to solve them are not taken now. For this reason, we acknowledge our responsibility and our privilege in teaching and collaborating with some of these future leaders at Harvard and Stanford. It seemed appropriate that these students and fellows at our universities be included in this Project, where they provided much of the necessary research, ideas, and constant prodding. They are listed on the bylines of chapters to which they made special contributions, and we wish also to thank them here: David Aidekman, Christiana Briggs, John Brown, Phil Ehr, Christopher Hornbarger, Marcel Lettre, Anja Miller, and Bruce Rember. We also thank those other collaborators who contributed in so many ways to the range and depth of our work, including Nurith Berstein at RAND, Thomas Longstreth at the Department of Defense, David Lehman and John Quilty at MITRE, and Shane Smith at Harvard.

Special thanks are due to consulting editor and publication manager Teresa J. Lawson, whose ability to elicit silk purse prose from sows' ears drafts is as remarkable as it was needed. The Preventive Defense Project Coordinator at Harvard, Shane Smith, kept the Core Group members focused and organized, in addition to making his own research contributions to the book. Gretchen Bartlett and Lillian Politser at Harvard and Deborah Gordon at Stanford somehow found time among all their other university and Preventive Defense Project responsibilities to administer this project with their typical perfection. We are deeply grateful to all.

Denis A. Bovin	*Judith A. Miller*
Ashton B. Carter	*Sean O'Keefe*
David S.C. Chu	*William J. Perry*
Victor A. DeMarines	*Brent Scowcroft*
John M. Deutch	*John M. Shalikashvili*
Jane Harman	*Elizabeth Sherwood-Randall*
Robert J. Hermann	*John M. Stewart*
Arnold Kanter	*John P. White*
Michael J. Lippitz	*Herbert S. Winokur, Jr.*

Core Group
Defense Organization and Management Project
Preventive Defense Project

1

Keeping the Edge

Managing Defense for the Future

ASHTON B. CARTER

Most advice on national security affairs focuses on the *ends* of our national security and foreign policy: on setting priorities among the almost numberless tasks that could be taken up by the world's leading power. Will China and Russia pose future threats, or can they be cooperatively integrated into the international system? Is preparing to fight two major theater wars still the appropriate organizing principle for overall forces and budgets? Is the defense budget large enough overall? When and how should the United States participate in peacekeeping and conflict prevention?

These are important debates, but equal attention and action should be directed at the *means* to implement policy priorities: the agencies and programs of the executive branch. There is mounting evidence that the national security establishment is deficient not so much in deciding what to do as in having the means to get it done. This book, prepared by a bipartisan Core Group of authors and advisers, therefore takes a different approach: it addresses the organization and management of the national security establishment, and especially the Department of Defense, to *implement* the policies the nation's leaders choose for it, to *manage* the programs they direct, and to *adapt* to a changing world.

When it comes to the means our nation now has to implement security policy, the situation is mixed. Our military is unmatched by any conceivable combination of foes, and will remain so well into the future under a wide range of assumptions about future trends. With its huge and growing economy, the United States can in principle devote economic resources to the pursuit of its foreign interests that are vast even in comparison to the scale of major world problems. We are constrained mainly by a lack of consensus about our role in the world. The powerful trends shaping the twenty-first century — globalization, commercialization, the information revolution — are so compatible with U.S. culture and interests that much of the world confuses them with "Americanization." Playing such a fundamentally strong international hand is far preferable to playing a weak hand.

But when we consider the state of the foreign affairs instruments of the executive branch of the U.S. government, we find that our cards are much weaker than they should be. Far less recognized than the perplexities of choice among the ends of U.S. strategy is the depletion of means. The military that brought victory in DESERT STORM, peace in the Balkans, and respect from friend and foe since the end of the Cold War is an exception in our government: the "point of the spear" is sharp and hard, but much of the rest of the national security establishment is deficient or broken.

Throughout the national security establishment there are systemic managerial and organizational problems. For example, critical post–Cold War national security missions — counter-proliferation, counter-terrorism and homeland defense, computer network defense, information operations, biowarfare defense, threat reduction and arms control, coalition warfare, peacekeeping and post-peacekeeping civil reconstruction, and preventive defense — are being accomplished in *ad hoc* fashion by unwieldy combinations of departments and agencies designed a half century ago for a different world. Too many of these new missions are institutionally "homeless": nowhere are clear authority, adequate resources, and appropriate accountability brought together in a clear managerial focus. Although it is widely understood and accepted that we need the means to accomplish the homeless missions — even if debate continues about when and how to do so — at this time the government is not well organized or managed to accomplish them when we choose to do so.

Critical underpinnings of quality performance in governmental functions are eroding. Top-flight people refuse to serve at all levels of government, from high political posts to the civilian and uniformed services, because the conditions of public service are often demeaning and frustrating. Quality people already in government are leaving, and those who remain often feel that their potential for creative leadership is stifled. Regulatory systems for auditing and accounting, contracting for weapons and services, export controls, and security classification and background checks today show all the signs of bureaucratic decline, applying an accumulation of rules rather than logic to their assigned missions. Policymakers attempting to oversee these systems often find themselves lost in the thicket of rules and give up trying to exercise direction over these critical functions, leaving the field to political fringes and interest groups.

The U.S. capability for joint military operations has not yet been affected by the pervasive managerial and organizational problems of the international affairs establishment. But even in the Department of Defense, a disturbing picture emerges if one looks at the "tail" instead of the "tooth." The infrastructure of bases and depots has not been reduced nearly as much as the force itself in the past decade, resulting in a large tail-to-tooth ratio and billions of wasted defense dollars. DOD acquisition personnel are still burdened with the Federal Acquisition Regulations, as thick as a big-city telephone book. Forces that are meant to fight jointly are still equipped, sometimes incompatibly, by the separate services and defense agencies. The research and industrial base upon which the distinctive American way of providing for security relies — with high technology that foes cannot match — is being transformed by the forces of commercialization and globalization, but DOD persists in many old habits regarding research and development (R&D), the industrial base, and acquisition. As a consequence, the U.S. military is not fully exploiting or even staying abreast of the information revolution. It is scarcely even in the game when it comes to biotechnology, whose implications for human conflict may be even more profound than those of information technology. The defense industry upon which the technological edge ultimately depends is suffering from difficulties raising capital and the flight of many of its talented engineers and managers. Trans-Atlantic defense industry cooperation, important for efficiency and NATO cohesion, presents a set of unsolved problems for all allied governments.

Despite these problems of DOD organization and management, the U.S. military is still far better than any other military anywhere in the world. But the government owes the public a military that is not just better than all the others, but one that is as good as the money we are spending can make it. By that standard, we will fall short if the continuing absence of imminent and galvanizing Cold War–scale traditional military threat causes us to be complacent and to avoid undertaking politically difficult reforms. Eventually these deficiencies will begin to affect the point of the spear itself. For these reasons and more, we must attend to means as well as ends in our national security strategy: to the "threat within" as well as to external threats. President Eisenhower said that the right system does not guarantee success, but the wrong system guarantees failure. A defective system will suck the leadership into its cracks and fissures, wasting their time as they seek to manage dysfunction rather than making critical decisions.

The transition to a new administration provides an opportunity to undertake change to counter the threat within, an opportunity that comes only every four or eight years. Early in a presidential transition, civilian jobs are not yet filled with officials who, once entrenched, might resist a change in their functions. The new administration has not yet settled into a pattern of making do with the system it inherited. Politically, the Congress and the voters are expecting change. Thus the time is right to address these chronic management issues.

Many of the changes we prescribe do not require creating new bureaucracies or eliminating old ones, although sometimes that may be needed. We do not, for example, recommend creation or elimination of cabinet departments or other large-scale structural changes in the executive branch agencies or congressional committees. But management values, incentives, processes, and procedures must change even if the United States keeps the basic organizational structure — the cabinet departments and National Security Council established after World War II, the four armed services, and the constellation of regional and functional Commanders-in-Chief (CINCs) in DOD. Thus our recommendations deal also with processes of analysis, decision, interagency coordination, and execution; with retaining and encouraging quality people, uniformed and civilian; and with incentives, rewards, and accountability.

We recommend evolutionary change where possible. Progressive paths to implementation avoid the kind of turmoil that could disrupt what is working as we try to fix what is not. Evolutionary change can also avoid opposition. Nevertheless, implementing the recommendations in this book will be a formidable task. Government organization and management, unlike policy formulation, is largely the stuff of low politics, not high politics. Resistance comes from inertia and complacency, from ingrained habits and entrenched interests and bureaucracies. Overcoming this type of resistance is sometimes harder than winning a spirited national debate on a major policy issue. Success will require sustained attention and support from the President and his top national security officials, and close cooperation with Congress, which must lend support and in some cases enact legislation to effect these recommendations.

The historical record of managerial and organizational reform is mixed. The broad outlines of the national security establishment were defined just after World War II and have changed little since. But there have been instances of sweeping and effective change. The All Volunteer Force successfully replaced conscription. The Goldwater-Nichols Act strengthened joint warfighting capabilities and the chain of command, where previously the armed services had sometimes seemed to be planning and waging separate campaigns. But elsewhere change has progressed, if at all, in fits and starts, as in efforts to close unneeded bases, make export controls more effective, and reform the Pentagon's cumbersome acquisition system.

The recommendations in this book reflect three kinds of need for organizational and managerial adaptation. The first need is maintaining the U.S. edge in areas where we are currently unrivaled but where future trends challenge our ability to preserve this lead. Examples include joint warfighting, military technology, application of information technology to national security, a near-monopoly in national intelligence, and keeping quality personnel serving in the armed services. The recommendations we make in these areas are intended to preserve the American edge under the new circumstances of the early twenty-first century.

The second type of recommendations focuses on the new era's demands for new capabilities to address post–Cold War priorities, such as counter-proliferation, counter-terrorism and homeland defense, computer network defense, information warfare, biowarfare defense, coalition warfare, threat reduction and arms control, peacekeeping and post-peacekeeping civil reconstruction, and preventive defense.

The third type of recommendations addresses chronic management problems that have long resisted change: closing unneeded facilities, outsourcing non-military functions to the commercial sector, improving the quality of DOD's civilian workforce, improving acquisition and logistics practices, and updating export controls and security practices.

Our focus is largely, though not exclusively, on the Department of Defense and the defense function of government. But organizational and managerial problems of the kind this book identifies are at least as severe in other parts of the national security establishment. We therefore believe that comparable remedial efforts are required in the Department of State, the intelligence community, and the Department of Energy.

The rest of this chapter summarizes this volume's key recommendations for action, highlighting the deficiencies in organization and management that prompted the Preventive Defense Project to undertake its study.

Preserving Key Strengths Under New Conditions

The recommendations under this rubric seek to preserve key strengths in the face of changing geopolitical, technological, and market conditions.

TAKING THE NEXT STEP IN JOINTNESS

The so-called Goldwater-Nichols reforms of 1986 were intended to insure that U.S. forces fought "jointly" rather than in separate Army, Navy, and Air Force campaigns. They gave Unified Commanders-in-Chief (CINCs) clear authority for joint operations, a strengthened Chairman of the Joint Chiefs of Staff to advise the President, and required joint assignments for officers to reach flag rank. They assigned organizing, training, and equipping the forces to the separate armed services as their principal mission under Title X of the U.S. Code. While operations are "joint," therefore, forces are still acquired severally.

Goldwater-Nichols has been a great success by almost any measure and account. But it did not answer the question of how joint forces could truly be produced from a non-joint acquisition system.

One option, which we reject, would create a truly joint acquisition process at the expense of the services' Title X authorities. This option would have the theoretical advantage of giving the power to configure and buy joint forces to their ultimate "customer," the warfighting CINCs. However, this option would weaken the services, which are proud, living institutions of which there are far too few in our government. It would undermine their proven ability to provide the best land, naval, air, and amphibious forces in the world. In addition, transferring responsibility for requirements, budgets, or acquisition to the joint CINCs would divert their attention from their principal tasks of maintaining alliance and other U.S. military relations in their areas of responsibility, planning for regional contingencies, and commanding operations. The CINCs have no staffs specialized in acquisition. The result of shifting most acquisition authority to the regional CINCs would be to weaken, not strengthen, program execution.

A second option would be to maintain the current system as the best balance between the demonstrated expertise of the services and the need for jointness. But maintaining the status quo is not a true balance because it perpetuates three critical managerial deficiencies that impede true jointness. First, the mechanism to ensure interoperability among forces and systems acquired by the separate services is weak. Second, a purely services-run acquisition system provides no clear mechanism to make difficult trade-offs among service programs and budgets. For example, is a given mission best executed by Army helicopters or by Air Force planes? Such issues are currently either unresolved or left to the most senior DOD leadership at the last minute in the budget cycle. Third, some key capabilities such as reconnaissance, surveillance, and information systems and logistics are inherently joint, and there is no strong voice in the current system for them. These deficiencies are too serious to leave uncorrected.

A third, middle-ground option, described in Chapter 2, offers the best chance for both sustaining the acquisition excellence of the services and giving appropriate voice to joint considerations in the acquisition system. Rather than involving all the CINCs in the acquisition process, the compromise is to give a single CINC — the Joint Forces Command (JFCOM) CINC —the capability as well as the authority to inject joint thinking into the acquisition process on behalf of the Chairman of the Joint Chiefs of Staff and all the other CINCs. This is, in fact, the option being pursued by the Department of Defense, but JFCOM has not yet been given the tools to do the job. Realizing the potential of this option requires four additional steps: first, CINCJFCOM should lead in preparing for the Chairman a broad roadmap, updated annually, for developing truly joint forces. Second, JFCOM should be given the personnel and resources in its Norfolk,

Virginia, headquarters to take on its new acquisition responsibilities. These should include some direct authority over resources devoted to inherently joint capabilities. Third, as the "joint and future forces CINC," the person chosen to be JFCOM commander should be a senior CINC, appointed from among those who have experience as CINCs or service chiefs or vice-chiefs. Fourth, CINCJFCOM should become a member of DOD's key decision-making bodies on acquisition matters: the Joint Requirements Oversight Council (JROC) and the Defense Resources Board (DRB).

EXPLOITING THE INTERNET REVOLUTION

The most important inherently joint military capability resides in command, control, communications, computers, intelligence, reconnaissance, surveillance (C4ISR in the current form of this lengthening acronym). But while the U.S. military is far ahead of any other military in exploiting the information revolution, the pace of commercial technological advance in this field is far faster than DOD's cumbersome requirements and acquisition procedures. Without change in DOD's practices, the information revolution that began in DOD will pass the Department by. This is a pervasive problem, and Chapter 3 recommends attacking it first where it counts most, in joint command and control systems that are used in contingency operations. The time it takes to "glue together" separate service command and control systems is too often incompatible with the required military action, resulting in lost military advantage. We build on the previous recommendation, to strengthen JFCOM's role in joint requirements, by urging that JFCOM undertake a well funded activity to develop a joint command and control system for contingency operations based on continuous exercising and experimentation ("expercising"). A Joint Blueprint Office should develop systems engineering architectural guidelines and lead to the acquisition of a common command and control infrastructure (the Global Information Grid). To accomplish this task, however, JFCOM will require additional resources and dedicated support from scientists and engineers outside the government, in much the way that both for-profit industry and Federally Funded Research and Development Centers (FFRDCs) supported early U.S. air defense and space programs.

A JFCOM activity of this type will make it easier to insert cutting-edge information technology (IT) into joint command and control, where it is most needed. However, the IT challenge is broader: it pervades DOD systems, yet defense systems no longer occupy the cutting edge in information technology. This place has passed from defense to commercial companies. It was DOD that pioneered the microchip, massive parallel processing, the Internet, software engineering techniques, and other information technologies, but these are now spearheaded by the well-financed commercial e-revolution. In the future, DOD will be a consumer rather than an originator of technology in all but niche areas of this sector.

Given this fact, Chapter 6 recommends steps to keep DOD at the forefront of the IT revolution. It is important for DOD to continue to fund R&D in this field, for three reasons. First, much commercial IT R&D is directed at near-term advances rather than the kinds of breakthroughs that have the most to contribute to national security. There, the government still has a role to play: sponsoring high-risk, high-payoff technology for defense and other national purposes. Second, only by being a participant in the ongoing information revolution can DOD remain a smart buyer of commercial technology. Finally, DOD has unique needs for research and development of new weapons systems, sensors, and other military-specific technology. In addition, DOD procurement practices, which have historically emphasized periodic block upgrades, have become obsolete: commercial practice emphasizes continuous, incremental upgrades and open-system architectures, and DOD's IT buying practices should adopt such practices. Finally, the uniformed and civilian workforces of DOD would benefit from the specification of new career paths for recruitment, training, and retention of technically competent information specialists (a so-called "Cyber Corps").

PRESERVING THE TECHNOLOGICAL EDGE

Information technology is an instance of wider changes in the technology base supporting defense. These changes have serious implications for a core pillar of America's defense strategy: the technological edge on which our "offset strategy" is based. The offset strategy was developed during the Cold War, when the United States decided it could not match the Warsaw Pact tank for tank or soldier for soldier. Instead, superior American technology would "offset" superior opposing numbers. The offset strategy secured deterrence of numerically superior forces and forced the Soviet Union to bankrupt itself in the pursuit of military technology it could not easily obtain from the West. The fruits of the offset strategy were demonstrated in DESERT STORM, where reconnaissance satellites, stealth aircraft, precision weapons, and other technologies unmatched by any other military made short work of Iraq's Soviet-equipped army. The technological edge on which the offset strategy depends remains the distinctive American way of defense, now applied to new post–Cold War missions.

But a challenge now looms to the preservation of America's technological edge from trends in the industrial and technology base. This base, once largely the creation of Department of Defense spending and almost exclusively American, is commercializing — the technology of central importance to national security increasingly originates in commercial rather than defense companies, without DOD sponsorship and outside its control — and it is also globalizing — leading technology companies are increasingly global rather than purely American in their outlook, ownership, workforce, and markets.

During the Cold War, defense technology originated in a defense technology base that was embedded in defense companies that resided in the United States, and that had DOD as their main market. In the future, defense technology will originate in a commercial technology base embedded in global commercial companies for which defense is but a niche market. In the past, military advantage was conferred by national possession of defense-unique leap-ahead technology that potential opponents could not get. In the future, military advantage will be obtained by adopting mostly commercial technology into defense systems faster than potential opponents who have access to most of the same technology.

Related to commercialization is *marketization* of the defense industry: defense companies must justify themselves to investors by the same standards of profit and cash flow as commercial companies. More and more, market forces are drawing capital away from defense firms and affecting the ability of these companies to be innovative and to attract talented personnel. The total market capitalization of the major defense firms today is about half that of Wal-Mart, just a quarter that of Microsoft. The list of premier U.S. industrial companies that have exited the defense market reads like a Who's Who of industrial America: IBM, Texas Instruments, Ford, Chrysler, GE, Westinghouse, and so on. Meanwhile the "new economy" companies are wholly absorbed in the pursuit of rapidly growing commercial markets rather than the slowly growing defense market.

Chapter 6 recommends two types of adaptation to help DOD preserve the technological edge in the face of commercialization and globalization. The first requirement is for DOD to align its own practices more closely with the market forces operating both on commercial companies that increasingly supply vital technology for defense and on defense companies that integrate technology into military systems. What is needed is not an "industrial policy" that props up weak defense companies and accentuates the isolation of the defense industry, but an approach that works with, rather than against, market forces, leveraging commercialization to secure the needs of defense. Acquisition and contracting policies that reward industry for delivering value as opposed to monitoring cost, as described in Chapter 7, are an important step in that direction. Chapter 6 describes three additional actions to align market incentives with DOD's needs. First, DOD should reward the defense industry when it follows sound business practices in pursuit of innovation and efficiency, including sharing savings from cost-cutting, facility closings, and other efficiencies between government and industry; allowing higher profits when industry performs successfully in terms of cost, schedule, and performance; expanding use of multi-year contracts with the approval of Congress; and adjusting "progress payment" practices for both contractors and their subcontractors. Second, DOD should encourage second- and third-tier companies serving both defense and commercial marketplaces to remain in the defense business. Third, DOD should encourage robust trans-Atlantic defense industry linkages, which will reinforce alliance solidarity (as described in Chapter 9) and, over the long run, will provide classic free-trade efficiencies to all allied militaries.

The second means to turn commercialization and globalization to DOD's advantage is to assure that the U.S. military remains the world's fastest adapter and adopter of commercial technology into defense systems. Potential opponents will also have access to much state-of-the-art technology since they can purchase it on the open global market. DOD must "run faster" than others, rapidly incorporating new technology from the growing global base into defense systems (and experimenting with concomitant changes in tactics and doctrine), rather than relying almost exclusively on its own sponsored R&D as it did during the Cold War. A key step in this direction is to encourage DOD to use commercial buying practices and commercial systems in defense procurement. If DOD persists in its idiosyncratic buying methods and cumbersome contracting procedures, it will always be a generation behind commercial practice, and many commercial companies will refuse to accept defense contracts. DOD must also continue to stimulate R&D on defense problems through direct contracting, prototypes and demonstrations, and especially by making R&D investments by defense companies as profitable as production so companies will have incentives to innovate.

PRESERVING THE INTELLIGENCE EDGE

National intelligence is another long-standing American strength in international affairs, amounting to a virtual monopoly on key security information of importance to the world community, especially in areas such as proliferation, crime, and terrorism. The U.S. national intelligence system was conceived after World War II as a unified effort combining secrets and openly derived information in integrated national analyses; supporting DOD's military operations as well as a broad range of needs from other agencies; and conceiving of engineering, collection, analysis, and dissemination as a single, unified effort. This unity of effort was not always achieved, but the management principle was that of "central intelligence."

Today's environment has some features that challenge this principle. More information and expertise reside outside of government than ever before. Commercial firms now collect information such as satellite imagery previously collected only by government. Military command and control and other governmental management functions are shifting to non-hierarchical models that leave both discretion and the need for intelligence to lower echelons. The pace of warfare and of all international events is quicker. The hierarchical unified system of the past is ill-suited to these changes. But other trends continue to favor the central intelligence model. Technology makes all information, whether signals intelligence, pictures, or open-source information, a common stream of electronic bytes. Wide-bandwidth communications permit rapid and widespread dissemination of information to all echelons simultaneously.

Chapter 4 and Chapter 10 argue that the model of central intelligence can still serve the nation best — indeed, can preserve intelligence as a key national security edge — with adaptations to network support for military operations (also described in Chapter 3), to expand international partnerships to avoid creating competing centers of intelligence expertise elsewhere around the world, to tap into expertise outside of the intelligence community, to manage collection and dissemination of technical intelligence in a common manner, and to embed more analytic capability at lower echelons.

KEEPING QUALITY PEOPLE IN UNIFORM

The All Volunteer Force has been a great success, largely through the DOD's commitment to quality and the continued application of sound management practices. Nevertheless, there are areas where improvements are needed in order to assure equal quality in the future. Military compensation policy has been subject to spasmodic across-the-board pay raises in response to political pressure. Chapter 8 argues that such blanket increases miss an opportunity for more effective management of the overall compensation system to give added incentives to the categories of military personnel we need most and to take account of the labor markets in which the military competes. A similar systemic approach is needed to "quality of life" improvements. Here DOD too often takes the approach of increasing government provision of amenities such as housing, a vestige of the nineteenth-century military practice of providing everything a garrisoned soldier needed through government supply bureaucracies. Today, however, quality of life can often best be assured by giving service members the resources to purchase amenities directly in the local economy.

Another important dimension of military personnel policy treated in Chapter 8 is adapting to demographic change. For example, the military's recruiting policies and career paths tend to force young people to choose between college and military service, yet two-thirds of American high school graduates now attend college. Thus recruiters are limited to a decreasing pool of high-schoolers who do not choose to go to college immediately. Competing in this market will require DOD to make such changes as opening up more career paths for promising enlisted personnel to move to warrant or commissioned status, and making college education compatible with a military career. Other demographic changes will also require adaptation in the personnel policies of DOD: the fact that Hispanics are a growing fraction of the U.S. population but have lower graduation rates than some other groups, the increase of two-career families, and so on. Personnel policies must go beyond a mixture of outdated bureaucratic procedures and bursts of "political correctness," to manage the human resources of defense to the standards prevalent in large civilian organizations.

Organizing to Accomplish the New Era's New Missions

The second type of recommendations we offer are focused on new missions of the post–Cold War era, which both call for new responses from DOD and, increasingly, cut across departments of the government, requiring a unified interagency approach.

NEW ISSUES THAT CUT ACROSS DEPARTMENTS AND AGENCIES

A key characteristic of the new missions for defense in the post–Cold War era — counter-proliferation, counter-terrorism and homeland defense, computer network defense, information operations, biowarfare defense, threat reduction and arms control, coalition warfare, peacekeeping and post-peacekeeping civil reconstruction, and preventive defense — is that they do not respect the boundaries between agencies and departments of government and between committees of Congress. Our departments and agencies were created in 1947–49 when there were sharper divides between war and peace, domestic and foreign threats, and security and economic issues than there are today. The National Security Council (NSC) is an effective means for policy coordination, but it has little capability for program coordination. For this reason, and because the Office of Management and Budget (OMB) is traditionally not strong in the security field, the White House has little influence in the allocation of resources to deal with a growing number of international problems that are interagency in nature. The current NSC has little ability to construct a government-wide program of technology, acquisition, and institution-building to correspond to its carefully coordinated policy, and few NSC staff have any programmatic experience, while cabinet agencies and congressional committees jealously guard their funding authorities. Yet if we are going to retain the current agency structure and at the same time deal with cross-cutting priority issues such as proliferation and catastrophic terrorism, we will need to have inter-agency program coordination at the White House.

A variety of solutions to this problem can be considered: a new "super department" of national security, various "czars" at the White House, a new staff organization for the President, new budget cate-gories, and so on. After carefully considering such options, Chapter 10 opts for retaining the National Security Council structure for pol-icy coordination, but strengthening its capacity for program coordi-nation, in concert with OMB. Under this mechanism, the NSC would devise multi-year, multi-agency program plans for key post–Cold War missions, and the Office of Management and Budget would as-sure appropriate funding within the agencies.

COUNTER-TERRORISM AND HOMELAND DEFENSE

An important example of the need for program coordination is the creation of a government-wide response to the danger of catastrophic terrorism involving weapons of mass destruction, cyber threats, dis-ruption of critical infrastructures upon which complex modern soci-ety depends, or attacks upon the institutions of government themselves. This is an issue that cuts across the boundary between foreign and domestic threats — a boundary deeply carved in Ameri-can government and cherished by its citizens. The specter of attack on their homeland is a new one in Americans' recent experience. In this century America's wars have been far away. Only after the Soviet Union exploded the atomic bomb in 1949 was a direct external threat of destruction posed to the American homeland. The impact on American thinking and institutions was immediate and profound. A huge and sophisticated strategic nuclear deterrent capable of retali-ating against the Soviet homeland was built. Vast programs of conti-nental air and missile defense were inaugurated. Civil defense shelters were built and drills conducted for schoolchildren. Think-tanks such as the RAND Corporation were founded by government to ponder the new security dilemma. Suspected spies and Soviet "sympathizers" were hunted.

It is likely that an incident of catastrophic terrorism on the U.S. homeland would spark concern and effort on a comparable scale. It is easy to see how the concern could escalate to hysteria, and how ac-tions taken in the angry aftermath of a destructive event could be counterproductive and corrosive of civil liberties. The aftermath of homeland attack is therefore as much to be feared as the attack itself. It is much better if government begins to organize for this future threat *now*, while considered judgments can be made about how best to protect the homeland and how to trade off protection against other social values. Chapters 5 and 10 address this question.

In the past three years, an effort has been made to craft an inter-agency response to the threat of catastrophic terrorism that bridges all the national security agencies and the law enforcement communities. "Lead agency" responsibilities were assigned to the Department of Justice and the Federal Bureau of Investigation, the Federal Emergency Management Agency, and the State Department to take charge in various circumstances where their historic charters and authorities make a lead role natural and appropriate. This policy was coordinated successfully at the White House, and it appears to be acceptable to all agencies. However, for the most part the agencies assigned lead roles have little existing capability and few or no new resources to carry out their assigned roles, which remain unfunded mandates. DOD, the Department of Energy, and the intelligence community, although they are appropriately not assigned lead roles, have most of the existing capabilities and the best base from which to build new technological and other capabilities. Even taking all the agencies together, current capabilities and plans for responding to such a fearsome event are not adequate. A multi-year, multi-agency program plan to build such a national capability over time is needed, and would provide a prime example of NSC program coordination.

ASYMMETRIC WARFARE, ESPECIALLY BIOWARFARE DEFENSE

Saddam Hussein's military in 1991 was in many ways a miniature version of the Soviet army in its equipment, doctrine, and tactics. This was precisely the type of threat against which the U.S. military and its coalition partners drawn from NATO had been practicing for decades. Faced with the hammer of the U.S. military, Iraq configured itself as a nail. The outcome was never in doubt. Slobodan Milosevic's Serb forces were similarly Soviet-like, as are Kim Jong-Il's North Korean conventional forces. Future opponents, however, observing the lesson of the 1990s, will make no attempt to counter the United States symmetrically. Instead, they will resort to asymmetric means: exploiting vulnerabilities in our elaborate but fragile C4ISR systems; using weapons of mass destruction; or bringing destruction to the U.S. homeland through catastrophic terrorism. Much of the DOD's spending goes to improving its capability for contending with symmetric foes quickly and with minimal casualties; too little goes to countering asymmetric threats.

Chapter 5 describes some specific steps to prepare better to counter asymmetric threats. In particular, DOD should make strong contributions to the interagency counter-terrorism and counter-proliferation programs recommended above. DOD should also develop a technology base in biowarfare defense (BWD) that is as strong as its base in nuclear proliferation. DOD and DOE have strong laboratories with thousands of personnel skilled in nuclear technology. But the national security community has few experts in the field of biotechnology, neither within its uniformed or civilian ranks nor in its affiliated laboratories and contractors. Biotechnology and pharmaceutical companies frequently decline to participate in BWD programs for fear of being "tainted" by defense work or because of the cumbersome contracting and accounting procedures required by the Pentagon. Yet the biotechnology revolution will have implications for security that will probably exceed those of the nuclear and information revolutions that preceded it. DOD will need to increase funding in the Defense Advanced Research Projects Agency (DARPA), U.S. Army Medical Research Institute of Infectious Disease (USAMRIID), and the Defense Threat Reduction Agency (DTRA) for biotechnology research, but this will not be enough. Government employment practices and the attractive private-sector employment opportunities available to biotechnologists mean DOD has little chance of retaining in-house expertise in this field. A university-affiliated government-owned laboratory (akin to the nuclear laboratories of the DOE) should be founded to give DOD a foothold in the BWD technology field.

ORGANIZE TO DEAL WITH INFORMATION WARFARE

Information technology is not only an enabler of traditional military operations, it is a weapon in its own right. Chapter 3 suggests that DOD needs to organize both offense (computer network attack, or CNA) and defense (CND) to give policy order to this area of importance to future international security. CNA's balkanized and overclassified activities need to be brought together in a functional joint command where the Secretary of Defense and the President can exercise policy oversight. CINCSPACE is the appropriate choice within DOD (supported by the National Security Agency as "force provider"), and CINCSPACE needs to be given the resources to do the job. For CND, the government shares the interests of private banking, e-commerce, and other businesses and of ordinary citizens in privacy and security for networks. A publicly funded but privately operated National Information Assurance Institute should be founded at a major research university, with initial funding from DOD.

BRIDGE THE GAP BETWEEN EUROPEAN AND U.S. MILITARY CAPABILITIES

European nations are far behind the United States in every dimension of modern military proficiency. The process of military reform in Europe will take many years, and it is not practical to "close the gap" between their militaries and ours in its entirety. However, as described in Chapter 9, it should be possible for one NATO Combined Joint Task Force (CJTF) to be equipped and trained to operate at or near U.S. standards and to interoperate fully with U.S. forces. If successful, this capability within NATO, though small, would have significant political effect, would shift some of the burden for small-scale contingencies from the United States to the allies, and would provide a stronger proving ground than European Security and Defense Identity (ESDI) for wider reform of Europe's militaries. The United States should also encourage trans-Atlantic defense industry partnerships.

STRENGTHEN OTHERS' ABILITY TO PERFORM PEACE OPERATIONS

Many Americans would prefer to see the United States attach a lesser priority to peace operations, but such operations must be performed by someone. Chapter 9 recommends a two-part U.S. strategy for dealing with this dilemma. The first part is to strengthen others, including international organizations, to perform certain selected types of peace operations. For example, the United States should appoint a defense advisor to the United Nations. Second, the United States should prepare for a supporting, specialized role emphasizing its areas of comparative advantage relative to other states, international organizations (IOs), and non-governmental organizations (NGOs). Examples would include restoring order in the early period of a peace operation rather than rebuilding institutions of civil society in the later period, and contributing transport and information systems rather than patrolmen to a policing operation.

IMPROVE THE CONTRIBUTIONS OF DOD'S MILITARY-TO-MILITARY PROGRAMS TO PREVENTIVE DEFENSE

DOD's military-to-military programs begin first and foremost with our key alliances, especially NATO and Japan. But the circle can be widened, as described in Chapter 9, through such programs as the military-to-military activities sponsored by the regional Commanders-in-Chief (CINCs), NATO's Partnership for Peace, and the Department of Defense Regional Centers. In Asia, these programs are a means to "engage" China and, more importantly, provide a U.S.-led mechanism to increase transparency and understanding among militaries in a region without NATO-like security structures. With Russia, military-to-military activities are a means to understand and, at the margin, to influence the attitudes of a key institution in Russia's ongoing revolution. With former Soviet states such as Ukraine and Uzbekistan, these programs are a vital lifeline to the West and provide strategic insurance for them and for the United States against a negative turn in Russia's revolution. These programs are both preventive and protective, and should be fostered.

EXPAND THE SCALE AND SCOPE OF THE NUNN-LUGAR PROGRAM

History has given the United States unique opportunities to reduce the threat of weapons of mass destruction (WMD) through cooperative programs. But Chapter 9 notes that the opportunities available are far more numerous than the current Nunn-Lugar budget can address. New programs are needed in the areas of chemical and biological weapons, assistance to non-Russian states, disposition of fissile materials, and implementation of possible future arms control agreements like START III.

Addressing Long-standing Management Problems

Perhaps most intractable are DOD's long-standing management problems, including management of its civilian personnel, reducing waste due to an excess of infrastructure, bringing government management practices up to the civilian standards characteristic of the recent economic boom, transforming the logistics system, and developing new ways to protect secrets in a changing world.

A NEW PERSONNEL MANAGEMENT SYSTEM FOR DOD CIVILIANS

The current DOD civil service system is badly in need of reform. It is out of touch with the labor market that supplies its people; it inhibits professional development and innovation by its work force; and it is incapable of responding to the changing needs of the DOD. A new system is needed to attract and retain high quality, innovative people who can implement and manage the new DOD described in this book. Chapter 8 argues that the DOD should manage the new human resources system outside of the civil service system. The new system would be better able to attract the right people because it would have more flexible pay and hiring rules, portable pensions, contracts for limited periods of government service as well as easier entry, exit, and re-entry into the system. It would be more effective because it would include performance-based compensation, interagency rotation, job grade attached to the person rather than the position, and extensive professional training. At the same time it would protect the fundamentals of the civil service system such as the merit system, equal opportunity, and absence of political influence.

REDUCE WASTED INFRASTRUCTURE

Infrastructure — bases, depots, test ranges, and the like — have not been reduced at nearly the rate of the forces since defense budgets peaked in 1985. As recounted in Chapter 7, Congress has ignored the current administration's call for two more rounds of Base Realignment and Closure (BRAC). Orderly, prioritized, and fair reductions require new legislation. The new administration should show its commitment to pursuing these needed economies by introducing a list of base closure candidates and making a commitment to a closure plan that comports with current law. This should drive the key players in both the administration and the Congress to the negotiating table in search of a new BRAC process. At the same time, the new administration should draft a legislative proposal in order to accelerate the inevitably difficult negotiations that will follow.

PURSUE THE REVOLUTION IN BUSINESS AFFAIRS

The current administration is introducing new business process reforms that reflect the principles of the Revolution in Business Affairs (RBA), but progress has been slow. We recommend that the new administration substantially increase the DOD's goals regarding competitive sourcing in order to capture its benefits, including the ability to focus on core competencies, take advantage of private-sector innovation, and obtain large cost savings. The Secretary should declare that the private sector is the preferred provider of goods and services. He should seek relief from the strictures (executive and legislative) of current competitive sourcing rules, and should greatly expand the kinds and types of functions to be assessed for possible outsourcing.

TRANSFORM THE LOGISTICS SYSTEM

Logistics agility is a key to maintaining our fighting edge. The DOD is moving in the right direction in enhancing the performance of its current logistics structures. But the need and promise of fundamental improvements in capability call for more extensive changes. The Secretary of Defense, with support from the President and Congress, should assign the Defense Logistics Agency as another component under the unified command for transportation (TRANSCOM). A National Distribution Center should be established under TRANSCOM, renamed Logistics Command (LOGCOM), and given enhanced staff to ensure that it has the ability to exercise the full range of its responsibilities. The Secretary should also direct CINCLOG to establish standing joint regional logistics commands in direct support of each regional CINC to replace the separate service commands. This should ensure that unity of effort and joint priorities are in place for all military operations, from peace through all stages of hostilities. In order to tailor and reduce the burden of logistics support, OSD should publish and keep current guidelines that set tough standards for size, weight, consumption rates, commonality in support equipment and parts, and other logistics parameters for all deployable pieces of equipment.

PROTECT SECRETS THROUGH AN IMMUNE SYSTEM RATHER THAN A HERMETIC SEAL

The United States must abandon the "hermetic seal" model of denying technology to others by seeking to put an impermeable barrier around the American defense technology base. Globalization and commercialization trends mean that crucial technology increasingly arises outside this barrier, and cannot be protected in this simple manner. It is also in the U.S. interest to have technology diffuse inward to defense from a globalized, commercialized base, and in these cases the hermetic seal approach would impede DOD from "running faster." Third, the unique sources of military advantage to the United States that will need to be protected will increasingly be systems engineering capability, rather than component or subsystem technologies. The latter will be widely available and increasingly difficult to contain. The U.S. export controls system must focus on unique sources of military advantage rather than technology across the board if it is to be truly effective at slowing the competition. Accompanying this new meaning of "secrets" must be new ways of protecting them. Much technology that is of foreign origin will find its way into U.S. defense systems and must somehow be made trustworthy. Meanwhile new network and compact data storage technologies make "insiders" as dangerous as "outsiders," as is commonly recognized in commercial industry. To deal with all these changes, the export controls and security systems must be capable of identifying and reacting to real security threats rather than applying simplistic and outdated bureaucratic rules. It should operate on analogous principles to the human immune system, which works not by trying to isolate the body from the environment, but by sensing dangers and combating the most dangerous ones selectively.

Chapter 6 recommends steps to make the transition from the hermetic seal to the immune system model. It supports the recent adoption by the U.S. government of a Defense Technology Security Initiative, streamlining and rationalizing export controls administration. It also recommends centralizing all administrative, training, and technical support for export controls licensing (but not policymaking) in a single entity funded jointly by State, Commerce, and Defense; providing the new entity with an automated licensing, intelligence, and enforcement tracking system; and increasing funding for intelligence support to export controls. But more fundamental steps should also be considered, including removing the distinction between munitions and dual-use items for regulatory purposes, widening employment of end-use controls, developing a control approach centered on systems engineering rather than underlying technology, and developing performance metrics common to those used in other government regulatory systems. In the area of personnel and industrial security policy, the most important steps to implement an immune system approach are to develop policy guidance covering the new threats and ambiguities introduced by technological change: the increased density of storage media (illustrated by the missing hard drives at Los Alamos Laboratory); network security (illustrated by recent widespread computer viruses and the allegations of data transfers by nuclear scientist Wen Ho Lee); and the integrity of software written outside the security boundaries. DOD and other government agencies should also expand their application of commercial techniques of security, privacy, technical monitoring, and human resources management to DOD personnel and industrial security.

Structure of this Volume

This book begins its exploration of ways of keeping the U.S. edge in defense with the "point of the spear," joint military operations. In Chapter 2, John M. Shalikashvili describes the need for evolution in the manner in which readiness, requirements, and logistics — all essential enablers of joint operations — are managed to keep the fighting edge. Chapter 3 by Victor DeMarines deals with two key aspects of the information revolution as it affects national defense: applying new information technology to joint operations, and organizing DOD's response to the fact that information technology is becoming a weapon in its own right. Chapter 4 by Robert Hermann expands the focus on information from warfare to national security as a whole, recommending ways of preserving America's near-monopoly on intelligence critical to international security under post–Cold War conditions. Chapter 5 by Ashton B. Carter and William J. Perry turns from keeping the edge in joint "symmetrical" conflict to developing an edge in asymmetric warfare if potential opponents, faced with a commanding U.S. lead in the former, turn to the latter.

Chapters 6, 7, and 8 deal with key supporting functions upon which success in dealing with future threats — symmetric or asymmetric — ultimately depend. Chapter 6 by Ashton B. Carter argues that the distinctive American technological edge in military affairs rests on a strong industrial and technology base, and urges adaptations to keep the technological edge as this base globalizes and commercializes. Chapter 7 by Michael J. Lippitz, Sean O'Keefe, and John

P. White argues that the business practices of DOD are in many places inefficient and wasteful, and that more resources could be freed for the "point of the spear" if the rest of DOD were better managed. Chapter 8 by David S.C. Chu and John P. White addresses the problem of giving thoughtful management to the most important resource of DOD: the quality of its uniformed and civilian personnel.

Chapters 9 and 10 deal with DOD's linkages to outside organizations with which it must ally to accomplish critical security missions. Chapter 9 by Elizabeth Sherwood-Randall observes that U.S. forces will almost always be operating in concert with allies, other security partners, international organizations, and non-governmental organizations, and that it needs to manage its interfaces with these bodies in a more deliberate manner rather than as an afterthought. Chapter 10 by John M. Deutch, Arnold Kanter, and Brent Scowcroft observes that the key national security challenges in the post–Cold War era cut across Washington's agencies and departments, and that DOD's role and capabilities need to be managed as part of an overall government team under White House direction.

The many recommendations of this book urge change — in many cases fundamental change. Change is never easy, especially in government, where broad consensus is usually a prerequisite. Some recommendations require legislative change, and all require the consent of Congress. Chapter 11 by Judith Miller addresses some of the legal and political considerations involved in implementing this book's recommendations.

Conclusion

The end of the Cold War left the United States with a substantial edge over every other nation in the world in matters of national defense. This volume is dedicated to keeping this edge in the future. While many in the United States and around the world might take the American edge for granted, the group that prepared this volume does not. The challenges to defense organization and management described in these pages are embedded in the practices and traditions of an enormous organization. They are not susceptible to solution by high-level policy decision alone, or by resolution of a policy debate. They are rarely the stuff of national debate. The mandate to make the needed changes we recommend must therefore arise from the natural insistence by citizens that their government function as well as the rest of the society they see around them, and from their growing awareness that an easy period in which security was inherited is giving way to one in which security will need to be earned. While change will not be easy, the mandate is there if the administration and Congress choose to use it.

2

Keeping the Edge in Joint Operations

JOHN M. SHALIKASHVILI

WITH BRUCE REMBER, PHIL EHR, AND THOMAS LONGSTRETH

In the last decade, America's military has demonstrated unmatched operational excellence in combat and in numerous demanding peacekeeping and humanitarian operations, from the stunning victory in the Gulf and the challenging peace enforcement missions so expertly executed in places such as Bosnia and Haiti, to air operations in the sky over Serbia, where we flew some 37,000 sorties and lost only two aircraft and not a single pilot. This chapter is about the steps that we should take to continue this operational excellence well into the twenty-first century. The chapter begins with some observations concerning the key strengths that have facilitated operational excellence to date, then highlights several potential shortfalls that, if not corrected, will undermine future operational effectiveness.

We want to express our thanks to the many individuals who found time to discuss issues with us, provide background information and other research materials to us, and in general to help us shape our final product. Unfortunately space does not permit us to thank everyone by name. Whether or not these individuals agree with us on the conclusions we reached, their contributions were invaluable to us as we considered a wide range of potential topics, issues, and recommendations that could improve future operational effectiveness for our military.

The views expressed in this chapter are those of the authors and do not reflect the official policy or position of the U.S. government or the Department of Defense.

The post–Cold War period has put the spotlight on peacekeeping and humanitarian operations. Such missions will almost certainly continue to occupy our military in the years ahead, although perhaps less frequently. But we should be careful not to reduce our fighting excellence by our efforts to increase our peacekeeping expertise. America's armed forces must continue to exist first and foremost to fight and win our nation's wars, even as we equip and train them for operations other than war.

While the exact nature and locations of future threats are unknown, it is certain that crises requiring military involvement will nearly all be far from our shores, and thus that power projection will continue to be the fundamental strategic concept of our future force. Properly sized and fully ready strategic air and sea lift will therefore be key to our ability to respond. Efforts to make our combat forces more strategically agile, and the footprint of our support forces and logistics considerably smaller, will yield large dividends.

Strengths to Preserve

Maintaining the U.S. fighting edge requires not only that we address our shortcomings, but also that we understand and preserve those strengths that have been a foundation of our operational excellence: high-quality people, demanding combat training and leader development, integration of cutting-edge technologies into the force, and the advances in "jointness" made possible by the reforms of the Defense Reorganization Act of 1986.[1]

1. The 1986 Defense Reorganization Act is more commonly known as the Goldwater-Nichols Act in honor of Senator Barry Goldwater and Representative William Nichols, the chairmen of the Senate and House Armed Services Committees. This act culminated a four-year effort begun by Chairman of the Joint Chiefs of Staff, General David Jones, and resulted in the most significant changes to the joint system since the National Security Act of 1947 established the Department of Defense. This act "greatly enhanced the authority of the Chairman, established the position of the Vice Chairman, bestowed wide new powers on the CINCs, and provided for actions and procedures to increase the prestige and rewards for joint duty in an attempt to improve the functioning of the joint system and the quality of joint military advice." Ronald H. Cole, et al., *The Chairmanship of the Joint Chiefs of Staff* (Washington, D.C.: Joint Chiefs of Staff, Joint History Office, 1995). For the text of the act itself see *Goldwater-Nichols Department of Defense*

PEOPLE

It is beyond argument that the foundation of U.S. military excellence has been the high quality of the people we have been able to recruit and retain. Thus, high-quality people must remain our highest priority, and under no circumstances should we lower our recruiting and retention standards just to "make the numbers." (For more on these issues, see Chapter 8 by David Chu and John White.) We must provide fully sufficient resources for the most promising recruiting programs, and take those steps necessary to retain the best and the brightest. Fortunately, after a few bleak years, there are signs that recently instituted programs are paying off and that all services will be likely to make their FY 2000 recruiting goals. But if in the end these steps still fail to keep the ranks filled, then we must be prepared to make the tough decision to reduce our force size further, rather than fill our ranks with lower-quality people. Reduction in the quality of people would only result in a second-rate military.

COMBAT TRAINING AND LEADER DEVELOPMENT

U.S. forces have enjoyed an enormous operational advantage as a result of demanding unit and leader training, capped by the tough combat-like experience they undergo in fully-instrumented combat training centers where units are pitted against professional opposing forces under the watchful eye of expert evaluators. But there are unmistakable signs that here the edge is wearing off. High operations tempo and funding constraints mean that units are not able to visit these centers as often as they used to; when they do go, their preparatory home-station training is frequently not what it should be. On occasion, material shortages and funding constraints have reduced the amount of training that crews are able to conduct, particularly with precision-guided munitions. In addition, we have not modernized our major training centers adequately and, as a result, their ability to conduct realistic state-of-the-art training has deteriorated. While there is consensus that we need to modernize our training infrastructure and capabilities, these tend to be sacrificed to pay other bills at budget crunch time. If we are to remain the world's

Reorganization Act of 1986, Statutes at Large 100 (1986). For an interesting retrospective analysis of the impact of Goldwater-Nichols, see Dennis J. Quinn, ed., *The Goldwater-Nichols DOD Reorganization Act: A Ten Year Retrospective* (Washington, D.C. : National Defense University Press, 1999).

best military, unit and leader combat proficiency must not continue to be treated as "bill payers."

CUTTING-EDGE TECHNOLOGY

Today, the United States is the leader in integrating the latest information-age technologies into our weapons platforms and systems (as Chapter 3 by Victor DeMarines details). This has given us unmatched battle-space awareness and an equally unmatched ability to gather, analyze, and distribute vast amounts of information to nearly everyone on the battlefield who might need it. We can strike from great distances day and night, in almost any weather, with far greater precision than was thought possible even during DESERT STORM. We have developed the world's most advanced stealth technologies that allow certain systems to operate virtually undetected in enemy-controlled space. These capabilities, now known as the Revolution in Military Affairs, or "RMA," have put us far and above any other military in the world.[2] But because many these technologies are increasingly available from commercial sources worldwide, we will keep this advantage only if, as Ashton Carter explains in Chapter 6, we manage to be faster and more imaginative in integrating these rapidly advancing technologies into our systems than any potential adversary.

JOINTNESS

Almost without exception, those who fought in DESERT STORM, and those who have watched over our military ever since, point to the changes brought about by the Goldwater-Nichols Act as the foundation of our current operational excellence. While each of our four military services has a proud heritage of operational excellence, our ability to achieve powerful synergies by combining the capabilities of the services in the heat of battle has in the past been due more to the personal relationships and ingenuity of commanders in the field than

---

2. The Revolution in Military Affairs is so called because of the fundamental changes in the nature of warfare made possible through a combination of new technologies, doctrinal innovations, and organizational adaptations. A concise and excellent discussion of the current RMA appears in James R. Fitzsimonds and Jan M. Van Tol, "Revolutions in Military Affairs," *Joint Forces Quarterly*, No. 4 (Spring 1994), pp. 24–31. Jane E. Gibish has compiled a thorough bibliography on the topic of RMAs, available from the Army War College library web site: <carlisle-www.army.mil/library/bibs/rma.htm>.

design. The failed hostage rescue attempt in Iran in 1980, and lessons learned during the rescue of American medical students in Grenada in 1983, underscored the need for more joint coordination among the services in all areas, from combat operations to doctrine to acquisition of new equipment. The most important contributions of Goldwater-Nichols have been to strengthen the ability of the Chairman of the Joint Chiefs of Staff to provide straightforward, undiluted military advice; to give the unified commanders the necessary authority over military forces assigned to them; and to set up officer assignment procedures to ensure that high-quality, properly trained officers are assigned to joint positions and that they remain there for an adequate length of time. There are those who would reverse these hard-won gains, arguing that jointness has gone too far, but to allow this to happen under the guise of fine-tuning Goldwater-Nichols would be a huge step backwards. To maintain positive momentum begun with Goldwater-Nichols, we should ensure that the United States Joint Forces Command (USJFCOM), formed in 1999 by redesignating the United States Atlantic Command (USACOM), has adequate resources and the senior-level support it needs to carry out its mandate.[3]

As we move forward, we should do so in accordance with our roadmap to the future. *Joint Vision 2020*, endorsed by the Secretary of Defense, the Joint Chiefs, and the unified commanders, lays out broadly the kind of human talent — the professional, well-trained, and ready force — and the operational capabilities that will be required for the joint force to succeed across the full range of military operations in 2020 and beyond.[4]

---

3. During the October 7, 1999, JFCOM "Stand-Up" ceremony, Secretary of Defense William S. Cohen charged JFCOM to "embrace your new mission to prepare for the future: To spell out the doctrine and refine the tactics that are going to guide and unite an increasingly joint warfighting force; to shape and educate and train so we will prepare the Total Force for this new art of warfare; to style and sustain the weapons and systems of the future; and to support domestic agencies in the event of an attack on American soil." Entire speech available at <www.defenselink.mil/speeches/1999/s19991007-secdef.html>.

4. U.S. Joint Chiefs of Staff, *Joint Vision 2020* (Washington, D.C.: U.S. Joint Chiefs of Staff, June 2000), available at <www.dtic.mil/jv2020>. This strategic blueprint is intended to guide the services and CINCs in developing future warfighting concepts and capabilities. It is an updated version of *Joint*

There are, of course, a variety of shortcomings that significantly affect our operational capabilities, both now and in the future. A number of these are topics of discussion in other chapters of this book, including intelligence, command and control, information warfare, countering asymmetric threats, and improving our ability to operate with allies.[5] However, improvements in the areas of readiness, the joint requirements process, and joint logistics will lay the foundation for maintaining our fighting edge and remaining the dominant military well into the future. These critical areas are the focus of the remainder of this chapter.

IMPROVING READINESS

Over the last few years, our services have experienced a nagging downward trend in people and equipment readiness. This trend is the result of a combination of factors: a decade-long downsizing, defense budget reductions, and a fairly high number of overseas operational deployments, both large and small. These, in turn, have produced frequent periods away from home and considerable unpredictability in the lives of our service members and, as most of them are married, their families. Fortunately, the FY 2000 and FY 2001 defense budgets halted and, in fact, slightly reversed the years of defense budget reductions. This made possible the funding of a number of important programs that promise to help correct some of these readiness problems. But it would be a serious mistake to assume that we have put our readiness problems behind us.

First, readiness has a number of components: personnel readiness, training readiness, and equipment readiness, each having two or more parts and each part confronting the Defense Department with unique challenges. Historically, our assessments of "readiness" have focused on how prepared units and individuals would be to execute

---

Vision 2010 (published in 1996), which focused on four operational concepts: dominant maneuver, precision engagement, full-dimensional protection, and focused logistics. To ensure success within these operational concepts, *JV 2020* emphasizes three critical factors: interoperability, innovation, and decision superiority.

5. See Chapter 4 by Robert Hermann on intelligence; Chapter 3 by Victor DeMarines on information warfare; Chapter 5 by Ashton B. Carter and William J. Perry on asymmetric threats; and Chapter 9 on managing relations with allies by Elizabeth Sherwood-Randall.

their missions if we had to go to war tomorrow. Many of the elements that contribute to this, such as training and spare parts, receive funding from operations and maintenance (O&M) accounts; consequently, O&M accounts have traditionally been thought of as readiness accounts.

Lately, however, we have also focused on two other kinds of readiness. "Joint" readiness is the unified commander's ability to execute his or her assigned war plans, given the resources that have been made available and the shortcomings as he or she sees them. "Future" readiness addresses those steps we must take today to ensure that we remain ready in the future, and thus concerns research and development (R&D) and modernization.

Maintaining a high state of readiness, however, does not mean that all units in the force could go to war tomorrow. The services have always had one form or another of "tiered" readiness. For example, in the Army, the XVIIIth Airborne Corps is expected to be able to go to war far more quickly than an Army National Guard division. "First to fight" units receive a higher priority for equipment and personnel than do units that are designated as later deployers. The Navy and Marine Corps have an elaborate cyclical program for the readiness of their carrier battle groups and their Marine expeditionary units, based largely on the demands of peacetime global presence deployments. The Air Force is moving toward a similar approach with its newly established Air Expeditionary Forces. The point is that all units, as a matter of course, go through planned phases when they are more ready or less ready. The challenge is for each service to refine these "tiered" readiness procedures to ensure that the force is as ready as necessary, at a manageable cost.

PERSONNEL CHALLENGES

The number one contributor to readiness is the recruitment and retention of high-quality people. This has become a significant challenge because our sustained, robust economy offers young people enormous opportunities in the civilian sector. Demographic trends also mean a shrinking pool of candidates, at least in the near term. A reduced propensity to enlist further squeezes recruiting, arising in part because fewer and fewer families have a military tradition, and in part because of the absence of a clearly visible threat. The problem is particularly acute in those areas where the services compete directly for people with the high-technology skills critical to today's high-tech military. The high operations tempo brought about by frequent overseas operational deployments further exacerbates the retention problem, but it would be a mistake to assume that reducing operational deployments alone would cure our personnel readiness problems: in fact, some of the highest retention rates are among personnel who have participated in various operational missions.

For now, what is required is a commitment to provide full resources for the most promising recruiting programs, and to sustain those programs that have proven to add significantly to the retention of high-quality people: programs such as adequate pay and retirement benefits, assured quality healthcare for service members and their families, decent housing and affordable childcare and, perhaps most of all, a challenging job with a fair opportunity for advancement and the feeling of belonging to the best military in the world. But in the end, we must recognize that we cannot forever treat these rising personnel costs as inevitable bills to be paid; rather, like the private sector, we must learn to treat them as costs to be managed.

INCREASED O&M SPENDING AND AGING EQUIPMENT

A significant funding dilemma facing the Defense Department is that although readiness spending, or O&M spending, continues to increase, we are not really buying increased readiness as a result. One reason is that aging equipment requires increasing amounts of money to maintain in combat-ready condition. Another factor is that O&M accounts are vulnerable targets for the payment of big new bills such as environmental clean-up, increased pay, and retirement and health care costs. Yet these issues are not readily apparent when simply looking at funding streams: the reality is that O&M spending is increasing in real terms at a rate of 1–3 percent a year. In FY 2001 it is about $110 billion, and our O&M spending per service member has never been higher.[6]

Next to its troubles of recruiting and retaining top-quality people, the greatest readiness challenge facing the Defense Department is the rapidly increasing cost of maintaining aging equipment. While some

---

6. Budget data are from DOD National Budget Estimates for FY 2001, <www.dtic.mil/comptroller/fy2001budget/fy2001grbk.pdf>.

modernization was accomplished in the 1990s, the bulk of modernization had already taken place in the 1980s, and much of that equipment is now in need of upgrading or replacement. This is especially a problem in the fixed-wing and rotary-wing aviation fleet. The dilemma is that the Defense Department has to devote increased resources to addressing the problems that affect aging equipment: parts break that did not often break before, others now break more frequently, the service life of platforms reaching the end of their design life must be extended, and the like. Yet every dollar that goes toward maintaining old equipment is a dollar that cannot be spent on replacing it with new equipment; it only postpones the inevitable day when it will have to be replaced. The answer is obvious but very painful. Unless more money is put into modernization and acquisition accounts — more than the $60 billion per year now planned for — and we start replacing aging equipment faster, the cost of material readiness will keep increasing, but material readiness will continue to decline. Perhaps additional acquisition and modernization funds can be freed up through the means described as the Revolution in Business Affairs (discussed in Chapter 7). But if not, then sustained increases to the services' modernization and acquisition accounts will have to be made by the new administration and the Congress.

Other aspects to readiness also require attention. Peacekeeping and humanitarian operations place a disproportionate demand on some "low-density" specialties (those we do not have in great numbers). This is particularly true of EA-6B electronic warfare aircraft, Airborne Warning and Control System (AWACS) aircraft, Joint Surveillance Target Attack Radar System (JSTARS) aircraft, U-2 high-altitude reconnaissance and surveillance aircraft, and the Army's Civil Affairs and Psychological Operations units. All are experiencing very high deployment rates, and as a result, excessive personnel turbulence is undermining crew cohesion and proficiency. Other factors adversely affecting readiness are significant reductions in spare parts inventories without a simultaneous increase in assured spare part deliveries, a shrinking pool of vendors who can rebuild or replace aging parts when they break, and a reduction in the Defense Department's skilled military and civilian labor force. All of these factors contribute to a downward trend in material readiness.

Today the services, the Joint Staff, and the Department of Defense all collect unprecedented volumes of data on everything from unit and personnel readiness and training readiness to material readiness and joint readiness. The Defense Department provides Congress with quarterly readiness reports that, with classified annexes, run to almost 500 pages. Yet all of this data falls short: what we need is a new system that allows for better assessment of readiness and a vastly increased ability to forecast readiness problems long before they occur, so that early preventive actions can be taken. A major effort to change the readiness reporting system along these lines would be a welcome development. But most crucial is the need to recruit and retain high-quality people and replace aging equipment.

RECOMMENDATIONS — READINESS

For now, the Department and the new President should put highest priority on funding and sustaining the more successful recruiting and retention programs. We should also put much more emphasis on managing personnel readiness by, for instance, reducing disincentives to retention as much as we can. Among those most often cited are broken promises about lifetime medical care and a fair retirement system, and frequent, short-notice relocations and repetitive operational deployments, which are particularly hard on families, and thus a major influence on whether a service member stays or leaves.

To arrest and reverse the rising cost of material readiness caused by aging equipment, the administration and Congress must provide sustained increases to the services' modernization and acquisition accounts.

WHAT ELSE NEEDS FIXING

Increasing funding for modernization, while a necessary condition for future readiness, is not alone sufficient for the task. Shortcomings in military modernization can result not only from inadequate funding, but also from inefficient business practices or a faulty requirement process. Shortfalls in annual funding can force delays or cancellation of some programs: even well-managed programs that meet valid military requirements may fall to the budget axe when services have to balance the books. Incremental reductions in modernization programs can be just as bad: program restructuring may reduce or extend production to the point that key programs become unaffordable. Likewise, inefficient business practices and overly burdensome acquisition regulations can be roadblocks to acquisition of much needed military capabilities. (In the latter area, the Department of Defense has already made significant gains, reducing reliance on military specifications and adopting commercial practices where feasible; Chapter 7 offers further suggestions for improving the Defense Department's business practices.)

However, neither funding increases nor improvements in business practices can adequately compensate for requirements problems such as lack of interoperability, or more fundamental disconnects between the concepts of operations for related systems fielded by different services. Thus, the key for maintaining the fighting edge in the future is reforming the requirements process so that it better encourages innovation and leads to the best possible equipment for employment by a joint force commander.

Logistics, the other major issue in this chapter, is equally critical for future operational capabilities. Many would consider America's world leadership in strategic transportation and in common and service logistics to be proof that the system needs no structural changes. The corollary to this view looks to new technology to provide all that is needed to improve logistics for the twenty-first century. Emerging information technologies will undoubtedly transform logistics, but the real question is whether we should anticipate this transformation and make logistic organization changes up front, or whether we should allow these technologies to mature within the confines of the existing mix of service, defense agency, and commander-in-chief (CINC) logistic organizations. This chapter argues that in order to provide more responsive support to regional CINCs and to capture the efficiencies and savings that additional centralization would bring, it is time to push change, even if that creates temporary tensions and raises opposition that others would rather avoid.

Improving the Military Requirements Process

Prior to World War II, the Army and Navy were completely separate organizations, each represented by a cabinet-level secretary. Each service received its own budget and procured its own equipment. Following World War II, the Secretary of Defense occupied the single defense post in the cabinet, presiding over the Departments of the Army, the Navy, and the newly created Air Force. With a small staff, the Secretary had the task of integrating and prioritizing the efforts of the three military departments; however, the tasks of generating requirements, budgeting for, and fielding new equipment remained with the individual services. During the 1960s, Secretary of Defense Robert McNamara instilled business discipline in the Pentagon's budget process by establishing the Planning, Programming, and Budgeting System (PPBS) to link spending better to strategy. Yet the initiative to start new programs remained with the services. Secretary McNamara's attempt to compel the Air Force and Navy to acquire a common fighter broke down when divergent requirements caused the Navy to withdraw from what ultimately became the Air Force's F-111.

The services maintained the initiative if for no other reason than that they retained most of the expertise for analyzing their respective requirements for what they needed in order to dominate their mediums of warfare. As discussed previously, however, the Goldwater-Nichols legislation initiated sweeping changes that elevated the role of the Chairman of the Joint Chiefs of Staff, and bolstered the support available from the Joint Staff. Since then, the individual service requirement proposals have come under increased scrutiny as CINCs, the Joint Staff, and the Office of the Secretary of Defense (OSD) have pushed for greater interoperability of new systems and better definition of joint concepts of operations.

This section argues that the Chairman should provide more detailed guidance to the services earlier in the requirements process by setting joint interoperability standards and shaping service initiatives, thus laying a foundation for future trade-off decisions both within and across service boundaries. To provide the best possible guidance to the services, the Chairman will benefit from CINC inputs, robust joint experimentation, and rigorous analysis. The Joint Staff has already taken steps down this path, which are to be applauded, but the bar should be set even higher. While some may dismiss this as "not bold," or an endorsement of the status quo, they should look at the progress that has already been made, and recognize that more radical alternatives — such as stripping the requirements functions out of the services, or even abandoning a requirements-based process altogether — are flawed, and risk breaking the force.

UNDERSTANDING THE REQUIREMENTS PROCESS

The requirements process should accomplish several key functions. First, it should generate and validate new requirements in order to address deficiencies in capability, replace or upgrade aging systems, or take advantage of emerging technologies. More often than not, ideas for new military systems come from the individual services, sparked by expertise in their respective competencies. Other organizations are also beginning to play an increasingly prominent role: defense agencies, especially those with combat support roles, propose requirements in areas such as logistics, intelligence, communications, and missile defense. Occasionally, the staffs of the Secretary of Defense and the Chairman of the Joint Chiefs of Staff, responding to inputs from the unified commanders and exercising their own top-down perspectives, identify requirements that may not fall within the unique core competencies of any particular service. In the future, JFCOM's joint experimentation efforts should also generate new requirements.

New major system proposals require Joint Requirements Oversight Council (JROC) validation prior to becoming actual programs. The Chairman of the Joint Chiefs of Staff is the chairman of the JROC, but has delegated its daily operations to the Vice-Chairman of the Joint Chiefs of Staff, the only person to whom the law allows the Chairman thus to delegate. The Vice Chiefs of the four services represent their Chiefs on the JROC. A common misconception is that these senior officers vote on proposals; in fact, no voting *per se* takes place during JROC deliberations. Decisions are usually the result of consensus reached during debate. A lack of consensus by the JROC members on an issue would be referred to the Chairman of the JCS for resolution. Thus, in much the same manner as with a corporate board, the rigor of JROC decisions partially depends on the individual characteristics of the JROC participants.

Initial JROC validation has historically been rather perfunctory following its original charter as a "clearinghouse" for service ideas. From the beginning, the JROC lacked the objective and rigorous analytical capabilities needed to show compelling cause for canceling a program over the objection of the sponsoring service and any associated political supporters. Recent years have witnessed significant efforts to address these shortcomings. The formation of the Joint Warfighting Capabilities Assessment (JWCA) teams in 1994 provided "analytically based insights designed to stimulate and inform discussions among the four-star JROC members."[7] The Chairman's recent direction to the JROC to make more decisions "up front" by guiding services toward the technology investments and system purchases that will achieve the highest payoff in terms of future joint warfighting capabilities is an especially significant step, but this will require much more rigorous joint analysis, testing, and experimentation during early program development.

A second key function of the requirement process is to apply a joint force commander's perspective to individual service initiatives, to assess how these capabilities might integrate with other service capabilities where applicable. This integration function requires a common joint vision of future warfighting. Integration also requires development of detailed overarching joint architectures — such as combat identification or the emerging global information grid — to provide sufficient up-front guidance to services and agencies to use when developing individual systems. Until recently, development of such detailed architectures has lagged behind development of individual systems. The services and agencies have frequently established their own unique architectures optimized for only their particular needs, with a resultant lack of Joint architecture and dysfunctional inter-service operation. As a result, integration frequently did not occur until joint exercises or actual operations. By then, seamless interoperability was vastly more difficult due to limitations of hardware, software, doctrine, and budget, to name just a few. This reactive integration could and should be avoided whenever possible and highlights why CINCJFCOM, as the "futures" CINC, should be intimately and proactively involved in the requirements process.

The Joint Staff is working to improve the timelines and detail of the overarching architectures that guide development of individual systems. One such example is the establishment of "capstone" requirements that detail interoperability guidelines for related families of systems and capabilities.[8] Additionally, increasing use of so-called

---

7. William A. Owens and James R. Blaker, "Overseeing Cross-Service Trade Offs," *Joint Force Quarterly*, Autumn 1996, p. 38.

8. Capstone requirements define standards — such as radio frequencies, fuel specifications, or software language — to ensure compatibility and interoperability for families of systems or "systems of systems." A Capstone

"knowledge management tools" helps capture and chronicle discussions and previous decisions, to create a transparent database to improve lateral coordination among services and agencies.

The third and final critical function of the requirements process is to help eliminate wasteful duplication and facilitate intelligent budget-driven trade-off decisions. Yet "wasteful duplication" is often in the eye of the beholder: what is to one person wasteful duplication is to another a hedge against uncertainty. The military, when preparing for an uncertain future, prudently adopts a natural bias toward the latter perspective. Except in cases of excessive technological risk or program mismanagement, program cancellation results primarily from budget-imposed restrictions that force difficult choices between very capable programs.

CHALLENGES FOR THE REQUIREMENTS PROCESS

Competition among the four services often sparks innovation, but it can also lead to a counterproductive competition for resources. That said, not all competition for resources is destructive. When it involves presenting the Secretary of Defense with several alternative capabilities from which to choose, such competition is very healthy. However, when it involves battles fought in the press or in the halls of Congress to circumvent decisions by the Secretary of Defense, it becomes very corrosive and counterproductive for the military as a whole.

While the Secretary of Defense has the undeniable authority to direct — or deny — service acquisition of equipment, or procurement of other goods and services, in practice the services exercise a great deal of autonomy. Certainly, services would have a great deal of difficulty fielding a new system without the approval of the Secretary of Defense, but they can and do find subtle ways to generate strong political support for their favored systems, and to derail top-down directed programs they do not favor. Furthermore, when facing funding shortfalls, services tend to give priority to features that sup-

---

Requirements Document (CRD) provides overarching guidance to the subordinate Operational Requirement Documents (ORDs) of individual programs. This was in response to criticism in DOD's Section 912C Report to Congress: "ORDs tend to be system specific and do not address interoperability within the same joint mission area." Department of Defense, Section 912C Requirements and Acquisition Study Working Group, *Section 912C Report: Requirements and Acquisition,* June 1999, p. ES-3.

port their individual operational concepts, over features that enhance support for other services or the joint force commander. Efforts to overcome incompatibilities in system or network design often come too late in the development process to be effective: even the best joint doctrine has difficulty overcoming the barriers of incompatible radios or data-link protocols. These integration efforts must begin prior to program validation, with the result that each proposal for a new program start should contain appropriate integration and interoperability details to show clearly how the system will interact within a joint family of related systems. Some systems may be service-specific and require little of this sort of information, but these will probably be the exception. Thus, as recognized by the Chairman of the JCS in April 2000 when he shifted the JROC's emphasis, a need exists to better shape inputs to the requirements process, rather than trying to cobble together the outputs.[9]

But achieving the next level of jointness requires more than simply making sure individual systems can work together; it requires a new approach to identify, develop, and advocate "inherently joint requirements." Many requirements typically provide an integrating or multi-service support function for the unified commander, and as such often do not compete well in the internal budget-priority decisions of the individual services. These types of capabilities usually benefit many customers, and may not fall neatly into the core competency of a single service, or may cross those of several services. Examples include command and control, theater air and missile defense, combat identification, and logistics.

The lack of rigorous advocacy for such inherently joint programs has allowed joint warfighting influence to lag behind service operational concepts. Greater advocacy for inherently joint capabilities requires more rigorous analytic assessments to provide insights into future requirements. The intellectual capital of Joint Staff and OSD analysis teams provides a good foundation that can provide a context for service initiatives. Yet traditional analytical tools have been unable to produce accurate forecasts of interactions and synergies of

---

9. As reported in Frank Wolfe, "Myers: Pentagon Needs JROC Influence Up Front," *Defense Daily*, April 5, 2000, p. 7.

"system of systems" or "effects-based targeting."[10] The Defense Science Board's recommendation that the Defense Department should acquire a greater capacity for systems architecture and systems engineering, in order to develop and field "born joint" capabilities, is thus right on the mark.[11]

The final challenge for the requirements process is the perceived lack of opportunity for CINCs to shape future warfighting requirements. The inherent difficulty in capturing CINC requirements is that each CINC's theater or functional area is different, leading to a unique set of priorities for each unified command. Thus, some theater-specific inputs are buried within the integrated priority list and do not receive the joint advocacy needed to compete well with other service-initiated programs. Compounding this is the difficulty CINCs currently have in seeing cost trade-offs between various requirements. While in theory CINCs have multiple opportunities to make inputs that drive future warfighting requirements, their short-term opportunity horizon and lack of staffs and resources for substantial requirement analysis effectively limit their influence. What is needed is a unified voice to help broker CINC initiatives, with an eye on future joint concepts and current budget constraints.

THE SEARCH FOR SOLUTIONS

The appropriate balance between a decentralized, service-dominated approach to generating requirements that favors innovation, and a centralized approach to integrating their respective efforts, will continue to be a topic of considerable debate. The penalties for shifting the balance too far in either direction are severe. The defense budget simply will not support all the initiatives advocated by each of the four services, and the nation benefits by ensuring that the forces of the four services can train and fight together effectively. While some degree of centralized direction to integrate the forces of each service is thus necessary, over-centralization of decision-making for invest-

---

10. See for example Booz-Allen and Hamilton, "Measuring the Effects of Network-Centric Warfare," Volume I prepared for Office of Secretary of Defense Net Assessment, April 28, 1999.

11. Department of Defense, *Defense Science Board Report on Warfighting Transformation* (Washington, D.C.: Office for the Under Secretary of Defense for Acquisition and Technology, September 1999), p. 25.

ments and operations, while producing process efficiencies on paper, risks the consequences of being wrong.

The JROC plays a central role in brokering the right balance between various service and CINC perceptions of requirements. High-quality data analysis and experimentation will be critical to maintaining this balance and garnering support from all participants in the process, including Congress. The recent charter for JFCOM as the Chairman's agent for joint experimentation provides cause for optimism.[12] With sufficient resources, JFCOM offers an unprecedented opportunity to develop synergistic concepts for cross-service battlefield operations and support. For example, while the Kosovo campaign demonstrated the utility of an air-heavy task force for some scenarios, it did not fit the traditional doctrine of having Army forces deployed in force to put pressure on hostile ground forces. Thus, attachment of an Army helicopter unit to an Air Force air expeditionary force to form a joint expeditionary force would make an excellent joint experiment. Joint experimentation can also address the thorny issues of eliminating wasteful duplication among overlapping service programs and making tough choices between complementary systems to meet the budgetary bottom line. Participation by the services is crucial to successful joint warfighting experimentation, not only to obtain their buy-in, but also — more importantly — to capitalize on their energy and resources. Joint experimentation that does not involve the services in a significant way risks becoming just one more "stovepipe."

Despite the promise of active JROC involvement, detailed overarching architectures, and joint experimentation, there are some who question whether the use of requirements *per se* is the best approach. Those who criticize the basic premise of a requirements-based approach point out the difficulties of a process that allows initial development of ideas and concepts in what they consider a budget-unconstrained environment, and later tries to fit the resulting programs within a budget. This criticism targets programs in which costs steadily increase to meet what are perceived as excessively rigid performance requirements. In actuality, implicit budget considerations

---

12. Sections 922 and 923 of the National Defense Authorization Act of 1999 detail a "sense of Congress" calling for joint warfighting experimentation and specify requirements in Section 485 of Title X of the U.S. Code.

do permeate the requirements process in practice, from use of "cost as an independent variable" in initial requirement proposals, to senior JROC deliberations that look for creative alternatives to accomplish a given mission rather than simply looking to replace specific systems. But there is room for improvement. While cost and profit-driven business models may not fully account for the unusual demands of combat or contingency operations, they can help articulate military requirements in a way that provides appropriate performance incentives for industry. (See the discussion of value-based acquisition in Chapter 7.) The bottom line is that a requirements-based system is compatible with flexible budget and technology trades. More importantly, the requirements process provides a key framework for checks and balances between the military's role in determining capability needs and civilian leaders' responsibility to weigh risks associated with funding shortfalls. The warfighter and taxpayer are both served by an ongoing dialogue between those who establish requirements and those who plan, program, budget, and develop specific capabilities to meet performance standards.

Others propose centralizing management of all military requirements in a joint organization, stripping out all other requirements bodies from the services and consolidating their analytic resources in a new joint requirements staff.[13] While this could reduce redundancy and streamline the process, it would also stifle innovation, both in system design and operational concepts. This would essentially be a large step toward unification of the services, and deprive joint force commanders of the flexibility and strength that flow from individual service competencies.

The desire to give CINCs a greater voice in the determination of future requirements has led to the suggestion to have the CINCs determine the requirements for the services to execute: in essence, the CINCs would become the JROC. Yet this suggestion would, even in an age of global telecommunications, seriously undermine a CINC's ability to carry out daily responsibilities within his or her area of responsibility. Moreover, CINCs' needs are too diverse to expect that, as a group, they would do any better than the Service Vice Chiefs in

---

13. William A. Owens, "Making the Joint Journey," *Joint Forces Quarterly*, Spring 1999.

making decisions. A related alternative to provide CINCs a greater voice would be to create additional Major Force Programs, such as for space, information, or logistics. Yet this would build additional "stovepipes" at a time when the need is to better integrate service, CINC, and defense agency efforts.

A call for balance is by no means an endorsement of the status quo: vigorous implementation of evolutionary changes to the military requirements process is essential as the U.S. military transforms itself to meet national security requirements in the twenty-first century. Recently, the Joint Staff has recognized that it must go beyond simply validating service requirement "outputs" by taking a much more active role in shaping "inputs." Yet ensuring a significant step forward will require a formalized process, beginning with guidance from the Chairman, supported by CINCJFCOM in his role as the "futures CINC." This guidance should not only address standards to ensure compatibility and interoperability of service systems within joint architectures, but also articulate the Chairman's priorities to address shortfalls in warfighting capabilities. The quality of this guidance will depend on rigorous analysis of data from operational lessons, joint experimentation, and advanced modeling and simulation techniques. Making CINCJFCOM the lead action agent for matters of jointness and future capabilities and increasing his participation in the JROC and Defense Acquisition Board (DAB) will appropriately strengthen overall CINC influence in the requirements process.

RECOMMENDATIONS — REQUIREMENTS

First, Congress should require in law that the Chairman submit to the Secretary of Defense, services, CINCs, and defense agencies a force development roadmap to guide development of the requirements that inspire and drive program development. The aim is the co-evolution of doctrine, organizations, materiel, training, leader development, personnel, and facilities. This roadmap should provide up-front guidance for requirements integration and overarching joint architectures, including, but not limited to, information operations, intelligence, precision strike, and logistics. This would strengthen the current Capstone approach and lead to more coherent development of overarching joint architectures and earlier, more effective, integration of individual programs. Further, this roadmap should also provide a prioritized listing of capability shortfalls or attributes needed by the joint force from the perspective of a joint force commander. Such guidance would change the focus: rather than beginning with a statement of service needs, it would place earlier emphasis on joint force commander needs. This would also provide critical input for earlier trade-off decisions.

As Chapter 3 details in its examples of information and communications interoperability, the current process lacks a mechanism to take the initiative in setting and enforcing interoperability standards or other aspects of overarching joint architectures. Better positioning the Chairman to drive trade-off decisions early in program development would lead to more strictly enforced interoperability standards and more appropriate budget priority for inherently joint requirements. (The increased role for the Chairman does not, however, alter the Secretary of Defense's decision authority for service, unified command, and defense agency initiatives.)

Second, the Chairman should establish CINCJFCOM as the lead action agent for matters of jointness and future capabilities, although all unified commands must continue to champion joint requirements. As the lead action agent, CINCJFCOM would support the Chairman in execution of his statutory responsibilities over joint doctrine, training, education, and requirements. CINCJFCOM would assist the Chairman by serving as advocate for the joint force, similar to a service chief's advocacy for his respective service's competencies and capabilities. To this end, he must remain fully cognizant of the views and priorities of the other CINCs. To strengthen CINCJFCOM's credibility and effectiveness as steward of future joint capabilities, Congress should establish the requirement that a prospective CINCJFCOM have previously served successfully as a unified commander or service chief or vice chief. Existing laws should be modified to include CINCJFCOM as a statutory member of the JROC so that he can properly execute his responsibilities as advocate for joint capabilities. For similar reasons, the Secretary of Defense should revise his directives to include CINCJFCOM as a member of the DAB.

The final recommendation is a call to improve the insights gained through rigorous analysis and joint experimentation. A tremendous opportunity exists to leverage emerging technologies to increase DOD's analytical capabilities. Such analytical tools must provide insights more closely linked to future joint operational challenges. If, for example, a theater objective is to deter or compel a certain enemy course of action, analytical tools must provide insights on the deterrence or compellence value of various alternatives, in addition to more traditional metrics such as blast effects, equipment losses, or casualties. These analytical insights will help identify shortfalls in future joint capabilities, guiding decision-makers in making trade-offs and inspiring proposals for new operational concepts and systems. With sufficient resources, JFCOM's oversight of joint experimentation should provide a level playing field for various service and defense agency proposals, both to test and integrate them and to explore new "born joint" initiatives. Even more than resources, however, JFCOM needs a free hand to pursue a balanced program across the range of near, mid, and far-term experiments. Because we often learn more by analyzing the results of unsuccessful trials and tests, JFCOM needs freedom to conduct experiments that fail.

A New Perspective on Logistics

One cannot talk about maintaining the fighting edge without talking about logistics. Confederate General Nathan Bedford Forrest's often quoted axiom to "Git thar fustest with the mostest" captures the essence of the warfighter's challenge. As we anticipate future scenarios for U.S. forces, getting there first has even greater importance than in Forrest's day. However, more important than the "most" is the *right* amount. Because we are increasingly an expeditionary force, we need to get to the fight as soon as possible, before our adversary can gain its objective and consolidate its gain. The price for getting there late is often a tougher fight and higher casualties. Thus, strategic agility is absolutely essential, and logistics responsiveness is key.

Some may assume our current system is already sufficiently agile, since our ability to supply and sustain operations in remote corners of the world and in the most austere environments is unmatched, and our strategic transportation system is the envy of the world. But that does not mean that it is good enough to meet the demands of tomorrow. Future adversaries, unlike Saddam Hussein, will not give us six months to complete our deployment. Considering that over 50 percent of the weight and cubic volume of deploying forces is support, it becomes clear that logistics can be one of the greatest impediments to rapid deployment.[14]

At the risk of oversimplifying a very complex issue, one can say that increasing logistic agility and operational effectiveness depends on dramatically reducing the logistic demands of military units and their various combat systems, and transforming the management of logistic resources. Demand reduction comes through acquisition of lighter systems, systems that expend less consumables, and systems that minimize dependence on unique support equipment or supplies. Logistics demand reduction must also include engineering greater reliability, availability, and maintainability parameters into weapons systems, thereby reducing time for overhaul and increasing mean time between failure. Most important of these is reliability. A few dollars focused early in weapons system development on greater deployed reliability pays life-cycle dividends in reduced ownership-cycle cost and a smaller required power projection and force sustainment footprint. Demand reduction begins with individual service acquisition programs. Setting tough standards for size, weight, consumption rates, and other logistics parameters will help reduce demand. Just as important, however, is the need to manage logistic resources dynamically: we need to improve our ability to synchronize logistics support in real time across regional and service boundaries. Enabling this effort are rapid advances in information technology that will undoubtedly have profound impact on current organizations and processes.

This is by no means a revelation to those who follow defense issues: the Department of Defense has already begun a well-orchestrated campaign to transform logistics, including the appointment of a logistics architect, the publication of a defense-wide strategic plan for logistics, and specification of transformation goals and timelines in a Defense Reform Initiative Directive (DRID).[15] This

---

14. Department of Defense, *Report of the Defense Science Board Task Force on DOD Logistics Transformation*, Vol. II (Washington, D.C.: Office of the Secretary of Defense, September 1998), p. 105.

15. The Department of Defense's Defense Reform Initiative Report (November 1997) provided a "strategic blueprint for business processes in the Department to adapt better business processes, pursue commercial alternatives, consolidate redundant functions, and streamline organizations." To carry out the reforms, DOD issued Defense Reform Initiative Directives (DRIDs) that required re-

emphasis on logistics transformation reflects the strong consensus of DOD leadership in the OSD staff, Joint Staff, services, and CINCs to operationalize and institutionalize the key "Focused Logistics" operational concept of *Joint Vision 2020*. All of the military services have made great strides through recent initiatives to streamline logistics. However, focused logistics will require additional organizational changes to be fully effective.

NEED FOR LOGISTICS TRANSFORMATION

Logistics agility is a key to maintaining our fighting edge. As noted by the Defense Science Board's (DSB) Study on Logistics Transformation, a failure to blend military logistics seamlessly with operations would be a showstopper for the Revolution in Military Affairs, since "an operational ability to plan and fight 'on-the-fly' means little if the movement and sustainment of that operational ability cannot be equally dynamic."[16] Highlighting the growing importance of agile logistics, *Joint Vision 2020* emphasizes logistics as a full partner in the joint warfighting process.

The logistics system inherited from the Cold War — especially the functions of transportation, supply, and distribution — was the most automated, worldwide batch-transaction processing and mass-movement capability in the history of the world. It literally moved "iron mountains," but it certainly was not agile. A predictable threat and a large presence overseas allowed vast amounts of equipment and large stockpiles to be pre-positioned both in the United States and overseas. In the post–Cold War environment, by contrast, when, where, and how the United States will have to fight is much less predictable. But we do know that we will have to be able to go anywhere in the world on short notice and arrive quickly, ready to fight. We can expect a broad range of expeditionary operations that require a global joint-support infrastructure versatile enough to support simultaneous operations in multiple unanticipated locations.

---

ports to the Deputy Secretary of Defense on the status of implementation of various initiatives. DOD's defense reform website contains a listing and explanation of all 54 DRIDs at <www.defenselink.mil/dodreform/directives-memorandums/directives/ index.htm>.

16. Report of the Defense Science Board Task Force on DOD Logistics Transformation, Vol. I, pp. v and 3.

The effects of new technologies, concepts, and business practices will reach from the foxhole to the national support base. Key to success will be confidence throughout the ranks that the right part will be at the right place at the right time. Traditionally, forward-deployed stockpiles of supplies and equipment provided this confidence, albeit at a large cost in terms of redundancy, strategic lift, and vulnerability to attack. In contrast, focused logistics involves a shift to a "pull" system. Information technologies coupled with more effective distribution methods will reduce the need for large stockpiles. Technology will also offer vastly improved tools for prediction of needs for fuel, munitions, and parts, and for real-time, automated communication of those requirements to logistic control nodes across an end-to-end supply chain, from factory to foxhole. The reduced size of the in-theater logistics footprint will result in faster deployments, a more survivable support base, and a more agile warfighting force.

Thus, the current logistics transformation is not simply another "do more with less" downsizing drill: it offers quantum improvements in logistics support concepts and capabilities. Ever-increasing bandwidth through multiple modes, means, and channels provides an unprecedented ability to link the front lines to any location on the globe in order to gain access to — and share — a virtually unlimited amount of data in real time. Similarly, interactive web-based logistics will offer huge improvements over the traditional single-transaction-based supply and requisition process. Such live interactive linkages with "customers" and the ability to make real-time flow adjustments will provide the confidence to make a transformed logistics "system of systems" work. Supply and transportation functions will increasingly overlap as new information technologies enable total asset visibility and predictive modeling for inventory management. However, to exploit the advantages of these new technologies, command and control arrangements must evolve by bringing supply, distribution, and transportation under one roof.

PROGRESS ON THE ROAD TO TRANSFORMATION

In its broadest sense, logistics encompasses all aspects of moving and sustaining forces. While every commander takes pride in his ability to take care of his own troops, unit logistics support also depends on a fully functioning logistics "system of systems" with active participation from the services, the unified commands, Defense agencies, the Chairman and the Joint Staff, and the Secretary of Defense and his staff. Each of these organizations is making significant progress toward focused logistics.

In accordance with their responsibilities under federal law, all services are aggressively pursuing more agile logistics through demand reduction and process improvements. The Army is in transition from a system that relied upon large stockpiles in theater to one dependent on rapid delivery, signified by the term "velocity management," and the new Army vision encompasses a significant Army Logistics Transformation component. The Navy's "High Yield Logistics Strategy" comprises efforts to reduce costs by leveraging technology and reengineering supply processes and regional maintenance. The Marine Corps' "Precision Logistics" aims to enhance distribution and improve logistics command and control. The Air Force's logistics transformation reorients the service to better support expeditionary aerospace operations represented in the Expeditionary Air Force.

Federal law and existing joint doctrine empower CINCs with authoritative direction over all aspects of logistics within their respective areas of responsibility. In crises or other critical situations, CINCs may use all facilities and supplies of all forces assigned to their commands, even directing cross-service support arrangements. But in peacetime, current practice limits the scope of logistic and administrative authority exercised by the CINC.[17] Budget processes further reinforce this distinction between wartime and peacetime. In wartime, funding is normally not an issue, as services would expect supplemental funding. However, in peacetime, reimbursement for cross-service support is problematic. Thus, the budget imposes a practical obstacle that hinders the goal to "train the way we fight." Solving some of these budget issues would facilitate better support across service lines on a daily basis, from peace through contingencies to war.

17. Although Title X of the U.S. Code makes no distinction between a CINC's peacetime and wartime responsibilities for logistics, joint doctrine recognizes the CINC's practical needs in peacetime to coordinate logistic decisions with the parent services of his components. Department of Defense, *Joint Pub. 4.0: Doctrine for Logistic Support of Joint Operations* (Washington, D.C.: Joint Chiefs of Staff, April 2000), provides guidance for dealing with disagreements between the parent services and the CINC.

Providing critical support to regional CINCs is the unified command for transportation, or TRANSCOM. TRANSCOM provides strategic common-user air, land, and sea transportation to deploy, employ, sustain, and redeploy military forces to meet national security objectives across the range of military operations. TRANSCOM's brief history illustrates its significance. TRANSCOM was created in 1987 in response to a recommendation from the Packard Commission to establish transportation "unity of effort" in wartime.[18] Recognizing the impracticality of delaying TRANSCOM-directed operations until commencement of hostilities, the Secretary of Defense in 1992 extended TRANSCOM's responsibilities so that it also oversees its components in peacetime, earning it the label "DOD's single manager for common-user transportation." This improved continuity between peacetime and crisis has allowed TRANSCOM to develop long-term contracts and leases to accomplish its mission; this is a significant advance, since the vast majority of strategic airlift flies under commercial contract.

Also providing key support to regional CINCs, as well as to the services themselves, is the Defense Logistics Agency (DLA). As a combat support agency, DLA provides common supplies and services to forces worldwide, including almost 100 percent of food and other subsistence items, clothing and individual equipment, bulk petroleum products, and medical supplies, and 90 percent of repair parts. Its Defense Distribution Center is DOD's single manager for distribution, storing, and local delivery. DLA also provides reutilization and logistics information management worldwide. Since the early 1990s, the Defense Logistics Agency has reduced inventories by 59 percent, logistics response times by 90 percent, and distribution workload by 20 to 30 percent.[19]

The Chairman of the Joint Chiefs, supported by the Joint Staff, provides a global perspective for logistical support of on-going operations. The Joint Staff prepares joint logistic and mobility plans to support strategic plans, and recommends assignment of logistic and mobility responsibilities to the armed forces in accordance with those

18. Ronald H. Cole, et al., *A History of the Unified Command Plan 1946–1993* (Washington, D.C.: Joint Chiefs of Staff, Joint History Office, February 1995), p. 101.

19. Department of Defense, *Dimensions: The DLA Vision* (Washington, D.C.: Defense Logistics Agency, 1999), p. 36.

logistic and mobility plans. The Chairman and the Joint Staff are actively developing the operational and logistic concepts necessary to maintain dominance against any potential foe in the twenty-first century. Joint doctrine calls for: "Focused logistics ... the fusion of logistics information and transportation technologies for rapid response, deployment, and sustainment, the ability to track and shift units, equipment and supplies even while en route, and delivery of tailored logistics packages and sustainment directly to the warfighter."[20]

DOD also established a Deputy Under Secretary for Logistics to serve as DOD's Logistic Architect to support focused logistics and to ensure integration of logistics transformation at the departmental level. DOD's Logistics Strategic Plan is noteworthy in its scope of effort to modernize logistics systems, cut costs, reduce infrastructure and cycle time, and improve overall support. To implement this plan, DOD issued DRID 54, providing overarching guidance to services and agencies to develop and submit logistic transformation plans. Its intermediate objectives are to accelerate progress in implementing improved customer wait time by FY 2001, adopt a simplified priority system by FY 2002 to provide time-defined delivery driven by the warfighter's required delivery date, achieve accurate total asset visibility through use of automated identification technology and automated information systems by FY 2004, and field a web-based, shared-data environment to provide seamless, interoperable, real-time logistics information for early-deploying forces by FY 2004, and for the remainder of the force by FY 2006.

Each of the preceding requirements is crucial to improved logistics support for the warfighter. Demand reduction will improve deployability, and better information flows will facilitate management and distribution of critically needed parts and supplies. Yet greater visibility of critical parts and supplies will not by itself result in better effectiveness: unit commanders in the dynamic uncertainties of combat would be extremely reluctant to offer up any parts, equipment, or supplies to another unit unless directed to do so. Similarly, supply chain integration and competitive sources offer significant advantages in many scenarios, but do not diminish the need for some measure of centralized control. Commercial vendors contracted to

20. Department of Defense, *Joint Pub 4.0*, App. D, p. D-1.

provide on-site support are subject to many of the same transportation choke points faced by the military, and thus will require prioritization at theater level. That is precisely why joint doctrine calls for a streamlined process for "global as well as theater distribution," and identifies the need for CINCs to "synchronize, prioritize, direct, integrate and coordinate common-user and cross-service logistic functions to accomplish the joint theater mission."[21]

PUTTING THE PIECES TOGETHER: GLOBAL LOGISTICS COMMAND AND CONTROL

Numerous historical examples show that without a pre-existing theater logistics command, effective management at a theater level rarely occurs. Logistic support during World War II, despite its successes, suffered from many difficulties that continue to be highlighted in after-action reports today. From congestion at port facilities, to lack of uniform procedures for supply accountability, these lessons appear to have been repeated in Korea, Vietnam, and DESERT STORM. Each of these conflicts demonstrated the difficulty of establishing a theater logistics command structure after a crisis begins. During Operation RESTORE HOPE in Somalia, arriving forces soon outstripped organic Marine logistics capabilities, but the Joint Task Force Support Command was not fully prepared to accept the theater logistics mission. Kosovo highlighted the insidious challenges faced by logistic planners: the conflict grew from limited strikes to an intensified air campaign with the potential for significant ground operations, yet had the latter been called for, the lack of an existing theater logistics command would have jeopardized timely execution of the joint campaign.

The problem is that an *ad hoc* approach to logistics command and control demands a significant change in operating procedures in the midst of the transition from peace to crisis, adding confusion to an already stressful phase of operations. By the time a newly formed logistics command is ready to take charge during a crisis, service components will already have established workarounds to meet their respective needs, making effective theater-wide management more difficult.

---

21. Department of Defense, *Joint Pub 4.0*, App. D, pp. D-2–D-4.

But fixing theater-wide command and control is not enough to provide strategic agility across theater boundaries. The security perimeter for U.S. forces has expanded both geographically and with respect to the nature and timing of threats. In the future, this trend will require ever greater global integration of logistics. Dynamic cross-CINC support will have to be routine. A RAND study of logistics support for expeditionary operations calls for a globally focused "logistics command and control system to facilitate decision making ... and enable the system to react swiftly to changes."[22] The report emphasizes that "decisions . . . must be made centrally for the entire system, so that mutual support between theaters can be leveraged." This argues for reorganizing our rapidly evolving visibility, decision-making, acquisition, distribution, transportation, and delivery capabilities across the spectrum of the supply chain: in short, a twenty-first century global logistics system.

The full benefit of focused logistics will not be realized without organizational changes to provide an integrated global logistics perspective that serves as a foundation for supporting individual needs of regional CINCs, Joint Task Force commanders, and operating units. A unified command for logistics would provide such a perspective, to ensure agile logistic support for U.S. forces around the world. This would be consistent with the thrust of Goldwater-Nichols, and thus part of the necessary evolution to continue to fulfill the Goldwater-Nichols vision. It can be argued that such organizational changes should await the full introduction of enabling technologies, but such an argument ignores the fact that the best forcing function to shape and quickly introduce such technologies is the establishment of a unified command with global responsibility and authority to implement change. The time to act is now.

Three considerations are paramount in developing specific organizational recommendations. First, to move toward focused logistics — and hence, strategic agility — we need to integrate better the connectivity and operational functionality across the logistics chain. This includes the functions of supply, distribution, and transportation. While TRANSCOM and DLA have performed extremely

---

22. Paul S. Killingsworth, et al., *Flexbasing: Achieving Global Presence for Expeditionary Aerospace Forces* (Santa Monica, Calif.: RAND Corporation, 2000), p. xxii.

well, there is no doubt that warfighting effectiveness will be improved and considerable efficiencies and savings will be realized from a single command and control arrangement. However, trying to bring the services under the same single command and control arrangement would create such a huge, complex, and unwieldy organization that the drawbacks would quickly outweigh any advantages. Second, while the regional CINCs already possess authoritative direction for logistics over forces assigned, they need a single logistics commander to be their action agent for all aspects of theater logistics. Third, to ensure that "we train as we will fight," CINCs' logistic command and control arrangements in peacetime should be the same as those in wartime.

RECOMMENDATIONS — LOGISTICS

The new Secretary of Defense, with the support of the President and Congress, should redesignate TRANSCOM as a unified command for Logistics (LOGCOM) and assign to it sufficient logistics and distribution specialists to enable its headquarters to supervise the full range of its new responsibilities; assign DLA as a component of this newly created LOGCOM; and expand the role of the Defense Distribution Center to that of a National Distribution Command, making it also a component of LOGCOM with the responsibility to manage all distribution requirements, including those of the services. As such, LOGCOM would consist of the Military Traffic Management Command, the Military Sealift Command, the Air Mobility Command, the Defense Logistics Agency, and the National Distribution Command. Additionally, it would be wise to consider assignment of the Defense Contract Management Agency to LOGCOM with the responsibility to manage contract performance, both for new weapons system acquisition programs and the entire range of life-cycle support, transportation, and force sustainment contracts. This will ensure the integration of contractual performance for the warfighter across the range of performance, from acquisition to power projection and support in the operating theater. As recommended by the 1998 National Defense Panel (NDP), LOGCOM would thus provide global logistic support through integrated procurement, supply, distribution, and transportation capabilities. "This command would improve our ability to more rapidly project forces with smaller logistic footprints, to leverage industry innovations, and to improve and reengineer business practices."[23] Such a command would not alter traditional service responsibilities for support, other than requiring the services to handle all distribution through the newly established National Distribution Command under LOGCOM to ensure central coordination of movement of goods and personnel to regional CINCs. CINCLOG would be responsible for defining a logistics roadmap that established standards for total asset visibility and forward movement, and for establishing and enforcing an associated logistics architecture.

An objection sometimes heard is that CINCLOG's span of control would be too great, and that a Joint Logistics Command would risk becoming a service-like organization over the long term. Similar arguments preceding the establishment of TRANSCOM, now regarded as an overwhelming success, proved unfounded.

The Secretary of Defense should direct CINCLOG to establish standing joint regional logistics commands in direct support of each regional CINC. An in-place organization would ensure that unity of effort and joint priorities existed for all military operations conducted within a CINC's area of responsibility, from peace through all stages and forms of hostilities. Having these joint theater logistics commanders belong to CINCLOG, but working in direct support of the regional CINCs, would ensure that they could fully leverage the global logistics system in support of the regional CINC's priorities. These commanders would be the joint logisticians responsible for integration of all general support missions. They would not have service logistics forces assigned to them, but rather would be empowered to ensure compliance with the CINC-approved logistics architecture and priorities, and to task for needed capabilities through each of the service component commanders. It is important to note that these organizations would not assume the traditional CINC J-4 functions of plans, policy, or programs, and that services would retain their statutory responsibilities for equipping and supporting their own forces. But these joint theater commands would have the responsibility for cross-level support to meet overall theater objectives. This cross-level support would not only be with service components, but also within the framework of Acquisition Cross

---

23. National Defense Panel, *Transforming Defense: National Security in the Twenty-first Century* (Washington, D.C.: U.S. Government Printing Office, December 1997), p. 72.

Service Agreements (ACSAs) currently being negotiated with the militaries of each eligible country in a CINC's area of responsibility. This will significantly accelerate the multinational emphasis of *JV 2020* Focused Logistics.

To better integrate and strengthen recent initiatives to reduce demand for logistics support, the Office of the Secretary of Defense, based on recommendations from the Chairman, should publish and keep current guidelines that set tough standards for size, weight, reliability, consumption rates, commonality in support equipment and parts, and other logistics parameters for all deployable pieces of equipment. Like industry standards that might be developed by federal agencies for transportation safety, clean air, or fuel efficiency, the logistic standards should set common benchmarks that, when met, will compress initial deployment timelines, reduce required throughput, and minimize the overall required theater logistic footprint.

Conclusion

The challenge before us is very different from that of the "hollow military" of the 1970s. The task of returning that military to operational excellence seemed nearly hopeless, but the need for change was obvious to all. Today, despite a number of significant shortcomings, the U.S. military is the envy of friend and foe alike, and the need for changes to keep it that way is much less obvious. Nevertheless, prudent changes are essential if we are to retain our fighting edge well into the future, particularly in the face of uncertain threats. Others will undoubtedly have studied our successes in DESERT STORM and in the sky over Serbia, not just to imitate us, but to learn how to defeat us with the more limited resources at their disposal. So to stay as we are is not an option: we must build on our strengths as we correct the shortcomings that would erode our fighting edge and keep us from reaching our full potential. This chapter has addressed three of the most urgent: readiness, requirements, and logistics.

3

Exploiting the Internet
Revolution

VICTOR A. DEMARINES

WITH DAVID LEHMAN AND JOHN QUILTY

Effective command and control (C2) capability — sometimes now referred to as C4ISR — is crucial to the successful execution of military operations and, in fact, to sustaining the U.S. military advantage in the information age.[1] The innovative application of information technology, in concert with the re-engineering of warfighting processes to exploit these technology enablers, is often called the Revolution in Military Affairs (RMA).

Over the last decade, a revolution in information technology (IT) has transformed business processes as well as many aspects of individuals' daily lives. The combination of cheap and powerful computers with effective networking has enabled commercial companies to increase greatly both the efficiency of their operations and the speed with which they can respond to new opportunities and challenges.

History shows that the same technologies and techniques that create economic growth can be turned to military purposes, that the military organizations that are quickest to exploit them can derive

---

1. The current term in vogue for command and control is "C4ISR." We believe the definition should revert to "command and control" (C2), because intelligence, surveillance, and reconnaissance are really support functions, while computers and communications are technology enablers. Logically, their inclusion would mean that other support functions such as weather reports, battlefield IFF (identification friend or foe), navigation services, and logistics should also be considered in any design of a joint command and control system.

substantial advantages from doing so, and that military power is most affordable when it rests upon a solid civilian economic base. We need only think of the centuries during which the British navy and the British merchant marine supported each other's leading positions, the exploitation of railroads by the Union during the Civil War, or the conversion of the U.S. automobile industry in World War II to the mass production of armored divisions.

However, the potential of the RMA — the potential for this commercially available IT to further improve C2 — while reasonably well understood, has not been fully realized. The United States has an enormous opportunity today to exploit its leadership in commercial information technologies in order to sustain affordable U.S. military power well into the future. If we do not seize this opportunity, we must worry that other nations may do so, at least in some selected aspects, thereby bypassing the existing U.S. lead in the military technology of the twenty-first century. One purpose of this chapter is to address how C2 can be enhanced and made "joint" through improving the DOD management of technological opportunities.

The rest of this introductory section outlines three salient characteristics of the Revolution in Military Affairs: it is incomplete, it has vast potential, and it has two sides — increased vulnerability comes with increased capability. Then, to promote a full understanding of the overall problem, the chapter provides a brief discussion of the evolutionary nature of joint C2 and the complexity of joint operations. It describes some lessons learned from past endeavors in joint acquisition and operations, and presents a set of recommendations on C2. A discussion of "cyber information operations" follows, with specific recommendations that focus on the different demands of computer network attack and computer network defense. The chapter concludes with recommendations to address the inescapable need for expert talent: the human factor that is crucial to the success of C2 and information operations.

THE REVOLUTION IS INCOMPLETE

A key example of a C2 technology that has created the RMA is the Global Positioning System (GPS). GPS virtually eliminates the age-old inability of troops in motion to know exactly where they are; it enables precision strike by autonomous weapons; and it allows a greatly expanded range of operational concepts and tactics in all terrain types. Precision strike, the first offshoot of the RMA to be applied in actual battle, is based upon information technology: databases, data fusion, networks and communication, navigation by means of GPS, visualization, and collaboration technologies. Precision strike was used to devastating advantage in DESERT STORM, with an impact analogous to the invention of the longbow, gunpowder, or the machine gun. Each brought about a change in range and lethality of weapons that enabled a dramatic change in combat tactics.

The overwhelming U.S. victory in DESERT STORM attests to the advantage of leading in the development and adoption of IT. The United States used GPS to guide cruise missiles precisely against air defense targets in the initial stages, thereby giving the allied forces immediate control of the enemy air space. A network of intelligence sensors located the enemy positions and movements, detected SCUD launches, identified moving targets, and found downed pilots. An enormous communications infrastructure sent this information ricocheting between support organizations in the continental United States (CONUS) and C2 in the field. Satellite imagery created thousands of highly accurate maps of Iraq. In essence, Iraq was blind and ineffective without IT-enabled C2, while the United States was nearly omniscient and therefore triumphant.

However, the penetration of IT into U.S. forces is incomplete and inconsistent, which leads to many time-consuming *ad hoc* arrangements in the field. True joint C2 requires not only that the force components from the various services be able to communicate with the Joint Task Force (JTF) headquarters, but that they also have effective tactical communications among each other. Mission planning systems and logistics tracking systems must be able to exchange information across service lines; for example, access to the Air Tasking Order should not require resorting to paper, as in DESERT STORM and Kosovo. Air defense capabilities from multiple services must cooperate closely in real time if friendly airspace is to be protected and fratricide avoided.

While the commercial world thrives on the basis of IT that enables the exchange of information among systems owned by separate companies — business-to-business commerce — jointness in military C2 has not yet been fully realized at the tactical level. As shown in Kosovo, many of the problems that plagued DESERT STORM still exist. Fundamental changes in command and control and fundamental changes to the joint acquisition of C2 systems are required to take full advantage of IT.

At the most basic level, commercial IT enables a new approach to what the defense community has termed "systems of systems," also called the enterprise. The system-of-systems approach knits together systems that were developed separately. With modern IT, the collection of systems can approach a single enterprise view with interoperable databases, functions, and user interfaces.

THE POTENTIAL OF RMA

The most exciting possibility is that IT could enable the U.S. C2 system to evolve from its traditional hierarchical decision-making structure to a more flexible and more distributed form. We find this potential transformation easier to understand through an analogy to team sports. Traditional military operations can be compared to football, in which teams attempt to carry out fixed plays, carefully designed and rehearsed in advance. A single decision-maker determines which play is best in a given situation, and each player carries out its assigned role in accordance with previously received instructions.

Compare soccer or hockey, in which each player has a position assigned on the basis of the player's distinctive capabilities. Within the general guidelines of the position, each player decides for himself or herself what to do from moment to moment. Players maintain continuous "situation awareness," so that their decisions about what to do next are based on an understanding of where the other players are and what they are doing from moment to moment. Good players learn through practice how to anticipate each other's moves, so that a pass is successful not because the receiver is where a playbook says he or she should be, but because the receiver is where the passer has figured out he or she is most likely to go, given his or her skills and the tactical situation.

We believe that modern IT enables the construction of a C2 system that would allow the U.S. military to play "soccer" rather than "football," maximizing the flexibility of individual elements responding to a situation. Actions would be based upon IT-enabled situation awareness and well-understood doctrine, rather than on detailed plans or explicit orders. This vision of the future has been called "network-centric warfare" because decisions about how to act are based on shared information and collaborative decision-making supported by a network of communications, rather than on communications up and down a hierarchical structure.

The great advantage of network-centric C2 is that it increases agility. As the experience of successful electronic commerce shows, there are two varieties of agility, both important. The first enables the organization to gather and process information rapidly in order to make quick decisions. The commercial system in which computerized cash registers send data to a system that can order accelerated production of the goods in greatest demand has its analogy in the military "sensor-to-shooter" systems. In each case, the use of IT enables faster response because information moves laterally rather than up and down a hierarchy. The second type of agility allows the entity to respond effectively to unexpected events. In a commercial situation, this might mean using the network to reconfigure supply chains rapidly in response to unexpected price competition. Analogously, the military could plan operations in response to a scenario never previously considered, on the basis of the full range of capabilities of the available forces, rather than the limited number of options in the "playbook." If it turns out that the enemy did not do what we had anticipated, or the weather did not follow our prediction, or our intelligence was not 100 percent correct, a network-centric C2 system could enable us to react much more rapidly to the unexpected opportunity or unexpected threat.

TWO SIDES TO RMA

IT also has its vulnerabilities, as evident in recent well-publicized hacker events. The pervasive use of IT and the ubiquity of computers and networks expose the C2 system to a new form of attack. Computer network attack (CNA) can take the form of denial of service, exploitation of the data within individual computers and throughout the network, or deception — actual alteration of the data within the computers and the networks, unbeknownst to the U.S. forces relying on the data.

Thus, the IT revolution can have two major impacts on warfare. First, it can transform the battlefield by solving the age-old problem of integrated, joint C2. This implies putting IT to work to allow rapid, distributed, accurate, and effective decision-making. Second, it can create a new battlefield: the cyber battlefield. To the extent that both sides utilize IT, each is exposed to computer network attack. To the extent that they are exposed, both must protect themselves from attack through computer network defense (CND). The United States must learn how to conduct both offensive and defensive information operations. This chapter addresses both of these impacts in turn.

Joint Command and Control: From Interoperability to Integration to Interdependence

The first step toward a genuinely joint C2 system that fully leverages the potential of IT is *interoperability*. Movement in this direction is well under way. The services have come to recognize that each C2 system must share information with the C2 systems of other services. This recognition has led to some standardization of protocols and data formats that allow the systems to exchange data, or at least enable users to view the data.

As they share more data more frequently, the services will recognize the advantages of further integration. An *integrated* system stores data only once, and does not duplicate functions. The individual service systems will access the same databases, and each service will be responsible for maintaining only the data that its own systems generate, avoiding the problems of data synchronization and integrity that plague systems today.

As the systems become integrated and the services learn to trust and depend on each other's systems, *interdependence* will evolve. Concepts of operations will change, eliminating systems from one service's inventory as it begins to deploy only with support from another service that supplies the eliminated function.

For example, tactical signals intelligence (SIGINT) is inherently a joint function. The sharing of intelligence data among the services creates a more complete picture of the threat and disposition of enemy forces. Today, tactical intelligence is provided by service-unique assets, such as surveillance aircraft from the services including the Air Force's RIVET JOINT, the Army's Guardrail, and the Navy EP-3 systems. While each of these systems individually satisfies some service-unique requirements, the bulk of the data collected is common to all services.

Years ago, at the prodding of the Office of the Secretary of Defense (OSD) and the Commanders-in-Chief (CINCs), the service-unique systems were made interoperable through the establishment of several processing centers and distribution networks. Now, anyone with a properly keyed satellite communications receiver has access to the combined data streams from the service-unique collection assets. The good news at this stage is that all users have a more complete set of SIGINT intercept data. The bad news is that this simple rebroadcast distribution creates redundancies, ambiguities, and correlation problems for every end user.

The Integrated Broadcast Service (IBS) program just entering development (again at the prodding of OSD and the CINCs) embodies the move toward the second step: integration of tactical SIGINT information. The primary goal of the IBS program is to create an integrated tactical SIGINT information management and dissemination service and an information repository based on processing inputs from service-unique as well as national intelligence assets. IBS would then distribute information from this repository to end users based on predefined profiles and knowledge of the bandwidth available to each user. The information distributed would thus be tailored automatically to end-user needs, free of the former duplications and discrepancies.

Possible evolution beyond IBS is, of course, conjectural, but might proceed as follows, with an emphasis on efficient data collection, rather than on efficient distribution. IBS central processing of SIGINT data would give rise to insights as to which sources provide the most accurate, timely, or detailed data under which circumstances. These insights would then begin to shape the tasking of these collection assets. The individual services would become more willing to concentrate on collecting more of "what they are good at," confident that the data they do not collect themselves would be available from the integrated information repository. As their confidence grew, the services would allocate their development and operations and maintenance resources to areas where their needs were not being met, so that overlap of SIGINT system assets would dwindle, along with the associated budgetary demands. Funds released would be used to increase capability and strengthen the defense-in-depth capability.

If we generalize from this example, we see that *interoperability* stems from the recognition that data sharing has advantages; *integration* comes from recognition of the need for further efficiency, speed, and collective application of resources; and *interdependence* evolves from trust and establishes optimal relationships for mission execution. The example also illustrates that each of these stages of evolution — interoperability, integration, and interdependence — involves two distinct processes: first, discovery of requirements and incremental improvement of the systems supporting the current concepts of operation, and second, radical change, with the creation of new concepts of operation enabled by the use of new technologies. It is important to recognize both of these processes and to manage them and their interrelations in developing joint C2. In fact, proper management to spur more rapid progress in the command and control of inherently joint activities may well require a separate organization dedicated to joint mission analysis, one that can experiment with roles and functions for each of the services within the context of an overall joint mission.

A PERSPECTIVE ON THE DIFFICULTIES

The fact that there are four separate services can create great difficulties for joint C2. The joint C2 system can only be configured from C4ISR system "building blocks" acquired and fielded by the individual services and Defense agencies. Interoperability becomes a constant challenge and, as noted above, evolving doctrine — and RMA expectations — go beyond interoperability, demanding integration and even interdependence.

The need exists, then, to ensure that the service- or agency-provided "building blocks" can not only support the parent service or agency needs, but also be an effective part of a coherent capability that transcends service or agency boundaries. Put differently, the building of the needed C2 capability is an inherently horizontal challenge in a world of inherently vertical service authorities and prerogatives which, while fully legitimate from service standpoints, create a tension between serving local interests and the broader common good as described here.

CASE STUDIES: SUCCESSES, FAILURES, LESSONS LEARNED

To illustrate the need for interdependence, we now turn to some real-world cases in which the United States has addressed the challenge of building and fielding inherently "horizontal" C2 capability, crossing organizational (and cultural) boundaries, and confronting inevitable existing controls and prerogatives in an inherently vertical world.

These cases are significant because they demonstrate that properly motivated activities, with adequate funding and personnel resources, can accomplish a great deal without major and painful structural changes to the organization of the DOD. We conclude this analysis of past activities with the lessons that lead to our recommendations.

Of course, no historical case has the full scope and complexity of the challenge addressed here; notions such as "transformation," "RMA," and "network-centric" joint warfare, taken seriously and broadly, go beyond our experience to date. However, these identifiable cases present, in microcosm, many of the difficulties of a "horizontal challenge in a vertical world."

The cases address both *infrastructure* and *application* (or operational mission/function) capabilities within the domain of C2: the DOD Intelligence Information System (DODIIS), an infrastructure success; the Single Integrated Air Picture (SIAP), an applications failure (to date); and the Special Operations Command (SOCOM), an important model of a functional command, with both an instructive history and unique features.

DOD Intelligence Information System (DODIIS)

The DOD Intelligence Information System, known as DODIIS, comprises a collection of people and information systems whose mission is to provide intelligence to the military command structure. It is a twenty-five-year-old worldwide network, originally based on Arpanet technology, which has developed into a modern intranet that allows the intelligence community to share information and collaborate on information production. Thus, DODIIS is not merely a system; it is also a process that has functioned and evolved for over two decades to improve information systems in response to the growing information needs of military commanders and the increased opportunities provided by the explosive advances in IT.

While DODIIS is far from perfect, it is fair to say that the process has worked. DODIIS has moved ahead as rapidly as the information technology that supports it; indeed, DODIIS was a leader in the deployment of a wide-area intranet. At the same time, DODIIS has remained largely interoperable across all of the defense intelligence community. If the overall military C2 system were as technologically agile, as well integrated, and as cost-effective as the DODIIS portion of it, we could be confident that it was capable of supporting the RMA.

A particularly striking success was the development and deployment in 1994 of a system known as "Intelink," which enabled unprecedented collaboration and sharing of information between U.S. intelligence organizations using the just-emerging World Wide Web technology. DODIIS had already created and maintained a worldwide secure network that was fully modern by commercial standards, and had built a community of technical experts who worked in close coordination with the producers and consumers of intelligence information. Funding procedures were in place that allowed a response to an opportunity without years of effort to define a "requirement." For these reasons, the community was able to deploy an intelligence equivalent of the World Wide Web within six months of the time that browser technology advanced to the point where this was possible.

The success of DODIIS has resulted from several factors. First, DODIIS has always supported the Defense Intelligence Agency (DIA) system of "delegated production," in which intelligence analysts located at the various major commands around the world are responsible for generating intelligence products relevant to the commands they serve. Thus, for example, analysts at U.S. European Command produced estimates of the Soviet order of battle in Europe, while analysts at the Strategic Air Command (later Strategic Command) produced estimates of the strategic nuclear threat. These analysts used data from national intelligence systems as well as theater systems, and had to supply their products to DIA. This created a continuing need for interoperability between DODIIS systems at the commands and DODIIS systems at DIA headquarters — not simply connectivity, but interoperability at the data element level. Two points deserve emphasis here. Interoperability was not just desirable, but essential, if the DODIIS users were to do their jobs. Also, interoperability was used and thus tested on a daily basis, not only during occasional conflicts or exercises.

Second, most DODIIS systems have been funded through the General Defense Intelligence Program (GDIP) rather than through the ordinary service budgets. This funding mechanism had three desirable impacts. First, while the GDIP as a whole must compete annually with weapons systems, operations costs, etc., for funding, individual items of value to DODIIS had to compete for funding only with other intelligence capabilities, and decisions were made by a staff that understood the value of DODIIS. Second, when funding shortfalls or technical difficulties required that some DODIIS requirements go unmet, the decisions on what to buy (or what not to buy) were made by a joint function rather than by a service, so that interoperability was less likely to be sacrificed. Third, when several systems with similar functions were available or under development by several different organizations, it was politically possible to choose a "best of breed" and insist that other systems migrate toward it.

Third, DODIIS systems were usually built, maintained, and used by a relatively small community of government and Federally Funded Research and Development Center (FFRDC) personnel who came to know each other and understand one another's perspectives. Regular meetings to address DODIIS issues enhanced this shared understanding.

Fourth, the leadership of DODIIS (including, significantly, the GDIP managers who controlled the money) believed in change, taking the attitude that "new technology represents opportunity" rather than "if it ain't broke, don't fix it" or "set requirements carefully and then leave people alone to allow them to meet the requirements." This leadership helped counter the risk that the small community of DODIIS experts would become responsive to each other's preferences rather than to the needs of the warfighters.

As a result, the system for managing DODIIS relied upon frequent incremental changes and the sharing across organizations of solutions to problems. This helped to keep DODIIS responsive to changing technological opportunities as well as changing user needs. It also provided a correction to the tendency of technical improvements to disrupt the interoperability of systems that change at different rates. It is symptomatic of this management approach that a revolutionary change — Intelink — was introduced as a rapidly and cheaply developed prototype, which then became operational in response to user demand. It is equally symptomatic that DODIIS standards were called a "reference model" rather than treated as something graven in stone that could dictate every decision.

Single Integrated Air Picture (SIAP)
For more than four decades, the U.S. military has been struggling to create a "single integrated air picture" — that is, a situation in which all U.S. forces concerned with a given region of airspace can know (and agree on) the track of each object flying there. The objective of

the SIAP is, informally, "a single track on each piece of metal in the sky." Despite years of effort, this objective has never been achieved.

Obtaining adequate data on everything flying in the airspace requires multiple sensors. Translating the raw data from these sensors into accurate tracks for airborne objects requires multiple communications links, multiple computer systems, and multiple command posts. But in practice, these multiple sensors and multiple data processing arrangements produce conflicting, competing, confusing, and redundant information. The fact that these sensors and processing systems are developed and owned by separate services compounds the formidable technical problems.

The crux of the matter is that no single sensor is perfect. Sensors and the associated communications and computers are designed with specific purposes in mind, and hence all of them see some things better than other things. Consider an enemy aircraft that is sensed by three different systems. One system may provide the most accurate information about its location, another about the type of aircraft, and a third about its velocity. If the data from all three systems are combined correctly, then we know what we need to know. If they are combined incorrectly, we may believe there are two or even three enemy aircraft — or worse still, two enemy aircraft and one "unknown" aircraft that might be friendly. The failure to obtain a reliable SIAP has three serious consequences: first, the failure to detect enemy activity early enough (for example, in using a ship-borne radar meant to cue a land-based interceptor missile); second, the risk of fratricide through misidentification of aircraft, or the risk of failing to attack an enemy aircraft due to fear of fratricide; and third, the inability to prosecute a battle on the basis of the clearest possible knowledge of what is going on in the battlespace.[2]

The failures that undermine interoperability have been called the "five deadly sins." They are:

• the lack of a common geospatial reference frame;

2. This ability is central to achieving "information superiority," a concept originally developed in a Joint Staff publication entitled *Joint Vision 2010* (Washington, D.C.: U.S. Joint Chiefs of Staff, 1996), and since used throughout the DOD to guide the evolution of C2 capabilities. The concept has been reaffirmed in the recent publication of *Joint Vision 2020* (Washington, D.C.: U.S. Joint Chiefs of Staff, July 2000).

- the lack of a uniform method for aligning platforms with true north;

- the lack of a common time reference among the platforms;

- the inability to correlate tracks from a local sensor with those from remote sensors; and

- the limited ability to use existing intelligence data to assist in the interpretation of observed data.

Each of the services has largely solved the first three problems — geospatial frame, compass alignment, and common time reference — for its own systems, but each has a different solution. The fourth and fifth issues — correlating data from local and remote sensors, and use of existing intelligence for interpretation — pose technical difficulties, but to achieve a SIAP, the tactical data links that carry and process the sensor information would have to be fully interoperable. Thus the services must arrive at common solutions to these technical problems as well.

In 1994, the Assistant Secretary of Defense for Command, Control, and Communications (ASD C3I) promulgated a standard called "Link 16" and directed the services to move toward implementing it. However, the interoperability problem has proven too complex to be dealt with by means of a single standard. At present, the Link 16 standard consists of several hundred pages of detailed technical information, but it still requires interpretation and technical judgments. Because no organization or mechanism exists to coordinate the judgments made by the many different programs implementing Link 16, different systems comply with the standard in different ways and cannot exchange data well enough to achieve a SIAP.

Recognizing that the individual requirements for individual platforms and systems do not include adequate demands for interoperability across systems and across services, the Joint Chiefs have created a Capstone Requirements Document (CRD) to address the need for interoperability. The initial CRD was relatively general in nature, and in 1999 DOD made an effort to centralize the funding needed to implement it under the sponsorship of the Ballistic Missile Defense Organization and the Joint Theatre Air and Missile Defense Organization. The services objected that this would impinge on their responsibility to procure systems under Title X of the U.S. Code.[3] In response, the Joint Chiefs are drafting a more detailed Capstone Requirements Document.

However, the experience of several decades suggests that the critical decisions will be the engineering trade-offs necessarily made in the course of developing or modernizing any state-of-the-art system. At any given moment in time, the constraints of technology, budget, and schedule always require that some performance objectives be compromised in order to achieve others. A more detailed Capstone Requirements Document is unlikely to change the priorities of the individual system program offices, which tend to assign the highest priority to functionality, the second to interoperability with other systems of the same service, and only the third to joint interoperability.

Thus, efforts to attain a SIAP have two shortcomings. First, they lack a system that would drive those who make these trade-offs to place a sufficiently high priority on the requirement for interoperability with systems developed by other services, even at the expense of functionality desired by the service developing the platform or sensor. Second, there is no mechanism by which departures from interoperability are observed and recognized very quickly, so that they can be remedied without extensive redesign.

Special Operations Command (SOCOM)

The U.S. Special Operations Command (SOCOM) was created in 1987 by congressional action, which also gave this command its own acquisition authority, independent of the services. Congress did this, over the objections of the services, because of two perceptions: first, that the services never had given and never would give adequate priority to procuring equipment designed for the particular needs of the special forces rather than the needs of the "mainstream" forces; and second, that the debacle of the Iranian hostage rescue mission had resulted from the inability of the special operations forces of the various services to make joint plans and conduct joint training. Taking advantage of this unusual degree of autonomy, SOCOM has succeeded in forging a generally effective C2 system. The operations conducted by SOCOM units have demonstrated that joint C2 has become a reality in SOCOM.

---

3. Title X of the U.S. Code is the federal law that gives the services the responsibility to organize, train, and equip their forces.

SOCOM has from its inception placed a very high priority on understanding the needs of the regional CINCs who actually employ the special forces that SOCOM trains and equips. This has led to a heavy emphasis on making its C2 systems fully interoperable with those of the CINCs, even at the expense of standardization. For example, a special operations unit that moves from the Pacific Command to the European Command may require two full days to modify its organic C2 systems (applications on ruggedized laptop computers, etc.). If the bad news is that this is necessary, the good news is that it is possible and commonly done.

Consequently, SOCOM's organic C2 is effective, but expensive. Today, a decade and a half after its inception, SOCOM is engaged in a major effort to rationalize its C2 systems, retaining their effectiveness and their interoperability with each other and with the systems of the "mainstream" forces, while reducing their cost.

The main lesson we draw from the SOCOM experience comes as no surprise: a high degree of C2 interoperability and effectiveness is achievable if an organization is guided by joint priorities. Whereas the services procuring C2 systems for mainstream forces usually have other, higher priorities than interoperability with the other services or interoperability with all of the regional commands, SOCOM's priorities have been driven by its structure as a joint organization, and its recognition that it must retain the political support of the regional CINCs to survive. Congress has been supportive of these priorities, and indeed has frequently added funds to the SOCOM budget requested by the President. Like DODIIS, SOCOM has also benefited from being a relatively small community, within which it is possible to attain and sustain mutual understanding.

Finally, another contributing factor is that SOCOM's forces have frequently been involved in real operations against real enemies. SOCOM likes to think of itself as the "911" of the U.S. military, and considers a high state of readiness and a high operational tempo to be normal. One consequence is that SOCOM's C2 systems are frequently tested in operational conditions, thereby ensuring that any failures of C2 interoperability will be noticed and also that such failures will be remedied on an urgent basis. This is another parallel with DODIIS.

LESSONS LEARNED

The first lesson we draw from these cases is that joint C2 is never easy but is clearly worth the effort. An effective horizontal function in a vertical world requires continuing effort, and success will never be complete or final, but much can be achieved. In addition, we can identify from these case studies a set of more specific factors that seem to have facilitated success.

"Continuous" Use Through Day-to-Day Operations and Frequent Exercises and Tests

C2 capability — as built from C4ISR building blocks — has at least two important attributes. First, it has no utility until combined with people and procedures in an operational context to perform a mission. Second, its set-up and operation are complex, and often "the devil is in the details." The first point drives a need for continuous use as part of continuous learning, leading to co-evolution of the systems, the people, and the doctrine. The second point also suggests the need for "mission thread testing," that is, testing the complex chain of systems that must operate together effectively to accomplish a mission.

A Substantive "Blueprint" for Centralized Guidance and Decentralized Execution

The notion of a "blueprint," substantive but not prescriptive in detail, is crucial. Decentralized execution within a common framework established by such a blueprint has established itself as a formula for success in at least some cases. It allows local flexibility to accommodate local needs, and enables innovation. As a corollary, the advocate of the blueprint must engage in follow-up activities with the developers responsible for the building blocks.

Dedicated Funds for at Least Core Activities and Implementations

Dedicated funds under the control of the organization responsible for the mission are a prerequisite to success in order to orchestrate and integrate CINC, service, and agency efforts successfully. This need not involve control of all funds in the domain (e.g., C4ISR), but should include control of funds to support core activities, such as exercise, experimentation, and interoperability or integration "augmentations" to CINC, service, or agency activities.

Technical Capability Committed to the Horizontal Challenge

There is a compelling need for substantial, broad-based technical capability within or attached to the organization responsible for the mission and for integrating the CINC, service, and agency efforts. This technical resource must be structured and provided with appropriate incentives to assure that it has no other interest than that of the government as a whole. This capability is needed for formulating a technically based blueprint, informing budgetary and programmatic decisions, and brokering user needs to developers.

Adding Value and Building Trust

It is crucial that the central authority take a strong user-support orientation, add value for the users, and develop trust over time. When pushing for the "common good" across organizational boundaries, two key ingredients for adding value are, first, appreciating and struggling to accommodate legitimate local interests, and second, providing funding for "common good" investments that would otherwise be viewed as unfunded mandates. If this is done well, another essential ingredient for success is created: a sense of shared mission and community.

Interoperability is a Process, Rather than a Decision

There is no such thing as a complete "specification"; in fact, total reliance on completely specified requirements will result in failure. Interpretation and interaction are needed for the ideas embodied in the requirements to evolve. Moreover, enforcement by dictum will not work; the community is too large, the topics too complicated, and the failure paths too many to issue "orders" as mandates and simply expect them to be executed.

RECOMMENDATIONS

We have outlined the problems plaguing joint C2: problems of inadequate readiness, the difficulty of achieving horizontal integration in a vertically funded world, and delays in implementing technological and doctrinal innovation due to a turgid requirements-based acquisition process. These issues could be alleviated if:

- a worldwide Joint Task Force (JTF) C2 baseline system configuration existed;

- the baseline C2 system evolved through continuous daily use and interaction between the developers and the users in a requirements discovery process;

- the commands and services practiced assembling, adapting, and operating these joint C2 systems for JTF deployment scenarios;

- the component systems of the C2 system shared an integrated technical infrastructure;

- the service systems that comprise the JTF C2 system were designed from the outset to be more adaptable and interoperable;

- detailed joint mission analysis developed a blueprint for integrated and interdependent service systems, leading to true specialization for service development activities, rather than today's redundancy; and

- acquisition agencies had a defined wartime support role and trained for deployment with C2 systems.

To achieve these ends we recommend four major organizational and management changes. U.S. Joint Forces Command (USJFCOM) looms large in these recommendations. The recommendation call for taking further steps along a path that began with giving the U.S. Atlantic Command (ACOM) significant functional responsibility in 1993 for training and providing CONUS-based forces to support the needs and operations of other CINCs. Effective in October 1998, ACOM was assigned responsibility for the DOD's Joint Experimentation Program.[4] This program calls for a broad range of experimentation activities to explore new ways of fighting using IT as a key enabler. That same year, a number of important joint activities were attached to them.[5] In October 1999, USACOM was rechartered as the U.S. Joint

4. Joint Experimentation provides for exploring and validating future joint operations and concepts that will drive changes to doctrine, organization, training and education, material, leadership, and people (known collectively as DOTMLP).

5. These joint activities included the Joint Warfighting Center (joint training and doctrine), the Joint Battle Center (joint C2 capability and interoperability), and the Joint Communications Support Element (rapid-response deployable communications in support of crisis and contingency operations).

Forces Command, with a broad set of responsibilities for supporting joint operations, including that of Joint Force Integrator.[6] However, these programs are add-ons to existing service and CINC C2 systems, not integral parts of them. The recommendations that follow call for a major increase in both the role and the responsibility of USJFCOM. They would give USJFCOM the responsibility, authority, and money to create a joint C2 capability and to test and train with it prior to deployment. The result would be a USJFCOM with a dominantly functional role, a strong focus on joint C2, and the teeth to carry out its joint force integration role.

Put a Single Organization — USJFCOM — in Charge of Joint C2 and Make It Accountable

DOD should make USJFCOM the supporting CINC for C2, and strengthen its role as Joint Force Integrator. When a regional CINC requires a joint operation, USJFCOM would be responsible for rapidly augmenting, assembling, delivering, and operating a properly tailored joint C2 capability at the operational level of command (CINCs and Joint Task Forces). Today a joint C2 capability does not come into existence until troops have deployed and solved all the interoperability problems, weeks or months later. Under this recommendation, one organization would have the responsibility for creating and enhancing the joint C2 capability during peacetime so that the capability is ready when needed.

Stated differently, the ability to exercise joint C2 effectively can be thought of as an issue of readiness. Like other dimensions of readiness, it requires constant effort, and it costs money. But it is essential if the United States is to have an actual rather than merely a potential military capability. Thus it is necessary to give a single organization the authority and accountability for developing horizontal joint C2 across the existing vertical realms.

As a result of the recommendations that follow, USJFCOM would be able to provide core suites of deployable C2 capability for rapid-response, early-entry operations, which would complement the communications capabilities of the Joint Communications Support Element; deploy rapid-response, expert C4ISR "tiger teams," com-

---

6. The 1999 Unified Command Plan (UCP-99) assigned the rechartered USACOM as USJFCOM.

prising USJFCOM personnel, service experts, or contractor personnel, to support the inevitable adaptations required during real-world situations; and provide tools and trained personnel to support a CINC or JTF commander with the crucial task of configuring and managing joint networks.

Create an Office in USJFCOM to Exercise and Experiment Continuously, to Ensure that Joint C2 Systems Work and are Ready when Needed

To make more rapid progress in joint warfighting, and to stay ahead of others who have the same access to emerging IT, the U.S. military must increase the rate of evolution by creating many more opportunities for the services to experiment and train in joint situations. Identification of requirements and changes in joint concepts of operations can occur more rapidly if organizational and management structures exist that enable the services to experiment, exercise, train, and equip for C2 functions frequently and together. With the right management structures and leadership the services, their systems, and their concepts of operations can evolve together from traditionally vertical service C2 systems into an interdependent horizontal dimension that supports inherently joint functions. After all, that is how they will fight.

Today, in a crisis, the service-unique components of the C2 system are deployed to the field and connected in *ad hoc* arrangements that attempt to fit the situation. The adaptation is often limited by the incomplete knowledge that the deployed forces have of these systems. In many cases contractors must accompany the systems to the field to make them work or to adapt them to the specific situation. New systems, not yet fielded but near enough to production to be useful, are also rushed to the battlefield with contractor support in the expectation that they will provide some additional advantage (as, for example, with JSTARS, a ground surveillance system, in the Gulf War). To complicate the situation further, coalition partners throw their own systems into the mix.

This chaos in times of crisis will never be eliminated, but it can be managed more effectively and can produce a more effective C2 system faster. To this end, we propose an activity that is a cross between an exercise and an experiment, for which we have coined the name "expercise." It would be both an experiment, in which many changes to C2 are tried and failure is allowed, and an exercise, in which warfighters are trained in assembling, adapting, and operating C2 systems. The exercise would consist of operating a joint C2 system in a scenario-driven environment on a daily basis. Warfighters would operate this system in realistic scenarios, and they would be accompanied by and interact with the IT specialists who developed the C2 systems. The warfighters and developers would incrementally improve the C2 systems by working out the technical interoperability problems in the "exercise" environment rather than in an actual crisis. They would also discover requirements through constant use of the system, learning how to make C2 processes more efficient and how to fix persistent interoperability issues. Constant use would be critically important. Like F-15 fighters who train daily to be the best pilots they can be, C2 operators must use their systems daily to become proficient at C2 and understand how the supporting systems can be improved.

A continuous exercise would mean the dedication of expensive resources — people and equipment — that must be funded and staffed properly. We therefore recommend establishment of an Exercise Office, located within USJFCOM, that would be responsible for:

- working with the regional CINCs to devise a range of CINC operational plans, and with the services to define a C2 system structure to implement the operation;

- creating a JTF C2 system that supports these operational plans;

- providing the means by which the JTF C2 system can measure performance of C2 functions and monitor their continuous improvement;

- managing the execution of these regional CINC-based scenarios, using the JTF C2 systems staffed with warfighters and developers described above;

- conveying the requirements learned from these exercises to the service acquisition agencies for implementation;

- appointing a service as the executive agent for the acquisition, on behalf of all the services, of a joint system for any entirely new capability that might be discovered;

- developing modeling, simulation, and instrumentation as needed;

- maintaining updated descriptions of the configurations; and

- establishing active liaison with all other joint exercise activities to garner the lessons learned and apply them to joint C2 acquisition.

If successful, the exercise process will create joint C2 systems for each CINC that offer good starting points for adaptation to a specific deployment. Furthermore, and perhaps more important, the staff running the exercise process will form a cadre of personnel trained to adapt the C2 system quickly to new situations.

The normal exercise would look like a command post exercise but should be augmented periodically with live exercises, in which the equipment and troops are actually deployed. The military organization supporting a given exercise must be complemented by a dedicated, strong technical work force on the order of a hundred people, with attributes that we discuss below. The exercise emulates for C2 the Intelink/DODIIS model of development, in which intelligence systems were used every day and thus evolved rapidly. The exercise must use scenarios and simulations, unlike Intelink, to create an environment for daily use, but only with such constant use can interoperability issues be resolved and requirements discovered and implemented. Infrequent exercises would allow the use of "work-arounds" that are effective only for the short duration of the exercise. In the exercise, by contrast, requirements would be derived from discussion between the users who are the real warfighters (rather than their representatives) and the developers. The exercise organization would then work closely with the service that would acquire and maintain the system to implement the requirement.

Use of the exercise would institutionalize, in the joint environment, the successes of the individual services. Examples of such successes include the following:

- The introduction of collaboration technology into the Air Force's Expeditionary Force Experiment dramatically decreased timelines for creating the Air Tasking Order by turning serial processes into parallel processes.[7] The reduction was accomplished by installing software on existing workstations that allowed geographically

---

7. The Air Force Expeditionary Force Exercise is an annual live-fly event in which the Air Force field deploys its C2 systems and experiments with new technologies and new concepts of operations.

separated individuals to work cooperatively and synchronously across a network.

- The Navy's command ship, the *Coronado*, was designed from the start to be reconfigured. Experimental systems are installed and exercised at sea, and then removed, refined, or made part of the operational system after the exercise.

- The Army's Task Force XXI experiment used "quick and dirty" installation of situation awareness displays on individual combat vehicles, along with digital tactical networks and collaborative technology for intelligence analysis, to prove the effectiveness of total situation awareness on the digitized battlefield.

In all of these service activities, innovation has been encouraged, technology inserted, and "failure" allowed. In none of them was the test community hovering around to pronounce the activity dead because some predetermined quantitative measure was not achieved. Instead, the services discovered requirements and took advantage of technological opportunities, emulating the commercial practice of shipping a product, learning from its users and the competition, and continually improving the product. The users who were trained on the systems and the developers who could adapt them teamed to make the systems work and to improve their functionality continuously.

Exercises would lead to constant interaction between the developers and the warfighters, who could thus continuously refine the interoperability, adaptability, and integration of the system and the concepts of operations prior to deployment. This model, in which discovering what the warfighter needs will lead to incremental improvement, more closely resembles the commercial relationship between marketing and product development, where new versions of products are churned out at a pace measured in months rather than years. In some cases, an exercise will identify an entirely new capability, and the exercise organization would appoint an executive agent to acquire it.

Establish a Joint C2 Blueprint Office Within JFCOM

The bottom-up, incremental improvement process recommended above, as well as the ongoing joint experimentation activity which seeks operational innovation enabled by technology, must be complemented by an activity which defines a C2 target architecture toward which to strive. We recommend that this be implemented in the form of a Joint C2 Blueprint Office that would be charged with defining and developing a common, adaptive, and agile C2 infrastructure, and with driving the evolution of service-provided mission systems toward the effective and efficient support of joint operations. The activity would focus on providing a robust and rich set of information services that respond to and support operational innovation, maximize the exploitation of rapidly advancing commercial IT, and provide the foundation for extensive data networking down to the tactical level. The mission capability effort would be focused on assuring that service C2 system developments support and respond joint operations needs, as defined by the top-down joint experimentation activity and the bottom-up exercise process, as well as by the results of service multilateral efforts.

The Office of the Assistant Secretary of Defense for Command, Control, and Communications and the Joint Staff (J-6) have adopted the concept of a Global Information Grid (GIG), and are implementing it as a framework for guiding service and agency developments. Operational and system architecture efforts have begun. The current focus is on information system infrastructure. These efforts are applauded. However, responsiveness to the needs of the joint warfighter would be substantially strengthened if responsibility for C2 capability evolution were put more in the hands of an operational command. Additional funding leverage is also needed if substantial progress is to be made in orchestrating the programs of the services and agencies.

The Blueprint Office recommendation targets these shortfalls. The office would be responsible for experimenting with commercial technologies and guiding how systems should be implemented with standards that enable interoperability and integrated systems. The underlying architecture would rely on the capabilities provided by standards-based commercial technologies that allow and promote data sharing (e.g., web-based technologies such as extensible markup language [XML] and application service provider models). The Blueprint Office would be responsible for understanding the technical trajectory of the commercial world and its implications for new systems and legacy systems. It would test new technologies and develop guidelines for program managers of new systems and legacy systems, to enable as much inherent interoperability among systems as possible. The architectures and guidance defined by this group would give the developers freedom to experiment in those areas of the technical architecture for which no single standard or solution is generally agreed upon among the commercial and military technical communities. From this diversity of approaches, clear winners would emerge and be included in new versions of the guidance.

In parallel with this focus on developing the blueprint for a common technical infrastructure, the Blueprint Office would build upon its JFCOM foundation (doctrine, training, experimentation/exercise, deployable capabilities) and work across the broader community to conceive, test, verify, and assure the acquisition of capabilities that support joint operations. The focus would be on a robust, modern infrastructure and mission systems that enable and support innovative doctrinal changes. Specifically, the Blueprint Office would, first, define concepts and drive the acquisition of C4ISR infrastructure and mission systems that would not otherwise evolve in response to the formal requirements process or the continuous joint exercise activity, but would be driven by potentially radical changes in joint warfighting concepts of operation emerging from joint experimentation or by new commercially based technology applied in innovative ways. Second, within this process, the Blueprint Office would identify common capabilities needed by CINCs or services whose acquisition could best be, but are not yet, managed centrally. The Blueprint Office would identify management options in such a case, such as a single service serving as the DOD's executive agent for acquiring particular capabilities. Finally, the Blueprint Office would place emphasis on maximizing adaptability and assuring interoperability in the technical infrastructure, by providing guidance regarding the design choices that the service acquisition agencies may make as they build and improve upon their systems.

This does not mean that the Blueprint Office would or should design a joint C2 system in detail as if it were simply a matter of specifying and executing. The lessons from past successes demonstrate that concepts of operations, system design, and implementations cannot be mandated or created top-down in organizations as large as the DOD or when problems as complex as C2 are involved. (See, on this point, Chapter 7.) The output of joint blueprint development should be minimally prescriptive but with appropriate incentives and enforcement provided for the fundamentals (e.g., adopting the Internet paradigm).

The Joint Blueprint Office thus would develop the concepts for a highly agile C2 system able to adapt to a given situation and theater across a wide range of scenarios and circumstances. The resulting infrastructure would enable radical changes: changes that would not occur automatically through the exercise process because of the attendant political problems associated with the adjustment of service responsibility. The Blueprint Office would work with JFCOM experimentation and recommended exercise activities, with the Joint Staff, and with the CINCs to identify the critical mission activities and functions that are inherently joint. Initially, a few inherently joint missions or capabilities, such as theater missile defense or the Single Integrated Air Picture (SIAP), would be identified as a basis for "mission thread" experimentation and analysis. The Blueprint Office would look for efficiencies enabled by technological innovation in C2, intelligence, or weapons systems, or by eliminating redundancies. This would be akin to the concept of disintermediation in Internet business models that eliminate "middlemen," whose functions are replaced by a more direct flow of information (as, for example, bookstores are disintermediated by Amazon.com); such concepts would be investigated in parallel within the Joint Experimentation program.

Returning to fundamentals, this recommendation is part of a larger mosaic whose objective is to place the responsibility, authority, and capability for joint C2 capability evolution — with exploitation of advanced IT as a central theme — into the hands of JFCOM, the warfighting command that has been given the Joint Force Integrator job, along with an important but incomplete set of tools for its accomplishment. The Blueprint Office, in concert with other elements of JFCOM and the broader community, would orchestrate an end-to-end process for C2 capability evolution, ranging from exploring new doctrine and concepts within the framework of the Joint Experimentation program, through analyzing C2 contributions to mission effectiveness, to driving service and agency acquisitions toward realizing the RMA. The notion of a Blueprint Office has been developed here to make the objectives, responsibilities, and activities tangible. Addressing the topic of whether such an "office," as such, would even appear on a JFCOM organization chart, and how it would relate to other DOD activities, would be an important next step if agreement could be reached on the basics. In any event, the recommended JFCOM blueprint activities would receive direction and ultimately derive delegated authority from both OSD — the Under Secretary for Acquisition, Technology and Logistics, and the Assistant Secretary for C3I in his or her capacity as Chief Information Officer — and the Joint Staff.[8]

Funding mechanisms as related to both enforcing and motivating all of this are addressed in the recommendation that follows. A later section deals with the other resource crucial to success: a skilled and dedicated workforce.

Centrally Fund Joint C2 Activities Through a New Joint C2 Integration Program Administered by CINC USJFCOM

Unfunded mandates for joint command and control would accomplish nothing. The money for the Expercise Office and the Joint Blueprint Office must come from a combination of a Joint C2 Integration Program, and the budgets for the services and the individual systems managed by the services. We propose the creation of such a new Integration Program, modeled after the General Defense Intelligence Program that provided the centralized funding that allowed DODIIS to succeed. The Commander-in-Chief of USJFCOM, as manager of the Integration Program, would balance the trade-offs internal to joint C2, free of service priorities and other entities competing for funds. He or she would annually allocate funds to requirements and recommend acquisition agencies. This funding would provide resources for the recommended new activities within JFCOM (the expercise process, the Blueprint Office) as well as for involvement in these activities by CINC and service C2 personnel and assets.

Additionally, this funding would be targeted on providing new or modified capabilities within service or agency programs to achieve the blueprint, thereby addressing the unfunded mandate issue. Much as the GDIP did for intelligence, it would create a C2 community, all

---

8. The Chief Information Officer (CIO) function was mandated by the Information Technology Management Reform Act of 1996 (P.L. 104-106). (This act and the Federal Acquisition Reform Act [FARA] of the same year are commonly referred to as the Clinger-Cohen Act.) It calls for a CIO position within each federal department or agency, and for performance-based management of IT investments and further streamlining of acquisition. The DOD ASD C3I is designated as the DOD CIO.

of whose members are dedicated to the same goal, with autonomy across the CINCs. This would allow each command to adapt the systems for its own situation and purpose. Ideas, architectures, and software developed centrally or by a CINC could be shared with and adapted by the other CINCs.

Thus, the Joint C2 Integration Program would fund the services' acquisition of joint requirements derived from exercises, as well as the exercise process itself, which needs funds for the exercise C2 systems, the USJFCOM personnel to operate them, and the regional CINC personnel to set CINC priorities, define scenarios, and judge usability. DOD has many activities underway to work on interoperable C2, some more effective than others. As this new process is implemented, DOD must examine the utility of these activities and either consolidate or eliminate them as appropriate.

Inherent in the exercise notion and funding model are two basic changes in the way systems are funded. The first change is that it allows managers to fund opportunity, not requirements. This notion is important; it is how commercial companies stay in business and prosper. When a new technology emerges, commercial companies invest in the opportunity to improve products, lower production costs, or extend themselves into a new business area. If the United States is to maintain a technological edge over adversaries, DOD must also be allowed to fund opportunity to speed the insertion of technology into defense systems. The Exercise Office and the Blueprint Office would have funding lines similar to the CINC Initiative funds to support experiments and the newly discovered requirements. Such unrestricted funding is not popular with Congress, but it is essential here in order to overcome one of the major obstacles to success: the funding handcuffs that hamper the acquisition community's agility to cope with rapidly changing technological opportunities.

The second change has to do with the funding cycle itself. No commercial company buys a network, maintains it until it cannot be maintained any longer, and then throws it away. Instead, companies have annual budgets to upgrade their networks and make trade-offs between maintenance activities and upgrades. As a GDIP-like funding source, the Integration Program would allow C2 systems to emulate this commercial practice. It would construct funding profiles that support incremental improvement of the software capabilities and recapitalization of the hardware on a reasonable schedule, and adapt them annually. In this way, the systems would improve faster, last longer, be better managed, and cost less. Again, this runs counter to current practice, and members of Congress would lose some ability to claim credit for new programs and new contracts in their states and districts because there would be fewer new starts. However, they would maintain oversight over how the money is spent.

These four recommendations — accountability, expercise, blueprint, funding — address the fundamental difficulties with rapidly evolving a robust, modern IT–enabled, joint C2 capability ready for rapid deployment. We now address the other side of the IT revolution — the cyber battlefield.

Cyber Information Operations

"Information operations" are defined in various ways throughout DOD, with different definitions offered by the services, CINCs, and agencies. The lack of an accepted lexicon has led to much confusion, and the diffusion of responsibility has led to duplication, inefficiency, and increased cost as well as missed opportunity. In this section, we address "cyber information operations" as a subset of information operations, defining the term to encompass the systems composed of computer networks used in critical warfighting operations, and not the general use of IT or the more traditional electronic countermeasures and counter-countermeasures. The discussion of the topic is divided into two portions, one concerned with so-called computer network defense (CND), and the other concerned with electronic attack through the use of techniques to disable, interrupt, or otherwise inhibit the enemy's use of its system, called computer network attack (CNA).

The previous section discussed the concept of network-centric warfare. This concept links weapons, sensors, and command centers as needed. The architecture permits components to be added or subtracted as circumstance change, and reach-back allows support centers and weapons that may be thousands of miles apart to operate in a single network. Therefore, CNA is directed not at a pre-specified set of facilities, hardware, or software, but at whatever is critical to the performance of a key warfighting function. CND must address the defense not just of the network as it functions today, but of all the configurations of the network that a commander might find useful.

COMPUTER NETWORK DEFENSE

Network-centric warfare offers dramatic advantages, but they carry with them the risk of a major loss of capability if the network is disrupted. The more the United States relies upon computer networks to get information to its warfighters, and the more our military concepts of operations exploit the advantages of having very good information, the more important it becomes to defend these computer networks.

In dealing with CND, we must distinguish between the "outsider" threat and the "insider" threat. Most of the effort in defensive technology has been devoted to dealing with the outsider — the hacker who seeks to penetrate the network or overwhelm it. The insider threat is potentially much more serious, because an individual with legitimate access to a critical node can easily disrupt the network, copy sensitive information, or (with greater difficulty) substitute false data for accurate data. The outsider threat requires technical solutions that involve the use of cryptography and related techniques whereas coping with the insider, while having technical aspects, puts demands on such practices as personnel assessments and periodic evaluations. (See the discussion of this issue in Chapter 6 by Ashton Carter.) In the commercial world, only the financial services industry has paid serious attention to the insider threat, driven by the principle that it should never be easy for its employees to steal money.

Constraints of budget and schedule mean that there are always trade-offs in building or upgrading an information system. Frequently a program manager must decide whether to spend time and money on improving system protection or instead on system functionality. In DOD, as in the commercial world, functionality is what sells a system, and therefore programs experience constant pressure to shortchange security and protection.

Within DOD, the current mechanism for ensuring that a cyber threat is given due consideration is the System Threat Assessment Report (STAR), a validated formal document that is intended to be reviewed within the acquisition process. However, because of the difficulty of validating cyber threat, the process is ineffective in stimulating program managers to spend money on countermeasures.

Knowledgeable observers know that electronic commerce is far too vulnerable to electronic attack. Such attacks will eventually take place in ways that could cause major companies to lose large sums of money, which will prompt industry to develop and deploy much stronger security measures than those in common use today. Through this process, the cost of effective security will decline as its availability increases. If this happens, DOD will of course purchase and make use of these new security technologies and products.

However, DOD cannot simply sit back and wait for industry to make network security affordable. First of all, with national security and the lives of our troops at stake, DOD cannot responsibly take the attitude that it must wait for a major disaster to create the demand for better security. Beyond that, DOD must assume that it confronts a far more sophisticated threat than that facing e-commerce. A foreign government bent on disrupting the critical warfighting networks of the United States can eventually obtain access to all the tools and techniques used by the hacker community, and it can develop additional CNA techniques that go beyond the hacker repertory.

A difficulty inherent in CND is that the attacker has the initiative, and the defender cannot know the time and place of the next attack. The standard military responses apply: vigilance and defense in depth. In the context of C2, defense in depth should include adopting the approach used by air traffic control. The designers of air traffic control systems know that bad weather will disrupt their systems, and that individual radars and computers will fail from time to time. They therefore design the overall system so that when failure or disruption occurs, there are procedures and systems already in place and fully tested that will permit continued operation even in a degraded mode. Air traffic control is designed so that even though bad weather or system failures may lead to delays, they do not compromise safety. C2 must be designed so that successful enemy attacks on our computer networks cause at most incremental losses of capability, but never a catastrophic failure.

COMPUTER NETWORK ATTACK

The ability to attack an enemy's critical computer networks will increase in importance as other countries modernize their warfighting information systems and move toward network-centric warfare. A critical characteristic of CNA, which creates numerous problems in planning its use, is its fragility. Many forms of CNA are most effective when the enemy does not realize that it is under attack, because they can readily be countered once the enemy learns exactly how the attack is being carried out. For this reason, research and experimentation into the techniques of CNA are very highly classified and tightly compartmentalized. We believe this has led to considerable duplication of effort within the DOD.

The fragility of most CNA techniques means that there is no way of knowing how effective they will be until they are tried. Consequently, DOD has an urgent requirement for techniques to assess the effectiveness of our attacks in near–real time. Furthermore, DOD must develop channels that will let our own commanders know the extent to which the enemy has been crippled by CNA, with minimal risk of leaking information that would cause the enemy to repair its systems.

A related problem is that the choice of CNA techniques will not always be easy. Suppose, as an illustration, that we have identified a communications channel through which enemy headquarters sends orders to its field commands. One method of CNA is to destroy or jam this communications channel at a critical moment in the conflict, decapitating the enemy just when it most needs effective C2. A second method is to listen in on the communications, feeding information to our own commanders about the enemy's intent. This would be less certain to work, but more effective if it did. A third method would be to introduce spurious communications into the C2 channel, leading the enemy to do what we want it to do. This would be the least certain, but the most effective if it succeeded. However, the successful use of any of these techniques may limit our options to attack the enemy's C2 communications channel, or others like it, in the future. Such choices should be made by the responsible parties in the DOD, but they may have difficulty in learning enough to make a timely and informed decision.

BALANCING CND AND CNA

There is an inherent conflict between the requirements for effective CND and the requirements for effective CNA. This conflict arises whenever we discover a potential vulnerability in a computer network. If we keep this vulnerability secret, and if a future enemy does not independently discover the vulnerability and protect against it, then we can exploit it for CNA. But if we develop a defense against the vulnerability and deploy it widely in our own networks, we make it highly likely that the future enemy will learn about the vulnerability and the defense, and we will be unable to use it for CNA. However, if a future enemy discovers this vulnerability independently, and we have done nothing to protect our own networks against it, the enemy can use it to attack us.

In principle, we should evaluate the likelihood that a future enemy will discover the vulnerability independently, and act accordingly. In practice, we tend to be overly proud of our own discoveries, and slow to predict that others may be just as clever. This leads to a bias toward CNA over CND. This bias is reinforced by the fact that CNA is much cheaper than CND; they require broadly similar research efforts, but deploying an attack capability is far cheaper than modifying extensive networks to eliminate a vulnerability. Moreover, there are many possible enemies if one looks far enough into the future, and they are at different levels of technical sophistication. Preserving the ability to attack a less sophisticated enemy (by not deploying our defenses against a promising attack mode) may leave us vulnerable to a more sophisticated enemy that is able to duplicate our research.

Realign Responsibility for CNA and CND

The role given to the Commander-in-Chief for Space (CINCSPACE) under the 1999 Unified Command Plan encompasses both CNA and CND.[9] The activities are clearly interrelated through the need to understand vulnerabilities and to deal with decisions that balance the needs of defense against the needs of intelligence. However, other serious considerations must also be taken into account in choosing how to allocate these responsibilities.

We recommend that CNA, a warfighter function, remain with a CINC — CINCSPACE — but that CND, which is an infrastructure development topic, be treated as a criterion to be considered by developers in the acquisition community. Policy for setting criteria for

---

9. The U.S. Space Command (USSPACECOM) was created in 1985 to advance and orchestrate the role of space assets and capabilities in support of national security interests. USSPACECOM coordinates the use of service assets and capabilities to perform missions ranging from launching and operating satellites to providing space-derived information to military commanders. The 1999 Unified Command Plan (UCP-99) assigned responsibility for CND to USSPACECOM effective October 1, 1999, with assignment of CNA responsibility to follow.

CND systems should be established by the Chief Information Officer (CIO) within OSD. The policy will need to be adjusted for different situations, to deal with systems that range from protecting business and administrative systems to warfighting.

In recent years, leadership for policy issues has been provided through the Defense Department's Chief Information Officer (CIO). Substantial progress has been made toward providing leadership to the service and agency CIOs on a broad set of information management topics, including defensive aspects. Clearly, much more needs to be done, but it is recommended that the CND policy-development function become a primary responsibility of the CIOs and stay within the office of the ASD C3I, and that appropriate measures be taken to deal with the interaction between CNA and CND (discussed below).

The CIO function in support of CND should include the following related responsibilities:

- provide information-operations strategy and develop policy;

- provide military representation to U.S. national agencies, the law enforcement community, commercial industry, and our allies on CND issues;

- act as the user in setting requirements for the information assurance aspects of systems, working through the Blueprint Office proposed above, and expanding upon current activity, which is unduly focused on the short term and is underfunded;

- create a DOD common threat analysis center, consolidating the various current CND activities; and

- identify, develop, and oversee employment of best practices within DOD organizations for managing IT assets.

Above all, the CIO must act as an advocate for adequate computer network defense measures, even though such measures do not add functionality and are difficult, time-consuming, and expensive to implement. CINCSPACE, which currently has responsibility for CND as well as CNA, is poorly placed, as a field command, to participate fully in the process by which budgets for thousands of information systems are drawn up. Further, given that CNA is cheaper than CND and that the choice between them depends in part on an estimate of our own efficacy relative to that of an enemy, the trade-offs between the two must be made at a very senior level.

Consolidate CNA Under a Single Organization

The development of USCINCSPACE as the DOD leader in cyber attack properly places responsibility at a CINC; it requires sustainable support. The organizational structure will take time to develop and will require not only funds, but also the attention of the key officials in DOD. Many related responsibilities of the services and agencies will require adjustment. USCINCSPACE may have to undergo the most profound change as it shifts its focus from conventional space activities to information operations. In our view, this new responsibility requires that CINCSPACE must:

- lead the effort within the DOD to reduce duplication of effort and consolidate resources, including clarifying the security and special access needs of information operations;

- establish minimum training, certification, and accountability standards for commanders with regard to CNA; and

- create a new functional component within CINCSPACE, which we would call the Joint Force Information Operations Component Commander (JFIOCC), to support Joint Task Force and CINC operations with respect to CNA.

The JFIOCC would represent a single point of contact to articulate CND and CNA activity to commanders in military terms (an improvement over the current situation in which commanders must deal with various intelligence agencies and service components, each with its own terminology). The resulting military-to-military interaction should provide significant improvement in effectiveness. In this role, USCINCSPACE would act as a supporting command, similar to the way in which it supports other functions, analogous to the way the Special Operations Command provides unique warfighting support. In its role of advising on military operations, the JFIOCC, in coordination with others as needed, would make the decisions to use CNA, balancing the various priorities against each other.

This consolidation also implies a critical set of actions regarding personnel: the creation of a highly trained group of officers specializing in CNA. These officers would have to bridge the gap between researchers on CNA techniques and field commanders whose own expertise is in more conventional forms of warfare. They should also be able to bridge the gaps across the various compartmentalized research efforts conducted by a variety of separate organizations, although this would involve subjecting them to extremely intensive security investigation and accepting the risk of trusting them with a very large quantity of critically sensitive information.

Focus CNA Development

We have proposed giving USCINCSPACE the task of managing the CNA function for budgeting, and for managing deployment and operations. Responding to CINCSPACE direction, the National Security Agency (NSA) would be the interface with the intelligence community and will coordinate the technical development, either directly or through its service cryptologic elements. NSA would thus become an acquisition arm for this function, acting much like the service acquisition organizations for CINCSPACE. NSA would provide leadership in the intelligence community similar to the way cryptologic activity is managed today. Other organizations would be tasked by USCINSPACE to provide support in their areas of competency.

Create a Laboratory for CNA and CND

One of the main arguments for keeping the CNA activity apart from CND is that many vulnerabilities are fragile, meaning that if they are revealed by the CND elements, the CNA efforts that take advantage of these vulnerabilities would be reduced in value. We recommend that a laboratory be established under USCINCSPACE to model realistic networks and explore techniques and countermeasures. This laboratory could develop countermeasures in parallel with the evaluation of a potential CNA. If a CNA technique were judged viable, then a decision could be made at that point whether or not to develop and deploy the countermeasure. The countermeasure would be deployed if doing so would not reveal the vulnerability. Even if it were not deployed immediately, it could be deployed later if needed. If a CNA technique were judged not to be viable, the United States could still deploy the countermeasure in case our enemies make a different viability judgment. The key to making this work effectively is to ensure that experts be made available for the evaluation, at least for a limited period of time.

Stimulate Development of Protection by Creating an Information Assurance Institute

The topics of cyber attack on the U.S. infrastructure and the role of the DOD have been discussed since the 1997 Report of the President's Commission on Critical Infrastructure Protection.[10] In response to the report, Presidential Decision Directive (PDD) 63 and PDD 64 mandated a number of actions, most notably the creation of the National Infrastructure Protection Center at the FBI. Other actions mandated by these two PDDs, such as encouraging private/public information sharing on such matters as cyber attack descriptions, have had only limited success. While commercial industry will eventually make the kind of investment necessary to protect information networks, government leadership is necessary because solutions cost money with little perceived immediate benefit. The denial-of-service attacks against eBay and others in early 2000 should have been a wake-up call, but industry will only make the investments in response to a known threat as it affects financial bottom lines.

The DOD must take the initiative on this issue, for several reasons. The ability to execute war plans successfully depends critically on the infrastructure industries, particularly transportation (air, rail, shipping), communication, and electric power. While the responsibility for dealing with these industries has been assigned to other agencies in government, DOD's dependency requires more action. It can also be argued that the DOD is the only agency in government that has the technical and management capability to form the kind of relationships necessary to stimulate action, and even that DOD shares responsibility for protecting the nation in the event cyber attack takes on the scale of warfare or catastrophic terrorism.

For these reasons we recommend that DOD help establish a nonprofit National Information Assurance Institute to build a bridge between the public and private sectors, including industry, universities, and not-for-profit companies that are involved in IT. The Institute should be placed in the private sector and not be a part of government or any infrastructure industry. Its activity would provide industry with a mechanism for sharing information assurance tech-

---

10. The President's Commission on Critical Infrastructure Protection was established in 1996 by Executive Order 13010; the Commission's report, "Critical Foundations," was completed in October 1997.

nology that poses no competitive threat, and it could serve as a single point of contact between industry and the national security and law enforcement communities. It would research and disseminate best practices, and improve the nation's ability to recognize and recover from cyber attack. It could be the mechanism for government to share sensitive intelligence about threats to the information infrastructure, and could be a conduit for sharing the results of research funded both by government and by others. The Institute would create a government-industry forum for coordinating federal policy, regulation, and other actions affecting infrastructure providers.

We are just beginning to understand cyber operations. The subject will grow in complexity and scope as IT is universally adopted. Many other issues will arise. The recommendations presented above are seen as first steps. We now turn our attention to the most critical element to power any change: well trained and dedicated people.

The Three Essentials for Success: People, People, People

Just as in real estate, where the value of a house depends on "location, location, location," the value of all of these recommendations depends on "people, people, people" to implement them. We have two further recommendations, therefore, to address the training of the military staff for command and control and information operations in the field, and to ensure that the technical work force is available to plan and design the enterprise. (This subject is addressed in greater detail in Chapter 8 by David Chu and John White.)

Create Recognized Military Career Paths in C2 and Information Operations
Creation of recognized military career paths in command and control and in information operations would not only build the expertise that the military desperately needs to conduct operations in the field, but would also create a sense of community that would help make integration work despite the various organizational constraints. The career path would include training, specialization, and certification in the chosen field of command and control or information operations.

An illustration of an earlier attempt from which we can generalize a solution is the Army's Task Force XXI experience with the "digital battlefield," when the Army recognized the need for a new role within its operations. The new role was designated "Military Occupational Specialty (MOS) 74B," and was effectively a specialist-class position trained in the network and system administration skills necessary for operations in the field. This new designation was established to correct the situation that developed when the Army began using signal officers and staff to manage systems and networks within the Tactical Operations Center (TOC). They got fairly proficient at network and system administration, but because the Army did not formally recognize the uniqueness of these soldiers, and treated them like any other signal soldier, it had difficulty retaining these specially trained individuals. The Army's decision to create the new position was accompanied by specialized training and, more importantly, specific slots within the digital TOC staff, to ensure that these responsibilities were not treated merely as "other duties as assigned."

It is imperative to recognize the importance and specialization of IT specialists in C2 and information operations, as the Army did in creating the role of the MOS 74B. The services should create specialist class roles for C2 and IO. Specific manpower allocations should be assigned at the proper command levels to ensure dedicated and proficient operations, and should be supported through specialized education and training. This role would be viewed as a specialized career path and offer the service member enough opportunities to retain the talent over time.

Support Both USJFCOM and USSPACECOM with Highly Trained Civilian Technical System Engineering Resources

The availability of a high quality, technically proficient civilian workforce is an absolute necessity for the activities outlined and it is enormously difficult to attract and maintain such expertise in today's environment. A recent Defense Science Board report lists many of the impediments to hiring and retaining civilians in the government.[11] This is also a problem for private companies, given the competitive market for IT talent. In fact, the companies that focus on DOD activity have a particularly difficult situation since they are not viewed by potential employees as providing growth opportunity comparable to IT companies.

---

11. The Defense Science Board Task Force, *Human Resources Strategy* (Washington, D.C.: U.S. Department of Defense, Office of the Under Secretary of Defense for Acquisition, Technology, and Logistics, February 2000).

However, the DOD must turn increasingly to the private sector for many services that involve the design, testing, integration, and support of hardware and software components. Of these, integration is the most challenging since the workforce must gain familiarity with a large number of independently designed systems and construct effective linkages to ensure interoperability. Success in this endeavor requires a relatively stable workforce that can only be achieved with business practices that provide incentives for companies to attract and retain skilled people.

The need for increased capability to support government decisions is an absolute necessity as well. A technically proficient workforce on the government side is needed for sound budgetary and programmatic decision-making and the design of overarching technical architectures. The attributes of this essential workforce include intimate knowledge of systems in use by the DOD, a long-term commitment to the process, the ability to be objective in driving technical solutions without conflict of interest and, most importantly, proficiency in understanding state-of-the-art information technology. One solution could involve the use of FFRDCs, which have worked very well in similar capacities for the last forty years.[12] Another would involve empowering a private company to provide this service, as has also been done in the past.

In addition, alternative innovative concepts can be tried for specific purposes. For example, the CIA has formed a private venture called In-Q-Tel to influence and funnel new, commercial technology

---

12. The DOD uses Federally Funded Research and Development Centers that account for 6,000 highly trained professionals. FFRDCs are managed by independent companies or are affiliated with universities. They have the ability to adjust the skills of the workforce as needed, offering incentives similar to those offered by industry. Sponsoring agreements between the DOD and the FFRDC provide for long-term support (typically five years), and restrict activity that would undermine objectivity, in return for government support to maintain a stable environment, provide access to critical data, and provide funds for independent research and development. FFRDC research and development is used to hone skills needed by the government and to stimulate research that would not otherwise be undertaken by industry.

developments to the intelligence community.[13] This model should be evaluated for possible applicability to DOD.

Four Trends for the Future

Today we are only beginning to see the future of information technology. Wonderful new commercial applications have appeared and will eventually be integrated, driven by four trends in the commercial world: ubiquity, simplicity, what we refer to as "zero and infinity," and interactivity.

First, computing platforms will be *ubiquitous* and take on many different forms. It is anticipated that by 2003 several billion computing platforms will be operational worldwide. The largest proliferation of computer technology will be embedded in other systems and invisible to the user. These computers will become extensions of the human being, able not only to respond to requests but to predict action.

The second factor is *simplification*. The human capacity to handle information has not changed since we started to measure it, and it is not expected to change in the near future, short of biomedical invention. It is this very important fact that motivates simplification to mask the inherent complexity of a growing, interconnected computing environment. Computers will become intuitive; they will be able to sense the environment through many more modes than just keyboard inputs, including voice, gestures, expressions, and pressure, and to respond with a variety of actions. Computers will continue to converge with the network but they will also, to an accelerating degree, converge with the user. This user convergence will offer deep personalization and customization.

The third factor we call *zero and infinity*. Equipment costs are being driven down toward a hypothetical "zero" cost, while capacity is increasing in the direction of being infinitely large. For example, fiber optic cabling now spans the globe and continues to be laid at remarkable rates. This fiber currently supports 8 to 16 wavelengths or independent signaling paths; it is predicted that within a year, the same volume of cable will be capable of supporting in excess of 800

13. In-Q-Tel, funded annually by Congress, has the goal of stimulating investments from innovative IT companies for products that the CIA can use and that are also applicable to commercial industry. It can enter into creative partnership and financing arrangements the DOD cannot.

wavelengths. One of these cable bundles can be expected to carry as much in an hour as three months of today's worldwide Internet traffic. These effects are tearing down barriers to entry and creating an asymmetrical effect in government, military, and industry, where otherwise small players can become dominant forces.

The fourth factor is *interactivity*. The next wave of services to be introduced on a large scale will be interactive services that will enable communities to band together in a virtual environment. The most rudimentary of these services, often referred to as "chat," is already in widespread use. With broadband technology, chat expands into a full collaboration suite to include shared applications, video, audio, and document sharing. It is projected that the number of software clients with on-line and interactive access will grow from 20 percent of all user applications today to greater than 70 percent of all user applications within the next few years. As technology matures and bandwidths increase, the desire for interactivity will lead to telepresence, or the ability to project virtually anything, anywhere, at any time.

These attributes will become available to the U.S. military, and, if embraced, will keep us ahead. To ride this inexorable commercial information technology wave, the DOD must reorganize and invest in order not to fall permanently behind.

4

Keeping the Edge in Intelligence

ROBERT J. HERMANN

The intelligence capabilities of the United States are an important consideration for any future Department of Defense. The projections of modes of military operations for the future that were presented by the Joint Chiefs of Staff in *Joint Vision 2010/2020*, and the outlines of a coming Revolution in Military Affairs, place a high premium on "information dominance."[1] The National Security Strategy advocates global engagement for the United States and is likely to continue to do so. This set of combined concepts places greatly increased demands on information gathering and analysis, and on the integration of these activities into the mission operations they support.

The burden of global engagement brings with it a need for global-scale sensors and the capacity for processing, analysis, reporting, and dissemination of the information they collect. This wide-ranging intelligence apparatus is essential for making national policy and conducting the affairs of state, and to support the deployment and employment of military forces on a global scale. The cost of these capabilities, however, is such that they will have to be shared by all functions and echelons of the national security structure, which creates major organizational challenges. This problem is already with us, and must be solved if the objectives of *Joint Vision 2010/2020* are to be achieved and the Revolution in Military Affairs carried out. Significant deficiencies must be addressed in current intelligence and

---

1. Joint Staff publication, *Joint Vision 2010* (Washington, D.C.: U.S. Joint Chiefs of Staff, 1996); *Joint Vision 2020* (Washington, D.C.: U.S. Joint Chiefs of Staff, July 2000). These are referred to collectively in this chapter as *Joint Vision 2010/2020*.

related capabilities, the analytic exploitation of these capabilities, and the integration of these systems with military forces.

This chapter begins by outlining the sources of the need for change. It is not intended to be a comprehensive treatment of the whole of U.S. intelligence issues, but to bring to the attention of a new Defense team the handful of most important needs. These are outlined in the next section, and a series of specific recommended actions are outlined in the concluding section of the chapter.

The Need for Change

The need for changes in our intelligence structure is driven by several factors. Chief among them is that, while the environment in which it must operate has changed, the national intelligence structure created in the shadow of World War II and developed during the Cold War has not kept up. Moreover, it is dominated by collection activities, while assessment of the information thus collected is inadequate to present and future needs.

THE ENVIRONMENT HAS PROFOUNDLY CHANGED

The information revolution has brought with it the means of proliferation of information and new technologies that fuel the economic and industrial growth of other nations around the globe. This has stimulated the global economy within which each nation, including ours, must compete for survival and well-being. It has also affected the technological and industrial base from which military systems, intelligence systems, and target information systems are drawn, permitting revolutionary approaches in each of these domains that have not yet been fully exploited.

Military Forces and Military Operations Have Changed

Dramatic advances in technology, particularly information technologies, have provided the basis for major changes in weapons systems, targeting systems, and communications systems. The concepts of *Joint Vision 2010/2020*, intended to exploit these technological changes, are revolutionary in scope; they place new burdens on the intelligence system and its related sensing systems.

One of the premises of *Joint Vision 2010/2020* is that the United States and its allies will establish "information dominance." To achieve this objective, force commanders will need a detailed understanding of the situation over the full range of their respective areas of responsibility, as well as of the situations affecting their ability to prosecute their specific missions. This permanent need for "situation awareness" will require that force commanders have access to a mix that includes both those globally capable sensor systems normally associated with "intelligence" and their own organic sensor systems.

Information dominance is also needed to support new weapons systems, which are designed to strike with precision from stand-off ranges and with a rapidity appropriate to a fast-moving conflict situation. Here, too, targeting these weapons and providing damage assessment will often require access to information from globally capable sensors. Their range, precision, and timeliness are appropriate and necessary to this modern mode of warfare, and must be available for this purpose.

The Current U.S. Intelligence Structure Was Established When Conditions Were Very Different

The structure that carries out U.S. intelligence activities is built around a set of agencies that have evolved since World War II, and are no longer well designed for generating a coherent product efficiently. First, the Central Intelligence Agency and its predecessors, which have primary responsibility for the production of national intelligence and the coordination of the U.S. intelligence activities, were initially formed during and shortly after World War II. The position of Director of Central Intelligence (DCI) was also established soon after the war. The National Security Agency (NSA), which has primary responsibility for collecting, analyzing, and disseminating signals intelligence (SIGINT), was first established as the Armed Forces Security Activity in the late 1940s. It was transformed into NSA in 1952 by President Truman, and given broad responsibilities for directing the nation's signals intelligence and communications security activities. These institutions, thus formed at the beginning of the Cold War, were shaped by the lessons of World War II. Both are now in need of modernization in their management and form.

The intelligence structure also includes the National Reconnaissance Office (NRO). Formed in response to Eisenhower's frustration after the U-2 shoot-down incident, the NRO became the vehicle for exploiting U.S. technological superiority in space. The NRO is not a complete mission agency: it has no substantive intelligence responsibility at the "front end" of the process where requirements are specified. It is charged with acquiring and operating space systems in response to requirements specified by the DCI; it is not expected to interpret these requirements, because it has no substantive analytic capability from which to draw independent substantive judgment. It also has no "back-end" role: it is not responsible for the processing, analysis, or dissemination of the output of its collection activities.

Processing, analysis, and dissemination of signals intelligence, including that collected by the NRO, is the responsibility of NSA. Over several decades, the NRO and NSA have worked out cooperative procedures for tasking and controlling satellites, processing the collected signals, analyzing the results, integrating this analysis with other SIGINT sources, and disseminating the results. However, investment in satellite collection systems is systematically given more emphasis than investing in processing, analysis, and dissemination. The director of the NRO, in response to the substantial requirements pressure for more coverage, more kinds of coverage (radar, infrared, imagery, etc.), more resolution, more precision, and more speed in delivery, proposes programs that are compelling and gain support in both the executive and legislative branches. Conversely, the director of the NSA must deal with the output of many other sources of material in addition to the satellites. In formulating NSA investment priorities, balance with the NRO is not the only criterion. Moreover, at this stage of the intelligence process, processing, analysis, and dissemination have an "infrastructure" connotation and are thus often not perceived as compelling as the systems "closer to the target."

The National Imagery and Mapping Agency (NIMA) was formed in the 1990s, with NSA as its model. It is responsible for coordinating all imagery collection as well as the processing, analysis, and dissemination of all imagery products. It was created by consolidating an earlier Central Imagery Office, the Defense Mapping Agency, CIA's Image Interpretation Center, and the DCI's Committee for Coordinating Image Exploitation (COMIREX). The difficulty of integrating an intelligence activity with a mapping agency, a CIA workforce, and a defense agency has hampered its effectiveness: it is not yet mature, and is having difficulty coping with its responsibilities.

Finally, the Central MASINT Organization (CMO), which has responsibility for measurement and signature intelligence (MASINT), is a very small coordinating group attached to the Defense Intelligence

Agency. Because of its small size and weak charter, it is unable to exploit the potential of this domain of activity.

These separate enterprises, formed in response to Cold War demands and built around Cold War–era technology, vary in their capability and execution. Moreover, each generates a fundamentally separate set of products relating to the same set of situations. This places the burden on their customers of creating a coherent picture, but often the customers do not do so either. In any case, the infrastructure of people and facilities needed in the customer domain to cope with these separate streams of information is duplicative and wasteful; such duplication also makes it harder to derive quality results.

THE SYSTEM UNDULY FAVORS COLLECTION AT THE EXPENSE OF ANALYSIS

Military commands are unanimous in their expressed need for more analytic support. The access provided by the current set of global and organic sensors has improved and does a better job at meeting the needs of operational commands; the shortfall is in the analysis of the data coming from these systems. The global reach of U.S. forces and the variety of threats and problem-sets they must address require at least as broad a set of analytic skills, languages, and specialized knowledge as were required during the Cold War, but since its end, the resources for this realm have been substantially reduced.

Most intelligence dollars are spent to acquire collection and processing systems, rather than analysis. While some imbalance might be natural, it is exaggerated in part by bureaucratic factors: the collection systems are championed by major collection providers such as the NRO, the Air Force, and the Navy, while the champions of analysis wield much less bureaucratic power.

Another issue is the increasing availability of valuable information in the public domain. During the Cold War years, the period during which many of the organizations, processes, and habits of the intelligence community were developed, most strategic intelligence information was derived from secret sources. The primary targets of intelligence activities were closed societies, and the questions needing answers required secret sources and methods. To analyze the data from these sources, a high premium was placed on people and organizations that were especially knowledgeable about the closed societies, the secret sources, and the special methods. These circumstances gave rise to extensive government organizations dedicated to analysis of secrets. Although public-domain data was used by these organizations, the problems were not amenable to solution through open sources, and the skills and knowledge needed to exploit the information were not generally available in the private sector.

In our current world, by contrast, many of the most important uncertainties for the United States are not so dominantly defined by secret data from closed societies. While estimating the future trajectory of Russia, China, India, Indonesia, or other foreign societies may require some access to secret sources and methods, the dominant prerequisite is knowledge of the society and familiarity with its public behavior. It is important for the United States to have access to the most knowledgeable scholars of these issues and to give them incentives to help the United States make the best estimates of the future. The organizations dedicated and staffed to address our Cold War adversaries are not likely to be the best ones for these purposes.

The regional military commands are now increasingly involved in many potential situations other than conventional military conflict. Peacekeeping, humanitarian, and other operations other than war require understanding of the substantial information available from open sources. The analytic activities supporting these commands need to make use of regional experts as well as classified information, in order to provide a complete and comprehensive picture.

Changes in assignment of analytic responsibilities, based on the discussion in the next section, would help facilitate these improvements. Ways to improve on the quality of the current system include improvements in linkages between collection activities and policy consumers, in support to military operations, and in covert and clandestine operations; greater use of open-source information; reduction of the number of organizations; establishment of a more realistic requirements process; and creation of a systematic assessment process.

Intelligence Strategy

Changes are necessary to support the strategic objectives of maintaining national dominance in intelligence, improving integration of intelligence into operational capabilities, and expanding international cooperation in intelligence.

RETAIN NATIONAL DOMINANCE IN INTELLIGENCE, RECONNAISSANCE, AND SURVEILLANCE

Support of U.S. policy decisions and support to military operations needed for U.S. leadership will require a superior intelligence, reconnaissance, and surveillance capability. Dominance in global awareness and in ability to apply military force intelligently is a primary national capability with a geopolitical impact in its own right. The United States currently has dominant capabilities in operational systems, systems integration, and industrial base. Ensuring that this strategic position is not lost over the next ten to twenty years will require continued investment in intelligence, structural changes, and initiatives in international cooperation.

IMPROVE THE INTEGRATION OF INTELLIGENCE INTO MILITARY OPERATIONS

One of the most difficult management challenges for the Secretary of Defense and the Director of Central Intelligence, both now and in the future, is how to share the extremely capable sensor, processing, and analysis systems that are now available under the rubrics of intelligence, reconnaissance, and surveillance.

A military commander must have a good picture of his or her area of interest. This "situation awareness" is derived from a wide variety of information sources, only a few of which are labeled "intelligence." Others, nominally "reconnaissance" or "surveillance," include air traffic control radars, warning radars, and command and control radar systems such as the Joint Surveillance and Target Acquisition Radar System (JSTARS) and the Airborne Warning and Control System (AWACS). The commander in the field has organic systems such as EW (electronic warfare) and ESM (electronic support measures) that have a substantial capability to sense and display information on the local situation. The commander also needs weather information, mapping and geodetic information, and locally derived information observable by the commander's own forces about enemy, friends, neutrals, and the terrain.

The integration of these various streams of information can only be done by the local commander: the only one with access to them all, and the only one whose organization can weigh the importance and relevance of each with respect to the capability of the commander's forces and with respect to the commander's operational intentions. It is very important, therefore, that the local commanders have the capability to perform their own assessments of the situation from all potentially useful sources of data. It follows that they must have the necessary information systems integrated in their units.

This formulation of the issue and solution are identical to the other "born joint" elements of command and control described in Chapter 2 by John Shalikashvili and Chapter 3 by Victor DeMarines, and should be thought of and addressed in the same way. The treatments outlined in Chapter 2 and Chapter 3 apply to the support provided by intelligence to military operations. They recommend ways to strengthen the joint elements of the Department for all aspects of force development, readiness, and investment decisionmaking. In particular, they recognize and applaud the current intention of the Chairman of the Joint Chiefs of Staff to strengthen the role of the Joint Requirements Oversight Committee (JROC) at the front end of the process. Under this concept, the JROC would concentrate its focus on shaping the requirements against which the armed services and defense agencies construct their program and activities.

They also outline significant new roles for the Joint Forces Command. They envision that this command, which already has a significant role in the joint force development process, will take on the responsibility of establishing a Joint Blueprint Office, to be charged with developing a common, adaptive, and agile command and control infrastructure including the elements of intelligence, reconnaissance, and surveillance. The Blueprint Office would provide an essential framework for the evolution of "born joint" functions. They also support joint demonstration, experimentation, and exercise ("expercise") activities by JFCOM for critical joint capability development, including intelligence. These are all steps in the right direction.

EXPAND INTERNATIONAL PARTNERSHIPS IN INTELLIGENCE, RECONNAISSANCE, AND SURVEILLANCE

Inherent in the current and expected future approach to security by the United States are major dependencies on other nations. This coalition approach to security poses many dilemmas, of which intelligence is one of the most complex. While the United States, as the sole superpower, must be prepared to act alone in some cases with a comprehensive military capability, more often it is likely to act in concert with others. In such cases, the decision to use or not use military force, as well as the effectiveness of the operation when forces are committed, will require some form of integrated information-sharing with the coalition partners. This requires specific planning before the fact with regard to intelligence and integration of information, just as with regard to use of forces.

The United States is the dominant player in reconnaissance, surveillance, and intelligence and must take the lead, both strategically and tactically, in preparing for shared use of these assets. This is not now a significant part of our preparedness activities, and it needs strengthening.

Recommendations

The foregoing analysis leads to three types of recommendation for the new President and his defense team: consolidation of collection activities; improving the capacity for analysis; and expanding international cooperation.

CONSOLIDATE THE VARIOUS INTELLIGENCE COLLECTION AGENCIES INTO A RESTRUCTURED NSA

The first recommendation is to consolidate the intelligence collection agencies — the NSA, the NRO, the CMO, and NIMA — into a single agency, the NSA. It would serve as the manager of a unified system of technical sensors, processing, reporting, and dissemination. The rest of this section explains why this consolidation makes sense. In brief, first, consolidation would improve the coherence and quality of the products that have been coming out of the separate agencies. Other reasons derive from the technological advances that have changed each of the separate agencies. Such a consolidation also offers opportunities to improve analysis as well as to increase efficiency.

The Technology of Imagery and Other Remote Sensing is Becoming Digital, Electronic, and Near–Real Time

In the early days of airborne and satellite imaging systems when the intelligence collection agencies were first formed, the film-based, batch-process style of conducting the imagery business would not have made it sensible to merge the various intelligence collection agencies, even if political imperatives had permitted it. Now, however, there are very few characteristic differences between a digital stream that represents a picture and one that represents a segment of multi-channel communications or a fine-grained electronics emission. The technical skills needed for the workforce, the industrial base to be used for these missions, and the information systems upon which the exploitation must be based are becoming identical for most aspects of the systems. This is an argument for consolidation.

The Functions Needed for SIGINT are the Same as for Imagery and Other Remote Sensors

The SIGINT system performs the same basic functions that now apply in all types of imagery and other remote sensing. These comprise needs identification, collection, processing, analysis, dissemination, interpretation, and feedback. SIGINT covers the technically different arts of communications intelligence, electronic intelligence, and foreign instrumentation intelligence. With changes in technology, imagery and the other technical sensor segments can be thought of in terms of the same functions. Moreover, the customer set for SIGINT is identical to the customer set for imagery and other types of intelligence. The current SIGINT system has an extensive doctrine and information system by which its customers can identify their needs for those who collect and produce the information, can exchange information with knowledgeable analysts, and can provide feedback to improve the performance of collection and analysis. An extensive set of cryptologic support groups (comprising 1500 people) work closely with many SIGINT customers to aid in their understanding and use of the signals intelligence that has been tailored to that customer's needs.

In contrast, the current Imagery system operating through NIMA has none of these characteristics; there is no reason to accept this shortcoming, now that it is a near–real time process. If these major segments of the intelligence system were not merged, it would be necessary to create a parallel and duplicative system for request, tasking, and dissemination for imagery data as well as for the other technical sensors. Concerns expressed by Congress, the DCI, and the military commands about Tasking, Processing, Exploitation, and Dissemination (TPED) for the imagery function are a manifestation of this issue. The fractionated responsibilities for these functions have produced inadequate investment in the TPED functions, and NIMA has not yet been able to turn this situation around. There is inadequate processing capability for the volumes of imagery that are truly needed; and a capable and practiced system for tasking these imagery systems by the users with a responsive feed-back mechanism does not exist. The systems engineering and project management capabilities of NIMA are not adequate to address these problems. The TPED problem needs the kind of project management that the NRO could provide in a consolidated agency (discussed below).

The Scope and Structure of the SIGINT Process is Appropriate for All of the Functions

Even though it has its own current technical challenges and management difficulties, the form of the NSA provides the best basis around which to create a more unified and streamlined approach. The SIGINT function carried out by NSA has proven to be the most robust over the years. The director of the NSA is an accountable executive responsible for using all of the capabilities and facilities of the United States in this functional area to best serve the nation. The director of the NSA is responsible for assuring the appropriate collecting, processing, analysis, reporting, and dissemination of the products of the whole SIGINT enterprise. A very robust set of management tools have been developed over several decades to guide and coordinate this effort. They are the most complete and effective available from any of the four agencies whose consolidation is recommended. Thus, many of the management elements for a single, coherent system of technical sensors already exist in NSA; with consolidation, they would not have to be recreated for each technical sensor area.

The Strong Systems Engineering and Project Management Capabilities of the NRO Should be Applied to this Larger Scope of Activities

The NRO should take over systems engineering and project management functions for the consolidated intelligence collection agency. The NRO is one of the U.S. government's best system acquisition managers, and is far superior in this respect to NSA, CMO, or NIMA. It already bears a significant share of systems management responsibilities for these three agencies. However, the bureaucratic strains created because they are separate entities hinders the creation of more effective whole-system solutions. Vertical consolidation of functions would give NRO full responsibility for systems management for all of the intelligence collection agencies.

Analysis Will be Strengthened and Efficiencies Achieved

By merging these separate functions, the way is open to integrate analytic functions now conducted separately. The analysts in each of the functions of SIGINT, IMINT (image intelligence), and MASINT are now, for the most part, directed at the same set of targets, for the same set of consumers, and with data of similar currency. Each is responsible for creating a product, which varies based on its functional access, about the same set of issues. Already these analysts often find it useful to coordinate their activities so that each can present a more complete picture. These separate sets of products must be integrated to provide a full and coherent picture, a task that now often falls to the user or consumer of these products. The current layered system provides some insurance, in that at least four sets of analysts are assessing the same events. It is, however, wasteful of analytic talent, which is already in short supply. Moreover it introduces, in some cases, time delays for product integration. Integration of these separate analytic functions should strengthen the quality of analysis, and reduce delays in product delivery. Finally, there are many parallel and duplicate sets of management overhead and infrastructure in these four agencies. Substantial reductions and resultant savings should be possible through consolidation.

STRENGTHEN ANALYSIS

The basic objectives of this set of recommendations are, first, to strengthen the analytic and interpretive capabilities of the mission departments and agencies of the government, so that the mission strategies and operations can become more closely linked to the analysis of information affecting these missions; second, to weigh the costs and benefits of information analytic expenditures more rationally; third, to develop a more intensive use of open-source information; and fourth, to strengthen the nation's overall information analysis function by creating a national assessment center that would draw from both classified and unclassified sources to analyze a select set of critical issues.

The Secretary of Defense and the Director of Central Intelligence should decentralize more of the analytic effort to bring the locus of analysis closer to the locus of mission responsibility. The majority of the nation's analytic and assessment efforts should be performed and paid for by the separate departments and agencies that have the primary executive-branch functions and responsibilities of the government. For the Department of Defense, which already has a significant analytic activity, the primary impact of this conceptual shift would be to strengthen the analytic activities that support its internal mission organizations. One particular need is to add to and strengthen the analytic effort supporting its operational commands.

The DCI should establish a "National Assessment Center" (NAC) to be the preeminent center for the U.S. government's analysis of selected issues whose assessment depends on the best possible information from all sources, open as well as classified. The information relevant to certain questions will often include non-secret sources as well as sensitive sources and techniques; the focus must be the integration of these different sources of information into a quality assessment. The premium will be on expertise in the subject domain, scholarship, and the credibility of professional reputation.

However, for the majority of critical issues whose analysis depends on sensitive sources and methods, the DCI should continue to rely upon the Directorate for Intelligence (DI) as the preeminent analytic organization. These include, in particular, many of the worrisome asymmetric threats that are dominated by secretive organizations, and which need increased attention by the DI. The intended relationship between the much larger DI and the small NAC is that of producer and consumer. The DI would be, as now, broadly responsible for intelligence product. The NAC would be selectively tasked to address a limited number of key issues, using its access to scholars on these topics and an organized open-source information collection system, as well as intelligence product.

It is envisioned that the National Assessment Center should be modest in size, perhaps 100–200 people. For the most part, these individuals would be from the private sector, people who have contracted to work for months or years on specific problems on the basis of their specific areas of knowledge. In some cases, substantial problems might be contracted out to eminent universities or private analytic institutions on the basis of their expertise.

The problems assigned to the NAC should be identified by the National Security Council both to limit the number of assignments and to establish their importance. The NAC's reports should be written for the President, the cabinet, and primary staff. The topics assigned should be those that are of strategic importance to the

United States, demand the highest level of scholarship, and require a mix of open source and secret information. For example, questions regarding the location and nature of the North Korean nuclear weapons development program would not be appropriate for the NAC, because the dominant issues are likely to require the understanding of secret sources and methods of closed societies. In contrast, an estimate of the course of Indonesian politics over the next few years would be appropriate, as it could best be accomplished with a mix of open and secret information in the hands of the country's most knowledgeable scholars on Indonesia.

EXPAND INTERNATIONAL COOPERATION IN INTELLIGENCE

The United States should establish itself as the leader of international consortia organized for cooperation in intelligence activities, which would form a collective umbrella under which a pooling of resources could occur when it is in the common interests of the participants. An additional objective is to make it attractive for major nations to join U.S.-led intelligence activities, so that they will not form competing and capable alternative groupings.

To achieve these objectives, the Secretary of Defense and the Director of Central Intelligence should develop a strategy and a plan for international intelligence cooperation. It should focus on a regional approach along the mission lines of the current regional areas of military responsibility, and should exploit the full range of bilateral, multilateral, and regional arrangements.

The consolidated intelligence agency proposed above can contribute to this effort significantly, by building upon the existing international structure and arrangements that the individual agencies have established. In some areas, the United States has for several decades been developing an approach to this strategy that could be used as a model. In the process, it has learned much about how to manage the complexities and has developed many of the management approaches necessary to success.

The Secretary of Defense should also task operational commanders to develop plans for information sharing with potential coalition partners in their areas of responsibility. These commanders will need the full support of the Joint Staff, the Assistant Secretary of Defense for C3I, and the DCI.

Progress in coalition intelligence will be accelerated substantially by the actions recommended by Elizabeth Sherwood-Randall in Chapter 9 with respect to U.S. cooperation within NATO, the United Nations, and with other potential partners. These would strengthen the basic coalition organizations to be served by a coalition approach to intelligence. Intelligence will always be strengthened by the quality of its customers. In addition, improved force planning, standards in security procedures, and the development of coalition command and control capabilities will enable early improvements in the intelligence processes.

Conclusion

The business of knowing what is going on in the world, where things are and what leaders intend to do, is essential for world leadership by the United States and security for the United States. Intelligence activities are an important part of meeting those needs for security strategy, diplomacy, development of economic policies and practices, and support of deployed and employed military forces. The roles of the current intelligence institutions need to change in response to the new environment and new technologies. The recommendations in this chapter are directed at implementing those changes.

5

Countering Asymmetric Threats

ASHTON B. CARTER AND WILLIAM J. PERRY

S addam Hussein's military in 1991 was in many ways a miniature version of the Soviet army in its equipment, doctrine, and
tactics. This was precisely the type of threat against which the
U.S. military and its coalition partners drawn from NATO had been
practicing for decades. Faced with the hammer of the U.S. military,
Iraq configured itself as a nail. The outcome was never in doubt. Slobodan Milosevic's Serb forces were similarly Soviet-like, as are Kim
Jong-Il's North Korean conventional forces.

The hammer that struck Iraq in Desert Storm was the result of the
second post–World War II "revolution in military affairs" (RMA), to
use a now-popular phrase. The first revolution began during World
War II and centered on the atomic bomb and the ballistic missile for
strategic bombardment. The second RMA, dubbed the "offset strategy" because it was begun in the 1970s to offset Soviet numerical superiority in conventional tactical forces, centered on air superiority,
dominant intelligence and communications, and precision weapons.[1]

Today the RMA continues, and organizing to exploit it has been
the subject of the preceding chapters. The tasks of implementing
jointness in procurement, exploiting the information revolution, and
improving intelligence support to national security, treated in Chapters 2, 3, and 4, are essential to keeping the U.S. military unmatched
by any other military in the world.

---

1. For a description of the origins and content of the offset strategy, and its
role in DESERT STORM, see William J. Perry, "Desert Storm and Deterrence,"
Foreign Affairs, Vol. 70, No. 4 (Fall 1991).

But we must also bear in mind that in mounting future threats to U.S. national security, opponents are not likely to make the same mistake as Saddam Hussein. Rather than take on the unmatched U.S. military with a symmetric conventional military force, they will seek asymmetric means to chase away or scare away the United States from protecting its interests. They will seek vulnerabilities in the technologically sophisticated, information-intensive, fully joint "system-of-systems" of the offset strategy whose development was described in the preceding chapters. They will employ weapons of mass destruction: chemical, biological, or nuclear. Rather than waiting for the United States to project power to a distant battleground; they will seek to bring destruction to the U.S. homeland.

As the previous chapters indicate, much of the U.S. defense effort is devoted to the projection overseas of sophisticated conventional military power. Proficiency in such symmetric warfare is necessary, but it is far from sufficient. A dedicated effort must also be mounted to counter asymmetric threats. Organizing that effort is the subject of this chapter.

Asymmetric threats are divided into three categories. First, there are vulnerabilities in the complex but fragile information technology (IT)–based systems-of-systems. Such threats as jamming communications that carry targeting information or the Global Positioning System navigation and timing signal, attacking reconnaissance satellites, or erecting decoy missiles to frustrate reconnaissance-strike systems are examples of challenges to the RMA for which countermeasures must be devised. The RMA military must be made more robust as it is made ever more sophisticated.

A second category of asymmetric threat is the potential use of weapons of mass destruction (WMD) — on the battlefield, at ports and airfields where U.S. power projection is taking place, or on the territory of allies the U.S. is trying to defend. This threat requires counter-proliferation capabilities such as protective suits and detectors, with accompanying tactics and doctrine for their effective use.

Third is the disturbing prospect that opponents will attempt to threaten the U.S. homeland with terrorism on a war-like scale. Catastrophic terrorism might result from the use of weapons of mass destruction, especially biological weapons; from attack upon the critical infrastructures upon which fragile modern society depends, including power, transport, communications, and finance; or from attack upon the persons and institutions of the federal government. The specter of attack on our homeland is a relatively new one; in this century, America's wars have been far away. The country is favored by geography, with oceans to the east and west, and friendly neighbors to the south and north. But globalization and technological change undercut the protection historically afforded by favorable geography.

In this century, it was only when the Soviet Union exploded the atomic bomb in 1949 that a direct external threat of destruction was posed to the American homeland. The impact on American thinking and institutions was immediate and profound. A huge and sophisticated strategic nuclear deterrent capable of retaliating against the Soviet homeland was built. Vast programs of continental air and missile defense were inaugurated. Civil defense shelters were built and drills conducted for schoolchildren. Think-tanks such as the RAND Corporation were founded by government to ponder the new security dilemma. Suspected spies and Soviet "sympathizers" were hunted.

In the coming years, an incident of catastrophic terrorism on the U.S. homeland would be likely to spark concern and effort on a comparable scale. It is easy to see how the concern could escalate to hysteria, and how actions taken in the angry aftermath of a destructive event could be corrosive of civil liberties as well as counterproductive. Because the aftermath of homeland attack could be as fearsome as the attack itself, our government should begin to organize for this future threat now, while considered judgments can be made about how best to protect the homeland and how to reconcile protection with our democratic values. The Department of Defense will, of course, play a role in homeland defense. Capabilities it possesses for battlefield use will find application in the event of homeland attack. But there are also limits to the role the military should play in providing domestic security. It is better for all if this role is defined in advance.

Countermeasures to Asymmetric Warfare

The history of warfare has always been a struggle between measures and countermeasures, and so it will be with asymmetric warfare. During the 1970s and 1980s, the U.S. offset strategy incorporated modern information technology in its weapons to offset the numerical superiority of the military forces of the Soviet Union. This strategy has come to be known as the Revolution in Military Affairs (RMA).

After the effectiveness of the new RMA weapons was convincingly demonstrated in DESERT STORM, nations potentially hostile to the United States began to seek "offsets to the offset strategy," i.e., countermeasures to America's RMA weapons. Since they are not able to copy U.S. weapons (indeed, even our technically advanced allies have been slow to do so), they are led to the development of asymmetric warfare techniques. More specifically, they seek to develop systems that can disrupt the information networks that serve the RMA weapons; their objective is to give the United States pause before it uses its superiority in conventional weapons. The Defense Department must, therefore, take steps to reduce the vulnerability of its RMA systems to these asymmetric measures.

There are many technical approaches to reducing the vulnerability of communication networks, including modification of circuits to make them more jam-resistant; designing protective shielding for circuits and cables; configuring critical networks with redundant nodes so that the loss of one node is not catastrophic; designing transmitters with frequency-hopping or frequency-spreading capabilities to make the intercept and jamming of these signals more difficult; and the use of radio frequencies in the high microwave band and with narrow beam widths to make them less accessible to potential jamming systems. A detailed discussion of how to reduce vulnerability to jamming and disruption would fill many volumes. The point to be made here is that although vulnerability reduction techniques are well known, they are generally expensive and difficult to implement, and often require changes in operating procedures. From this we draw important conclusions regarding future DOD programs.

First, countermeasures must be seen by the Defense Department to be a serious threat; otherwise, the actions necessary to reduce vulnerability, which are not easy or cheap, will not be taken. Second, many of the techniques for vulnerability reduction are best done when the communication network is designed or installed; therefore the commitment to reduce vulnerability needs to be made before the threat of countermeasures has been manifested by an actual attack on the network. And finally, reducing vulnerability is not just a matter of equipment design; most importantly, it affects tactics, doctrine, and training, all of which should be developed with explicit consideration of countermeasures. All of this is lacking in today's military, which has been lulled into a false sense of complacency. This complacency has arisen because Saddam Hussein's military forces were so taken by surprise by the effectiveness of RMA weapons that they were not able to mount an effective countermeasure program. But since then, Iraq and many other nations have learned the lessons of DESERT STORM and are seeking ways to counter the RMA. In the meantime, America's military forces have come to depend more and more on RMA, and therefore on the reliable operation of their information networks, but have done little to reduce their vulnerability to asymmetric attack.

We believe that this deficiency is so serious that it calls for dramatic changes in the way the U.S. military forces train. Robust countermeasures should become a required part of military exercises; at present they are often excluded because they "disrupt" the exercise, but of course this is exactly the point of having them. An even better approach, and the one we recommend, would require a significant modification to the major national training ranges such as those at Nellis Air Force Base and Fort Irwin. Special facilities should be added to these ranges that allow the robust application of countermeasures during exercises and the "scoring" of their effectiveness. The "Red Teams" that are resident at these ranges should develop countermeasure tactics as a part of every exercise, and the team being tested should be scored on how it responds to the countermeasures. This would serve to illuminate, first of all, the inadequacy of our present approach to countermeasures. More importantly, it would train American troops how to deal with countermeasures as best they can with present equipment and tactics. What is essential, however, is that it would lead to the development of improved tactics and doctrine, and to the establishment of requirements for the development of information networks with inherent resistance to countermeasures.

Counter-proliferation

In recognition of the fact that potential opponents in regional conflict might not play by the same rules as Saddam Hussein did in DESERT STORM, the U.S. Department of Defense launched a Counter-proliferation Initiative in 1993. The objective was to integrate preparations to counter weapons of mass destruction into U.S. capabilities for power projection and joint operations. A great deal of progress has been made since 1993, including the creation of a Counter-proliferation Council chaired by the Deputy Secretary of Defense and the establishment of the Defense Threat Reduction Agency (DTRA) to bring together a number of WMD-related technology and field operations efforts. However, DOD's technology and systems acquisition capabilities are still fragmented, and WMD preparations are still incompletely integrated into planning for joint operations. These efforts will require the continuing attention of the Secretary of Defense.

The greatest deficiency in counter-proliferation, as in other cross-cutting issues described in Chapter 10, lies in interagency program coordination, however. An interagency program planning mechanism is needed for counter-proliferation, similar to the one described below (under "Homeland Defense") for countering catastrophic terrorism.

A second challenge for counter-proliferation is the improvement of our international cooperative efforts. One such effort is the Nunn-Lugar program, which should be expanded in scale and scope as detailed in Chapter 9. Cooperation with key allies and friends is also important: even if U.S. forces are adequately protected, allied forces and allied populations near a war zone cannot be left vulnerable to WMD attack. The new administration should, therefore, support and sustain the NATO Senior Defense Group on Proliferation and the bilateral counter-proliferation "Working Groups" with the United Kingdom, the Republic of Korea, Japan, Israel, and the Gulf Cooperation Council.

A third urgent need for U.S. counter-proliferation efforts is development of a technology base in biowarfare defense (BWD) that is as strong as our base in nuclear non-proliferation. The United States has strong DOD and DOE laboratories with thousands of personnel skilled in nuclear technology, but few experts in the field of biotechnology, neither within DOD's uniformed or civilian ranks, nor in its affiliated laboratories and contractors. Biotechnology and pharmaceutical companies frequently decline to participate in BWD programs for fear of being "tainted" by defense work or because of the cumbersome contracting and accounting procedures required by the Pentagon (a problem discussed further in Chapter 6). Yet the implications of the biotechnology revolution for security will probably exceed those of the nuclear and information revolutions. DOD must do more than increase funding in the Defense Advanced Research Projects Agency (DARPA), the U.S. Army Medical Research Institute of Infectious Diseases (USAMRIID), and DTRA for biotechnology research, although this is also necessary. A university-affiliated government-funded laboratory (akin to the nuclear laboratories of the DOE) will need to be founded to give DOD a foothold in the BWD technology field, and to compete for talent despite the drawbacks of government employment practices and the attractive employment opportunities available to biotechnologists in the private sector.

Homeland Defense

New technology means that smaller and smaller groups of people, well below the scale of nation-states, will be able to inflict war-scale violence. This poses a fundamental long-term problem for global society. Appropriate and effective counters to this danger are likely to take a long time for the United States government and others around the world to devise. The question is where and how to begin.

When to begin should not be in question: the time is clearly "now." Even though an instance of catastrophic terrorism has not yet occurred, such an event seems inevitable. Not only is mass destructive power becoming more available, but society is becoming more vulnerable through the complexity, interdependence, and global reach of its supporting infrastructures. Some groups that turn to terrorism are motivated by vengeful and messianic rather than political agendas, inclining them to drastic acts that more "mainstream" terrorist groups would regard as excessive or counterproductive. The United States may be a prime target, precisely because its conventional power is so great that asymmetric means such as catastrophic terrorism might seem the only method available to those who would challenge U.S. policies by violent means.

The aftermath of the first event of catastrophic terrorism would be the wrong time to take preventive action. In an atmosphere of fear and hysteria, we are unlikely to achieve the delicate balancing among competing social objectives that such an effort requires. Because the effort involves protecting the homeland rather than foreign interests, and because terrorist groups might well include or even be composed entirely of U.S. citizens, this problem straddles the divide between the agencies in our government that are dedicated to fighting domestic crime and protecting civil rights and those that are devoted to countering foreign threats. The required effort will also involve agencies of the government that are not normally involved in security issues, such as the Department of Health and Human Services and the

Department of Agriculture. Preparations must extend well beyond the federal government to the state and local government bodies that respond to emergencies and provide essential services. Protecting critical national infrastructure must also involve the private-sector providers of these infrastructures.

A cross-cutting issue such as catastrophic terrorism therefore calls for an unusually broad concert of government departments. In recent years, the U.S. government has begun to put this concert together. This effort has been organized by the White House National Security Council and the existing departments and agencies, rather than by designating a single existing agency as "lead agency" or by creating a new "department of domestic security." Progress has been made in parceling out "lead agency" and "supporting" assignments, and setting policy on "who's in charge" in a given circumstance involving catastrophic terrorism. These assignments are consistent with the historical roles and other duties of the existing cabinet departments, with due regard for other social values such as civil rights. For example, lead federal agency responsibility for responding to imminent threat of catastrophic terrorism (called "crisis management") was assigned to the domestic law enforcement agencies, the Department of Justice, and the Federal Bureau of Investigation, rather than to national security agencies such as the DOD or the Central Intelligence Agency.

This arrangement is appropriate and can work, but its current capability falls far short of what is needed to counter catastrophic terrorism. In many cases the agencies assigned lead roles have few or no capabilities for carrying them out and little funding, technology, or institutional base to build new capability. The result is a host of unfunded mandates. Other agencies, of which DOD is the prime example, are assigned only supporting roles, but have preponderant capability because of their other missions, including, in DOD's case, counter-proliferation, force protection, and defense information network protection. The result of this management plan is that if an incident of catastrophic terrorism occurred in coming years, the federal government agencies would arrive on the scene with an orderly system of command and control but with capabilities that are inadequate: a "come-as-you-are" party.

We have finished the period of assigning roles, and now it is time to begin an era of capability building. Now that the National Security Council (NSC) has coordinated interagency policy for catastrophic terrorism, it must begin to coordinate interagency programs. We need a national program covering technology, doctrine and techniques, law and regulation, research into the underlying causes of catastrophic terrorism, and institution-building. This program should cover all phases of the "life cycle" of catastrophic terrorism: intelligence, prevention and deterrence, warning, protection, crisis management, damage mitigation and cleanup (called "consequence management"), forensics and attribution as the basis for prosecution or retaliation, and "lessons learned" to prevent future events.

The NSC has not performed this type of program design and coordination in its recent history (for more on this point, see Chapter 10), as it is mainly a mechanism for policy coordination, not program coordination. It has little clout in determining agency budget allocations or internal management, while the Office of Management and Budget (OMB) does not play a very strong role in interagency budget coordination among the national security agencies compared to its role in domestic policy matters. NSC staff are typically selected for their foreign policy and international experience rather than experience managing large operating agencies or technical programs. In this weak NSC program coordination system, program decisions coordinated at the NSC are easily ignored by departments or overturned by congressional committees that have even weaker mechanisms than the executive branch for coordinating cross-cutting activities.

The problem of program design, planning, and coordination is common to many post–Cold War new missions that are cross-cutting and where new capabilities are required. As discussed further in Chapter 10, this problem can be addressed within the existing NSC and departmental structure through a strengthened White House mechanism. Specifically, we recommend a new NSC arm, headed at the level of a Deputy National Security Adviser, with a small staff experienced in program and budget management. This entity would have the charter to draw up a coordinated program plan for catastrophic terrorism, counter-proliferation, peacekeeping support, and other cross-cutting issues on behalf of the President. OMB would play an essential role in this new arrangement, ensuring that agencies reflect the President's cross-cutting program plan in their budget priorities and in their internal organization and management. In comparable efforts in the past, an active role by the Vice President, the only official besides the President who stands above the cabinet secretaries, has also proved valuable.

DOD's role in the national program for homeland defense is appropriately not a lead one. But DOD should play a strong supporting role, especially in the interagency program to build capability. Much of the needed effort can be an offshoot of DOD's existing missions of counter-proliferation, force protection, and protection of its own information networks.[2] For example, as DOD seeks information dominance through the application of network technology as described in Chapter 3, it will become increasingly important that its information systems remain secure. Through the National Security Agency and other DOD components, the Department must conduct a strong program to develop and deploy security technology such as public-key cryptography, and techniques such as requiring two cleared persons to perform key network control functions (akin to the "two-man rule" long in force for personnel who handle nuclear weapons). Due to DOD's sheer size, this effort will dwarf any comparable effort that other agencies can mount, and it should therefore be conducted as the core of a national effort. For example, DOD could take the lead in funding a National Information Assurance Institute, a government-funded but private organization dedicated to developing best-practice information assurance techniques and technology in partnership with the private sector.[3]

Conclusion

The very strengths of the U.S. military could also create vulnerabilities unless we begin, now, to recognize them and to plan appropriate protections and countermeasures.

---

2. The ingredients of a DOD program to contribute to the national effort against catastrophic terrorism were detailed in Ashton B. Carter and William J. Perry, *Preventive Defense: A New Security Strategy for America* (Washington, D.C.: The Brookings Institution, 1999).

3. The National Information Assurance Institute concept was described in Carter and Perry, *Preventive Defense*, pp. 164–165.

6

Keeping the Technological Edge

ASHTON B. CARTER

WITH MARCEL LETTRE AND SHANE SMITH

Rather than attempting to match the Warsaw Pact tank for tank or soldier for soldier during the Cold War, the United States evolved an "offset strategy" whereby superior American technology would counterbalance greater opposing numbers.[1] The offset strategy had two components. The first was to field superior technology through aggressive pursuit of military R&D, and developing a high-technology defense industrial base. The second was to deny opponents that technology through a system of export controls and protection of technological secrets.

This strategy of superiority and denial worked: the offset strategy secured deterrence of the numerically superior forces of the Soviet Union and its allies, and forced the Soviet Union to bankrupt itself in the pursuit of military technology it could not easily obtain from the West. Elsewhere, denial slowed proliferation of weapons of mass destruction. The success of the offset strategy was demonstrated in 1990–91, in a war no one had anticipated: in DESERT STORM, U.S. reconnaissance satellites, stealth aircraft, precision weapons, and other technologies — unmatched by any other military — made quick work of Iraq's Soviet-equipped army. Americans liked the offset approach, and superiority and denial remain the distinctive American

The insights and information provided by Denis Bovin, Herbert S. Winokur, Jr., and Philip A. Odeen are gratefully acknowledged. They bear no responsibility for errors of fact or judgment.

1. William J. Perry, "Desert Storm and Deterrence," *Foreign Affairs*, Vol. 70, No. 4 (Fall 1991).

way of defense, now applied to the post–Cold War era's new missions.

But a challenge looms to the preservation of America's technological edge in the post–Cold War era. The challenge results not from new types of military threat, but from trends in the industrial and technology base that undergirds the U.S. technological edge in military affairs. This base, once largely the creation of Department of Defense (DOD) spending and almost exclusively American, is increasingly becoming commercialized and globalized. *Commercialization* refers to the fact that the technology of central importance to national security, especially information technology, increasingly originates in commercial rather than defense companies, without the sponsorship of DOD and outside its control. Related to commercialization is the *marketization* of the defense industry: defense companies must justify themselves to shareholders by the same standards of profits and cash flows as civilian commercial companies, and the industry is today having difficulty withstanding the market's pressures. *Globalization* is the related trend whereby leading technology companies are increasingly global rather than purely American in their outlook, ownership, workforce, and markets.

The United States cannot accomplish the national security objectives its people expect without the offset strategy, but the Pentagon cannot carry out the offset strategy without access to a strong industrial and technology base willing to serve its needs. Maintenance of this base in the face of commercialization and globalization requires that the Defense Department adapt its approaches toward maintaining U.S. technological superiority. Meanwhile the denial component of the offset strategy requires a new definition of the "secrets" that must be protected if it is to remain effective. This chapter describes three types of adaptation that should be encouraged by the new U.S. administration and its defense team. The first two seek to preserve the *superiority* dimension of a continuing offset strategy: first, aligning defense procurement practices with market forces, and second, remaining the world's fastest and best integrator of commercial technology into defense systems. The third adaptation is meant to preserve the *denial* dimension: protecting secrets by means of an "immune system," rather than a hermetic seal as during the Cold War.

ALIGNING DEFENSE PROCUREMENT PRACTICES WITH MARKET FORCES

DOD must have access to an industrial base to which it can turn for superior military systems. Commercialization requires DOD to align its own practices more closely with the market forces affecting the commercial companies that increasingly supply vital technology for defense, and the defense companies that integrate technology into military systems. This is emphatically not a call for an "industrial policy" that would prop up weak defense companies and accentuate the isolation of the defense industry. Instead, the United States needs an approach that works *with* rather than *against* market forces, leveraging commercialization to secure the needs of defense. Globalization means facing the implications of trans-border and especially trans-Atlantic links within the defense industry.

REMAINING THE WORLD'S FASTEST INTEGRATOR OF COMMERCIAL TECHNOLOGY INTO DEFENSE SYSTEMS ("RUNNING FASTEST")

Second, the U.S. military must be the world's *fastest* adapter and adopter of commercial technology into defense systems. Potential opponents will also have access to much state-of-the-art technology, since they can purchase it on the open global market. Thus DOD must "run faster" than others, rapidly feeding on the global base rather than relying almost exclusively on its own sponsored R&D as it did during the Cold War.

PROTECTING SECRETS THROUGH AN IMMUNE SYSTEM RATHER THAN A HERMETIC SEAL

Third, the United States must abandon the "hermetic seal" model: denying technology to others by seeking to put an impermeable barrier around the American defense technology base. Globalization and commercialization mean that crucial technology now arises *outside* this barrier as well as inside, and cannot be protected by a simple barrier. Second, it is in the U.S. interest to have technology diffuse *inward* to defense from a globalized, commercialized base, and in these cases the hermetic seal approach impedes DOD from "running faster." Third, the unique sources of U.S. military advantage that will need to be protected will increasingly rely on U.S. systems-engineering capability, rather than component or subsystem technologies. The latter will be widely available and impractical to contain. The U.S. export controls system must focus on unique sources of military advantage rather than technology across the board if it is to be truly effective at slowing the competition. Finally, accompanying the new meaning of secrets must be new ways of protecting them. Much technology that is "foreign" will find its way into defense systems and must somehow be made trustworthy. Meanwhile the new technology of networks and compact data storage make "insiders" as potentially dangerous as "outsiders." To deal with these changes, rather than applying simplistic and out-dated bureaucratic rules, export controls and security systems must be capable of identifying and reacting to real security threats, just as the human immune system works not by trying to isolate the body from the environment, but by sensing dangers and combating the most dangerous ones selectively.

The magnitude of the conceptual challenge to America's techno-logical edge, and the profound nature of the adaptations needed in these three areas, can be seen from Figure 6-1, which contrasts the technological context of the Cold War's offset strategy with the world toward which commercialization and globalization appear to be car-rying us, which differs from the Cold War world in virtually every determinant of superiority and denial.

Can the offset strategy and America's technological edge be pre-served in the new world? While commercialization and globalization create a strange new world for defense, on balance they are strongly favorable. Riding the commercial technology tide provides DOD greater capability at lesser cost than it could have by "going it alone." Defense systems based on commercial information technology enjoy nearly continuous upgrades: the commercial "cycle time" to produce new products is typically 18 months or less, compared to a program lifetime in DOD that might be years or even decades. DOD also saves money by outsourcing functions that are more efficiently performed by the commercial sector, where natural market adjustments replace pain-ful political adjustments. Strong market forces, if properly harnessed, can be used to keep the defense industry innovative and efficient (for more on this point, see Chapter 7). Since our allies in both the Atlantic and the Pacific are drawing on the same globalized technology base as we are, alliance interoperability both the Atlantic and the Pacific are drawing on the same globalized technology base as we are, alliance interoperability — the capacity to fight as a coalition — and political solidarity will be strengthened.

Figure 6-1.   COLD WAR .... ⇨ .... FUTURE

Defense Technology	Defense Technology
▫ originates in defense technology base	⇒ originates in commercial technology base
▫ that is embedded in defense companies	⇒ that is embedded in commercially driven companies
▫ residing in the United States	⇒ that are global
▫ for which defense is main driver.	⇒ for which defense is niche player.

Defense Industry	Defense Industry
▫ is a multi-tiered system of national (U.S. and European national) companies, primes, and subs;	⇒ is centered in a few large prime contractors that are:
	either separate U.S. and pan-European continental champions protecting home markets and competing in third markets (Fortress America, Fortress Europe);
	or fully merged trans-Atlantic primes competing across the Atlantic and globally;
	or U.S. and pan-European primes united by joint ventures, strategic partnerships, and teaming arrangements; and competing across the Atlantic and globally;
▫ that develop defense-unique technology and embed it in components	⇒ that buy commercial technology and components
▫ from which they engineer systems.	⇒ from which they engineer systems and systems-of-systems.

Export Control and Industrial & Personnel Security Policy	Export Control and Industrial & Personnel Security Policy
▫ A hermetic seal,	⇒ An immune system,
▫ based on denial of access,	⇒ based on risk assessment and flexible response,
▫ surrounding a well-defined defense technology base	⇒ operating in the midst of a global industrial organism
▫ that is American,	⇒ that has no national identity,
▫ protects technology ("secrets"),	⇒ protects systems architectures and unique military capabilities ("secrets"),
▫ trusts Americans,	⇒ trusts no one without checking,
▫ accepts dependence only on U.S. citizens.	⇒ but depends on everyone.

Military Advantage	Military Advantage
▫ is conferred by national possession of defense-unique leap-ahead technology that potential opponents cannot get.	⇒ is conferred by rapid adoption and integration of (mostly) commercial technology and components into defense-unique systems-of-systems more rapidly than opponents (who have access to most of the same technology).

Commercialization and globalization are both inexorable, so it is a good thing that they can be beneficial for national security if they are embraced rather than resisted by DOD. But if DOD were to persist in old approaches to superiority and denial, the new trends will both erode the technological edge and open up new vulnerabilities. Even under the best of circumstances, the scorecard can be positive for the offset strategy only if the increased benefits can be made to outweigh the undeniably greater risks of the new world. It is a policy choice whether the United States will fully avail itself of the benefits and fully mitigate the risks. If it does not, the alternative is a bleak one: when the Pentagon turns to industry to support the offset strategy, it might find no companies willing or capable to do so.

Commercialization

Commercialization is affecting defense in two ways: first, most new technologies of relevance to defense originate in the commercial sector. Second, defense companies are undergoing marketization — or increased focus on shareholder value — and are consequently under intense pressure in a competitive industrial marketplace that is demanding higher margins, valuations, and growth.

GROWTH OF THE COMMERCIAL TECHNOLOGY BASE

In the days of the Cold War, new technologies of importance to defense usually arose from research conducted under DOD sponsorship within defense companies, think-tanks, and universities located in the United States. Today new defense systems tend to arise when defense companies embed commercially developed technology into weapons.

To appreciate the facts, contrast the situation in 1980 with the year 2000. According to the National Science Foundation, the amount of money spent on scientific research and development in the then-western world in 1980 was about $240 billion in today's dollars, evenly divided between the United States and its G-7 partners.[2] The U.S. Department of Defense sponsored about $40 billion, or one-sixth of the entire total. In the year 2000, by contrast, the corresponding global total for R&D spending is $360 billion, half again as much, in

2. National Science Board, *Science and Engineering Indicators—1998*, NSB 98-1 (Arlington, Va.: National Science Foundation, 1998), pp. 4–5, 4–24, 4–37.

constant dollars, as in 1980. The United States still accounts for half the total, about $180 billion. But today DOD furnishes only one-twelfth of the total: half its 1980 share.

Moreover, there are indications that this shrinking portion is not being used to press the technological frontier. Much more of DOD's R&D spending is being used for downstream engineering of mature systems than for research into new enabling technologies: that is, more "D" than "R" (88 percent development and 12 percent research in 2000, compared to 69 percent and 31 percent, respectively, in 1980).[3] In terms of applications, much defense R&D today goes to keep old "legacy" systems going or to prop up faltering programs, rather than launching new leap-ahead military systems. Independent research and development (IR&D), conducted within defense companies and cost-shared with DOD, used to be a means for keeping defense companies innovative; this, too, is declining, amounting in 2000 to only half its mid-1980s value.[4] All these indices point to one fact: tomorrow's defense innovations will largely be derivatives of technology developed and marketed by commercial companies for commercial motives.

---

3. Ibid., p. 4–23.

4. Independent R&D (IR&D) refers to basic or applied research, development, or systems or other concept formulation studies devised and conducted within industry. Each year the company proposing an IR&D program submits its plans to DOD. When DOD agrees that a portion of the proposed program contributes to DOD's purposes, it permits the company to include that portion in its indirect costs (overhead) on its contracts. In other words, DOD reimburses industry for a portion of industry's own R&D. The overall amount of IR&D has been declining. More seriously, over time the government is tending to dictate more of the programs, making them less truly the result of the independent judgment of non-government scientists and engineers. See John D. Moteff, *Defense Research: A Primer on the Department of Defense's RDT&E Program,* Congressional Research Service Report 97-316, May 5, 1998; Frank Lichtenberg, "U.S. Government Subsidies to Private Military R&D: DOD's IR&D Policy," *Defense Economics,* Vol. 1 (1990); Testimony of Under Secretary of Defense for Acquisition, Technology, and Logistics Jacques Gansler before the Military Research and Development Subcommittee, House Armed Services Committee, March 1, 2000; and Defense Science Board (DSB) Task Force Report, *Preserving a Healthy and Competitive U.S. Defense Industry to Ensure our Future National Security,* Summer 2000.

A telling example is software. Since the defense market is a small portion of the overall software market, it has no alternative but to adopt the most popular software systems. The alternative is to develop its own hothouse software, which would inevitably be inferior and more costly than the widespread commercial versions. In all but narrow custom niches, DOD has no alternative but to ride the tide of commercial development.[5]

The cases of information technology, biotechnology, and space technology show the variety of challenges posed by commercialization. As the software example highlights, the cutting edge in information technology (IT) has passed from defense to commercial companies. Once upon a time DOD pioneered the microchip, massive parallel processing, the Internet, software engineering techniques, and other technologies that are now spearheaded by the well-financed commercial e-revolution. In all but niche areas, DOD will be a consumer rather than an originator of technology in this sector. But at least in the IT sector, DOD has strong engineering capability in its own laboratories and industry, a legacy of its earlier preeminence. In biotechnology, by contrast, there is no such legacy. The biotechnology industry has no tradition of working for defense. Indeed, in some cases biotechnology companies have exhibited an aversion to working on defense applications, citing onerous federal acquisition rules and sometimes fearing damage to their reputations. Yet biotechnology poses fearsome possibilities for biowarfare and bioterrorism. Indeed, it is likely that the biotechnology revolution will prove to be as profound as the information revolution in altering the possibilities for armed conflict, both offensive and defensive. The United States has rightly foresworn offensive biowarfare, but DOD will need protective devices such as detectors and vaccines. For these technologies, DOD must establish a working relationship with the new biotech industry. A third example is that of space technology, which occupies a position between IT and biotechnology in terms of the impact of commercialization. DOD and NASA still occupy a commanding position in this field, but the number of commercial communications, imaging, navigation, and launch services busi-

5. Defense Science Board studies in 1987 and 1994 analyzed the issue of software management, and other DSB studies on international arms cooperation (1996), information warfare (1997), and globalization and security (1999) have continued to draw attention to the software challenges for DOD.

nesses is growing. The flow of technology, which has run from DOD to commerce since the Space Age began, will in time begin to reverse direction.

To benefit from commercialization, DOD must buy from commercial companies. This sounds easy enough, but current rules and procedures governing the spending of public monies frequently get in the way. These rules impose accounting burdens on companies selling to defense and frequently involve contracting vehicles that are foreign to commercial practice. Some commercial companies, simply unwilling to tolerate DOD's eccentricities, refuse to sell to the Pentagon. Their place is taken by specialized defense-only companies adapted to the arcane ways of the Federal Acquisition Regulations (FAR); they generally pass on their high costs and inefficiencies to the military. This problem has long been recognized, and in recent years a determined start has been made at acquisition reform.[6] However, the process is unfinished. At stake is much more than simple budgetary efficiency. If the U.S. military cannot "run faster" than other militaries, it cannot sustain the technological lead that is the key to its preeminence.

MARKETIZATION OF THE DEFENSE INDUSTRY

For companies specializing in engineering defense systems, whether using commercial or defense-developed technology, the business climate has changed as dramatically as the international environment since the end of the Cold War. In the mid-1970s, then Chief of Staff of the U.S. Army Edward C. Meyer warned that the United States had a "hollow army." There is now more reason to fear a hollowing out of the industry upon which America's technological edge depends.

The U.S. defense industry is still by far the world's largest and most technologically proficient. The U.S. defense budget, $279 billion

---

6. Calls for acquisition reform began in the 1980s. See Packard Commission, *A Quest for Excellence*, Final Report by the President's Blue Ribbon Commission on Defense Management, The White House, June 1986. See also Chapter 6 of Ashton B. Carter and William J. Perry, *Preventive Defense: A New Security Strategy for America* (Washington, D.C.: Brookings Institution Press, 1999); and Steven J. Kelman, Michael J. Lippitz, and John P. White, *Reforming the Department of Defense: The Revolution in Business Affairs*, Preventive Defense Project Publication Series, Vol. 1, No. 4 (1999). See also Chapter 7 in this volume by Michael J. Lippitz, Sean O'Keefe, and John P. White.

in FY 2000, is at least 20 percent larger than the aggregate of all its European and Asian allies.[7] Moreover, this budget is increasing, whereas Europe's budgets are flat or declining. The critical investment portion of the defense budget, covering procurement and R&D on new weapons, is $92.5 billion in FY 2000, and is growing more rapidly than the overall budget. This is about 50 percent more than is spent on defense investment by all the U.S. allies combined. However, the U.S. defense industry has shrunk dramatically during the 1990s, as the rest of the economy has grown robustly. Today's defense budget is only 69 percent of its 1985 peak (measured in FY 2000 dollars), and investment is only 55 percent.[8] The FY 2000 defense budget consumes 3 percent of gross domestic product (GDP), just half of 1985, when it consumed 6 percent of GDP.[9] Employment in the defense industry had dropped to 878,000 in 1999, from 1.4 million in 1990 (a decline of well over one-third).[10]

DOD and the industry attempted to contend with the shrinking market by consolidating the prime contractor base. By 1999, just eight consolidated primes existed where there had been 36 in 1993.[11] The shakedown has begun to affect the lower tiers of the defense industry — companies that supply the primes with subsystems and crucial

---

7. *Department of Defense Annual Report to the President and Congress*, 2000, Appendix B: Budget Tables; Office of the Undersecretary of Defense (Comptroller), *National Defense Budget Estimates for FY 2001*, Table 1-1 (March 2000). For allied defense expenditures, see *World Military Expenditures*, Center for Defense Information, at <http://www.cdi.org/issues/wme/>; *CIA World Factbook*, January 1, 1999, country listings at <http://www.cia.gov/cia/publications/factbook/country.html>; country summaries in *The Military Balance 1999–2000* (London: International Institute for Strategic Studies, 1999); and Loren B. Thompson, *The Post-Deconstruction Defense Industry: Now What?* Lexington Institute, September 9, 1998.

8. Office of the Undersecretary of Defense (Comptroller), *National Defense Budget Estimates for FY 2001*, Table 6-1 (March 2000).

9. Office of the Under Secretary of Defense (Comptroller), *National Defense Budget Estimates for FY 2001*, Tables 6-1 and 7-7, (March 2000).

10. Bear Stearns, *The Consolidation of the Defense Industry: Winners and Losers*, February 7, 2000.

11. Bear Stearns, *The Consolidation of the Defense Industry: Winners and Losers*; and Bear Stearns, *The Consolidation of the Aerospace Industry/Defense Merchant Supplier Base*, April 17, 2000.

technology. The number of these companies has decreased by about half since 1993, from 85 to 44. But further consolidation at the second and third tiers is needed: many of these companies are too small by themselves to provide the critical mass that is necessary for innovation. They should be encouraged to merge with each other or with units spun off from the primes (units regarded as "non-core") as the latter rationalize their portfolios.

Accompanying the dramatic change in industry structure is an equally important change in the types of products DOD is asking these firms to produce. An increasing share of the procurement budget goes to upgrading the electronic and weapons systems aboard aircraft, ships, spacecraft, armored vehicles, and intelligence and command centers, rather than to new procurement of the platforms themselves. These subsystems are themselves more complex: they are truly systems in their own right and not just "black boxes" added to the platforms as if in afterthought. The electronic "innards" are an increasing share of the value of new platforms. For example, the electronic warfare suite aboard tactical aircraft now under development is a complex system uniting radar, targeting, communications, electronic countermeasures, and attack warning functions previously attached to the aircraft system as separate subsystems.

The cost of developing defense systems is high because of their increasing complexity, and these costs can rarely be recovered by contractors, as they once were, in long production runs. In the 1980s, contractors absorbed losses on R&D contracts in the expectation that they would recover the losses in production contracts: every dollar of defense R&D in 1985 was followed by three dollars of procurement spending on the weapons developed. Today these losses cannot be recovered: only about $1.50 of procurement follows each dollar of R&D.[12] The companies accordingly perform less R&D.

Today's defense *systems* — platforms, weapons, and sensors — are being incorporated into synergistic *systems-of-systems*.[13] For example, a reconnaissance aircraft might spot a target — perhaps an air defense battery — and give its coordinates to a precision weapon, which then destroys the air defense battery. Elimination of the air de-

12. Office of the Undersecretary of Defense (Comptroller), *National Defense Budget Estimates for FY 2001*, Table 6-1.

13. The term "system-of-systems" was coined by the Defense Science Board in 1990.

fense in turn makes the collection of further targeting data by the aircraft easier, and the cycle continues. The key skill this requires of defense companies, therefore, is systems engineering: making defense-unique systems and systems-of-systems (for the primes) and complete subsystems (for the second tier) from a base of underlying technology that is increasingly commercial. Both military advantage (the offset strategy) and economic value to the industry (cost of the program and, accordingly, profits) therefore increasingly inhere in the systems engineering rather than in the technology underlying individual components.

Firms attempting to stay in the defense business in the face of these changes must do so under increasing market pressures. On the whole, of course, the decision by the United States after World War II to rely on the private marketplace to serve most of its national security needs has been vindicated. Nations that opted to preserve government-owned and operated arsenals have regretted that decision. However, DOD's needs for a healthy defense industry to preserve the offset strategy are not now well aligned with the market forces pressing on the industry.

First, the defense industry must compete in the stock market for capital. Here the signs in recent years are negative. The newly consolidated prime contractors, saddled with debt as a result of overpaying during their consolidation binge, have seen their credit ratings plunge. A stock market looking for high margins, growth, and predictable cash flows has observed that the primes have been subject to increasing government pressure on profits, abrupt terminations of programs, and flat or decreasing defense spending for a decade. The result is sunken market capitalizations of the major defense companies, during a period of overall rapid growth in stock market valuations. The total market capitalization of the defense industry had become, by the end of 1999, about half that of Wal-Mart and a quarter that of Microsoft.[14] There is plenty of blame to go around for this predicament. The big primes paid too much to acquire one another, and the resulting giants are deep in debt. They are having difficulty managing centrally the ungainly portfolios they have amassed. DOD promised to share the savings from consolidation

14. Market capitalization figures as of the end of calendar year 1999 are from Defense Science Board Task Force Report, *Preserving a Healthy and Competitive U.S. Defense Industry*.

with industry, but the efficiencies realized were smaller than hoped and DOD reneged on its pledge to share them. Finally, the defense industry has suffered along with other "metal-bending" industries from the stock market's infatuation with "dot-coms." In this climate, defense companies cannot afford to make investments in future defense systems: they are concentrating on making it through the next quarter. They often see little market incentive to emphasize innovation and efficiency: in contrast to the commercial market, innovation rarely feeds further market growth, while the DOD or Congress either blocks plant closings or captures the benefits of cost-cutting measures for itself.

Second, marketization implies that managers, directors, and stockholders have alternatives for the capital they are devoting to defense. Large conglomerates that formerly pursued both defense and non-defense businesses voted with their feet during the 1990s: the list of premier U.S. industrial companies that have exited the defense market reads like a Who's Who of industrial America, including IBM, Texas Instruments, Ford, Chrysler, GE, and Westinghouse. Meanwhile, the "new economy" companies are wholly absorbed in the pursuit of rapidly growing commercial markets rather than the constrained defense market.

Third, defense companies compete in a labor market where executives are rewarded with stock options and engineers want to be on the cutting edge. Here too, the market appears to be working against defense. The drop in defense stocks has wiped out the fortunes of many of its top and middle managers. They, like their stockholders, are wondering why they should remain in the defense industry. Scientists and engineers who relish the challenge of systems engineering will still find defense work rewarding, but those whose skills are focused on the underlying technology (especially information technology) are leaving defense for commercial industry.

Defense must find ways to align its needs under the offset strategy to the market forces in which industry must survive. Properly aligned, market forces will harness the dynamism of the modern American economy to its national security needs as well as its material welfare. The alternative would be an isolated and increasingly backward defense industry that will not support the offset strategy.

Globalization

The industry that will provide the underlying technology to support U.S. defense in the future is not only increasingly non-defense, as described above, but increasingly non-American. Defense prime contractors still tend to be national or regional — American, European, etc. — in their orientation. But their suppliers of technology and subsystems are increasingly globalized companies; their markets are global; and even their ownership is globalizing. Each of these trends to globalization has important implications for DOD.

Once again, software provides an important example, this time of the globalization of suppliers. For example, India is fast becoming the world center of software engineering.[15] India may soon far surpass the United States in lines of computer code it produces that find their way into widespread commercial — and thus perforce defense — applications furnished to DOD by supposedly "U.S." companies.

Globalization of defense markets is occurring more slowly, but perceptibly. Since the Cold War ended, the worldwide arms market has shrunk by about one half. U.S. defense companies, however, have increased their market share, and with Pentagon procurement budgets shrinking or flat until the past few years, many firms have looked to overseas sales as a key source of growth. Still, U.S. firms are far less dependent on exports than are European firms. The U.S. defense sector exports about one-quarter of its production, whereas European firms tend to sell half to three-quarters of their output abroad.[16] European firms are eagerly eyeing the U.S. defense market, which is large and, unlike European acquisition budgets, growing (although

---

15. In 1999, the Indian software industry posted revenues of $3.9 billion, of which $2.7 billion were accounted for by exports. The number of engineers graduating in the field, a current force of 200,000 software engineers, and the country's comparative labor advantage in low wages pushed industry growth at annual rates in excess of 50 percent through the 1990s, and an Indian national task force has called for building it up into an $85 billion per year business by 2008 (predictions that struck some as overly conservative). See Pankaj Ghemawat, Murali Patibandla, and William J. Coughlin, "The Indian Software Industry at the Millennium," *Harvard Business School Case*, N9-700-036, September 7, 1999.

16. *Report of the Defense Science Board Task Force on Globalization and Security*, December 1999, pp. 9–11.

slowly). Market globalization creates two sources of trans-Atlantic tension. First, U.S. companies and European companies compete with each other for sales around the world. Second, disagreements between European countries and the United States about which foreign customers might end up as foes rather than friends are amplified by the market pressure on both U.S. and European companies to sell enhanced versions of weapons to third countries. Air defense systems and anti-ship systems are two categories of military systems where the capability that can be procured on the open market has increased dramatically in recent years because the United States and its partners have not been able to agree on restraints.

Globalization of ownership is the slowest of the trends to affect the defense industry. While globalization of ownership of commercial companies is far advanced and inexorable, ownership of defense companies in Europe is only now completing the shift from the state to private hands. The corresponding process occurred decades ago in the United States as the arsenal system was dismantled. Whether the U.S. and European defense industries, all dependent on a globalizing commercial technology base, can stand apart from the globalization trend in ownership is the topic of fevered speculation.[17] The outcome has important implications for defense policy.

At one extreme, as shown in Figure 6-1, the defense industry might not follow commercial industry in the globalization trend. The result would likely be national defense companies in the United States, on the one hand, and on the other, pan-European defense companies (resulting from mergers and acquisitions among British, French, German, Italian, and other firms under the pressure of the European Union), all acting with their governments' help to protect their home markets, and competing ferociously for the export market. An economic rift within the North Atlantic Alliance, and a parade of charges that one side was selling weapons to the potential opponents of the other, would likely follow. This outcome would

---

17. See, for example, "Pentagon Mulls Overseas Sale of Lockheed's Sanders Unit; Deal May Test Limits," *Defense Daily*, June 19, 2000, p. 1; John D. Morrocco, "Consolidation Poses Transatlantic Quandary," *Aviation Week & Space Technology*, July 24, 2000, p. 4; Pierre Sparaco, "U.S., Europe Explore Transatlantic Partnerships," *Aviation Week & Space Technology*, September 13, 1999, pp. 37–40; Howard Banks, "Foreign Entanglements," *Forbes*, September 6, 1999, p. 5.

probably also widen the gap between U.S. and European defense capabilities, to the further detriment of Europe.

At the other extreme, extensive trans-Atlantic mergers and acquisitions might result in a defense industry consisting at the prime contractor level of several trans-Atlantic giants competing among themselves for both the Alliance markets and global markets. The result would be a melding of continents and a knitting-together of NATO's military capabilities: a politically significant reinforcement of Alliance solidarity in the realm of political economy.

An intermediate outcome seems most likely. While there might be some additional trans-Atlantic mergers and acquisitions among the large primes, there will surely be a host of other relationships that will tend to join continents and reinforce alliances: joint ventures, strategic partnerships, teaming arrangements, and consolidation of second and third-tier sectors. In addition to its political benefits, evolution towards a trans-Atlantic industry serving all allied defense establishments will also provide the classic economic benefits of free trade.

To enjoy the benefits of this form of intermediate globalization, the United States will have to work around three problems that are certain to arise. First, there seems little prospect of entirely free and open competition for U.S. and European defense dollars. National protection of jobs will require offsetting purchases every time the Pentagon buys weapons made in Europe (even if by an American-owned company), and vice versa. Cutting costs by combining manufacturing operations is usually a key economic motive in industry consolidation, but governments want to share work out among plants in different countries. Clearly the pressures to "buy American" or "buy French" will inhibit the business motives that lead to consolidation. Second, U.S. policy sharply limits offshore companies from exercising "foreign ownership, control, or influence" (FOCI) over defense companies that deal with classified information. The rules are especially strict when the U.S. company acquired by a foreign company does work on highly classified compartmented or "black" programs. This problem is a matter of trust in the ability of allies to protect secrets. A third problem sorely tests this trust: the United States and an ally with whom it has a defense business alliance might not agree about sale to a third-country destination of items produced jointly. Such items are, in essence, re-exports of U.S. technology from the foreign company or joint venture. Are such re-exports subject to U.S. or rather allied export controls regulation and enforcement? Unless the nations agree on what arms and secrets should be controlled, and on destinations to be denied certain arms, international business ventures can be the source of inter-allied tension rather than solidarity.

New Meanings of "Secrets" and their Protection

The right-hand column of Figure 6-1 describes a world in which the very foundations of export controls policy are undermined, especially controls on items with inherent dual-use applications.[18] We are not yet in the future world to which current trends seem to be carrying us, but it will not be long before we are closer to it than to the world that became familiar during the Cold War.

In the future world, it will still be possible to describe defense *applications* of technology, but increasingly meaningless to speak of defense *technology* as such: most technology used by defense will be drawn from the commercial sector.[19] Moreover, that technology will not come exclusively from U.S. companies, but from a global base. Thus, permanent U.S. denial of such technology to all potential enemies is impractical. Rather, opponents will have access to the same technology, and U.S. military advantage must therefore come from being better and faster at *adapting* technology to military use, rather than trying to retain exclusive use of technology.

In the future world, secrets will not inhere in the underlying technologies but in their military applications. In the future, the basis of the U.S. edge in military technology will be the defense-unique systems and systems-of-systems — made mostly from commercial technology ingredients — and the systems engineering skills that go

18. For challenges stemming from these trends already faced by U.S. export control policies, see William A. Reinsch, "Export Controls in the Age of Globalism," *The Monitor: Nonproliferation, Demilitarization, and Arms Control*, Vol. 5, No. 3 (Summer 1999), pp. 3–6; and *Report of the Defense Science Board Task Force on Globalization and Security*, December 1999.

19. An example of the difficulty of distinguishing military from commercial technologies came in early 2000: Sony's new mass-marketed gaming console faced Japanese export regulations because its technology was deemed to be usable in a missile guidance system. "Sony Game Sparks Fears: So Powerful It Could be Used to Guide Missiles," *The Gazette* (Montreal), April 17, 2000, p. B-4.

with them. It is their architectures and modes of operation that will be the secrets that need protection. This circumstance will stand on its head the principle of Cold War export controls, that the object of control should be component technologies. It also makes obsolete the "hermetic seal" ideal for the export controls system of the Cold War. Then it was practical to think of placing an ostensibly impermeable barrier around the technology underlying defense applications, since most such technology arose in facilities directly or indirectly controlled by the United States government; indeed a great deal of it originated in DOD-controlled laboratories under government sponsorship.

Intense debate during the Cold War revolved around how much of this defense technology should be allowed to diffuse *out* of defense and *into* international commerce; in effect, the issue was where to place the barrier in order to balance security risks against the commercial benefits of outward diffusion.[20] But the flow of technology is increasingly in the opposite direction: technology diffuses *into* defense, *from* international commerce. The institutions generating this technology are not directly controlled by government, nor are they exclusively American. The issue in the new world is not simply balancing security and commercial interests. Instead, a host of new and more complex issues emerge that the export controls system inherited from the Cold War is ill-prepared to address. New approaches are needed.

One challenge is to define which items are still "controllable" in practical terms. Laptop personal computers, for example, are obviously useful items for potential military opponents, and most control candidates (such as North Korea) are unable to make such items indigenously for their own military applications. It is surely desirable to deny engineers working on the North Korean missile program the

---

20. For historical and Cold War perspectives on export controls, see Richard T. Culpitt, *Reluctant Champions: U.S. Presidential Policy and Strategic Export Controls* (New York: Routledge, 2000); Gary K. Bertsch, ed., *Controlling East-West Trade and Technology Transfer: Power, Politics, and Policies* (Durham: Duke University Press, 1988); and the report from the National Academy of Sciences Panel on the Impact of National Security Controls on International Technology Transfers, *Balancing the National Interest: U.S. National Security Export Controls and Global Economic Competition* (Washington, D.C.: National Academy Press, 1987).

use of powerful laptop computers. But even if the United States were to attempt to control all international sales of such computers, it could not stop the North Korean missile engineers from obtaining them: laptop PCs are sold in such large numbers around the world, in countless retail stores, that clandestine procurement by the North Koreans could not be stopped. It is evident that applying export controls to PCs is futile — attempting to control the uncontrollable. Since PCs become more potent every day, a real security price will be paid for their ubiquity in the future world. The rising tide of technology eventually raises all boats, including those of potential opponents.

Still, all is not hopeless for making some export controls effective. What is needed is not a hermetic seal, but a more discriminating system that might be likened to the human immune system. The human body does not attempt to isolate itself from all pathogens: it is not possible to breathe, eat, and come into contact with the rest of the natural world without encountering health risks. Rather, the immune system is a highly sophisticated system for detecting risks and for responding to them in a proportional and discriminating manner. The same type of approach is needed for export controls. It requires a better capability to assess the levels of technology that are widely available.[21] Such an analysis will indicate that, for some defense items (but less and less often for "technologies"), it will still be possible to configure a hermetic seal that prevents potentially antagonistic states from acquiring them. Increasingly, that seal cannot be applied around the United States but must instead be placed around the group of nations that manufacture and market the items in question. The key here is to arrive at agreement among those nations about which items to control and which countries to deny. Elsewhere, regulators will necessarily have to permit widespread sales of sensitive items, but should require exporters (backed by government inspectors) to certify that the end user of particular items is not a proscribed foreign military destination. By refocusing scarce intelligence and enforce-

---

21. In determining controllability, the Commerce Department's Export Administration Regulations (Part 768, "Foreign Availability Determination Procedures and Criteria") currently focuses on an item's foreign availability: whether it is readily available "without effective restrictions" from sources outside the United States, and is in "sufficient quantity" and of "comparable quality" so as to render a control "ineffective in achieving its purpose."

ment resources on the truly threatening transfers rather than on the "uncontrollables," security will be better protected.

The current export controls system has few of the attributes of the immune system model. It shows all the signs of a government regulatory system in distress. Morale, training, and workforce skills are low.[22] Bureaucratic battles consume more attention than program execution. Slow processing of paper copies persists, even two decades into the era of office automation. Where there should be an underlying logic to guide the regulators' actions, instead there is layer upon layer of complex and arcane rules, many embedded in statutes written by different congressional committees and administered by different agencies.[23] Enforcing the rules takes precedence over accomplishing their purpose of stopping harmful transfers. Senior policymakers attempting reform cannot get a logical handhold; overwhelmed by the tangle of rules and put off by the intense infighting of the bureaucracy, they give up in frustration, leaving the field to political fringes and interest groups.

The export controls system can still serve a vital security function if it is properly adapted to the commercializing, globalizing new world of defense. The system must modernize and streamline, define a new conceptual basis for control, employ better intelligence concerning threats and assessment of foreign availability, emphasize enforcement as much as licensing, and make better use of other control tools such as end-use controls.

---

22. For example, recent reports from the Inspectors General of the controlling agencies noted frustration among their personnel resulting from such concerns as resource constraints, overlapping priorities, increasing responsibilities, and lack of guidance. An interagency report stated that nothing better than "on-the-job training was the primary training available" for licensing officers. Offices of the Inpectors General of the Departments of Commerce, Defense, Energy, State, Treasury, and the Central Intelligence Agency, "Interagency Review of the Export Licensing Processes for Dual-Use Commodities and Munitions," Report No. 99-187, Vol. I and II, June 18, 1999.

23. Currently, export controls are established by several different statutes: the Arms Export Control Act is administered by the State Department, the Export Administration Act by the Commerce Department, the Trading with the Enemy Act by the Treasury Department, and the International Emergency Economic Powers Act by the Treasury and Commerce Departments.

Fighting against traitors, spies, and saboteurs is not the usual stuff of high-level defense policymaking, but here too the changing technological context will require basic adaptations directed from the top. The Cold War security model here, too, was simply based on the hermetic seal. Once it was applied (after some controversy in the 1950s) to the communist bloc, the hermetic seal model became ingrained in the industrial and personnel security system. The system did not work perfectly, but the model was generally understood and accepted. The key attributes that signified trustworthiness were U.S. citizenship and, for those working in defense institutions, a security clearance. But in a globalized, commercialized world, many of the people who will make important contributions to maintaining the U.S. technological edge in defense will be outside both perimeters. At the same time, technology is changing the nature of the threat to information security. As shown by recent sensational cases — nuclear scientist Wen Ho Lee's downloaded files at Los Alamos, the computer hard drives that went missing at the same laboratory, and the "Love Bug" Internet virus — entirely new security risks are emerging. In the future world, secrets will be hard to define and even harder to confine. Globalization and commercialization present difficult problems. The hermetic seal approach to personnel and industrial security will be increasingly unable to protect secrets in the new environment. A very different and more discriminating approach is needed, and the immune system model is the appropriate one.

The way changing technology is posing new risks is perhaps illustrated best by the risks in the information technology area of cyber traitors, cyber spies, and cyber saboteurs, all of which are very different from their Cold War counterparts. For example, a computer network might be used for sharing intelligence information among analysts, for planning contingency operations, or for designing a secret weapon. A spy trying to get access to information on the network is barred from doing so by a system that controls access, such as by requiring passwords and by preventing workers who are using the network from tapping into information they do not need to know. Some workers have higher clearances than others, with senior managers having access to all the information. However, it is well known that the greatest security risk in this system is not the senior managers with the highest clearances, but rather the systems administrator who installs and operates the safeguards. That individual might be able to alter the software that controls the system of passwords, allowing an accomplice broad and completely undetected access to the network.

Even having a completely reliable administrator to run the system does not provide full protection. The software that controls the passwords is part of an enormous network management program consisting of millions of lines of computer code. Increasingly, this is commercial software, even in the most secret defense networks. DOD cannot develop such complex software on its own (and it should not, since superior software in wide usage, periodically upgraded, can be bought cheaply). Substantial parts of this software are likely to have been designed in foreign countries by individuals without U.S. security clearances. Since the cost of computing and storage are falling so rapidly, developers have little incentive to streamline software, and so problems are often fixed by adding a new layer of software rather than redesigning from scratch. Since software is easy to change in this way, it is changed frequently and by many people. The result of all these factors is complex, opaque, "bloated" code. Software engineers agree that systems of this nature are so complex that there is simply no way to "verify" the software, that is, to make certain that its designers or modifiers have not embedded changes that would allow an outsider to get access to a network it controls: neither by scrutinizing all the lines of code, nor by insisting that all its authors have security clearances. Instead, some other means must be found for thwarting cyber saboteurs. Such methods do not follow the hermetic seal model. One method is to operate the software for a time, deliberately accepting the attendant risk, to see whether certain pieces of the software show suspicious patterns, e.g., are not called into use during normal operations and might have been added solely to permit clandestine penetration. A more radical method would be to open the software to the "hacker" community: if after a year or so this highly motivated and competent community has not penetrated the system, one may conclude that it is "secure" enough to begin using it for classified operations.

If information is difficult to confine in the networked world, it is also difficult to detect or even to destroy. Workers can download enormous amounts of information onto a high-density medium and walk out of the office with it. Early in 2000, two hard drives were reported missing from a vault at Los Alamos National Laboratory.

These two small devices reportedly contained all the data on U.S., foreign, and hypothesized makeshift bombs that would be required for protection against nuclear weapons terrorism and accident; such information would be invaluable to a terrorist. This incident illustrated the new problem of *density*: enormous amounts of information can be stored in compact media. Erasing stored data on such media does not destroy it; subtle traces remain on a hard drive that could allow information to be recovered. Even physically smashing a hard drive does not help: tiny fragments of the drive can contain large amounts of information, enough, for example, to reveal the nature of a secret project.

The ultimate challenge to *defining* secrets in the information age is presented by the unclassified World Wide Web itself. DOD has found that well-meaning information officers had placed on the Web seemingly innocuous and clearly unclassified information that, nonetheless, posed a threat. For example, a video walking tour through the home of the Chairman of the Joint Chiefs of Staff was, for a time, accessible on the Web, potentially giving terrorists just what they would need to plan an attack. In the past, it would have required painstaking and risky work for terrorists to collect such information, and without it, they would be far less capable of mounting a successful attack. While no one would suggest that all such information should be classified, the fact remains that the very volume of information on the Web and the ease of access to it poses a security threat. Once again, a hermetic seal is not possible; a more subtle immune system approach must be designed and implemented.

Finally, information is available to opponents to a greater degree simply because, during the 1990s, the U.S. military has been employed much more frequently and visibly than during the Cold War. These operations have given potential opponents an unprecedented view of U.S. defense systems and concepts of operations. Operational security is hard to maintain in the glare of modern media. Balancing the need for allies and the public to be informed about ongoing operations against the revelation of capabilities to potential opponents is a task that is only now beginning to be addressed.

Recommendations to the New President and the New Defense Team

Recommendations for preserving the U.S. technological edge revolve around three principles: the United States should align its defense procurement practices with market forces; it should remain the world's fastest integrator of commercial technology into defense systems; and it should abandon the "hermetic seal" model of protecting secrets in favor of an "immune system" model.

ALIGN DEFENSE PROCUREMENT PRACTICES WITH MARKET FORCES

Commercialization and globalization are ineluctable: DOD cannot escape or "manage" them through command-and-control regulation of industry. Powerful market and technological forces drive these changes. Resistance is futile; instead, DOD can achieve many of the nation's goals for the offset strategy by aligning its own procurement practices with the forces at work in the global economy as a whole. Where a regulatory approach would ultimately result in a weak and isolated defense industry, propped up by the government, that falls short of prevailing standards of innovation and efficiency, a market approach will give DOD the ability to ride the tide of the dynamic global world industrial economy.

Reward the Defense Industry When it Follows Sound Business Practices in Pursuit of Innovation and Efficiency

Too often the incentives given to private industry by the government are adverse to the government's interests. DOD should share with industry the savings from cost-cutting, facility closings, and other efficiencies. On most current defense contracts, higher costs lead to higher profits, giving industry an incentive not to cut costs. If the government does not share the returns on investment, industry managers will not invest in new factory equipment or make other cost-cutting investments. DOD should take steps to reverse this perverse incentive.

DOD should allow higher profits when industry performs successfully in terms of cost, schedule, and performance. Under current procurement rules, poorly performing companies too often enjoy the same profits as those that deliver superior value.

DOD should (with the approval of Congress) expand use of multi-year contracts. Multi-year contracting is common practice in commercial industry, with the period of the contract adjusted by the customer to enhance value to itself. Congress has begun to permit exceptions to its general requirement of annual reauthorization of budget authority; this should be expanded. Such exceptions can result in enhanced program stability, lower costs, efficiencies due to load-leveling of employment, and greater capital investment by industry.

DOD should adjust "progress payment" practices for both contractors and their subcontractors, with the goal of having their cash flows match defense industry historical levels and more closely approximate related industry standards. DOD reimburses contractors for costs of operation through progress payments. Historically, these progress payment rates were in the range of 80–85 percent, but in the past decade they have declined to 70–75 percent. As a result, industry must borrow or cut internal investment in innovation to make up for the reduction in cash flow, neither of which serves the government's interest.

DOD should educate program managers and acquisition policymakers in commercial management and finance practices, not just the Federal Acquisition Regulations, so they can better align their management practices with market forces. It is not surprising that managers who have spent their careers mastering the government's unique business practices are sometimes not familiar with commercial best practices. They are therefore not able to advocate changes in regulations that would increase value to the government, nor to apply better practices when existing regulations would permit them. In recent years training in commercial practices has been made more available to the acquisition workforce through courses in DOD institutions such as the Defense Acquisition University, the Industrial College of the Armed Forces, and the National Defense University, as well as civilian business schools and distance learning.[24] These programs should be expanded, and tailored instruction should be made available at the

---

24. See Testimony of Under Secretary of Defense for Acquisitions, Technology, and Logistics Jacques Gansler before the Readiness and Management Support Subcommittee, Senate Armed Services Committee, April 26, 2000. Examples of curriculum descriptions can be seen at <www.ndu.edu/ndu/icaf/curriculum9.html>.

highest levels of the acquisition system, where the need and potential benefits are greatest.

The Secretary of Defense should provide an annual statement to Congress on the state of the defense industry and technology base and its ability to support the offset strategy. Preserving the offset strategy through a market approach to the defense industry and technology base is a shared responsibility of the Secretary of Defense and Congress. A dialogue between the two branches on such matters as contracting policy would acquaint senior policymakers on both sides with the issues and would foster joint solutions. The personal delivery by the Secretary of Defense of an annual statement on the "industrial force structure" to the relevant committees of Congress would provide a focus for policy thinking and action on both sides of the Potomac River.

Acquisition Practices Should Foster the Health of the Second and Third Tiers of the Defense Industry

Second and third-tier companies, more often than the primes, combine both commercial and defense businesses; they thus are an important conduit by which commercial technology can find its way into defense systems. A number of steps could be taken to help ensure their continuing good health.

First, DOD should encourage lower-tier companies serving both defense and commercial marketplaces to remain in the defense business. This objective can be attained by reducing the administrative barriers to selling to the government, and by encouraging the primes to manage their subsystem suppliers in the best practices of commercial supply-chain management.

DOD should encourage continued consolidation of firms in the lower tiers, including units spun off from primes. DOD should make clear that it encourages consolidation in the cause of greater efficiency at the second and third tiers, and should provide clear guidance on issues of competition, anti-trust, and security policy to companies pursuing consolidation.

Program managers should encourage prime contractors to buy rather than make subsystems themselves, when better value could be obtained by buying from a lower-tier company. The large primes created in the consolidation wave of the 1990s sometimes have internal incentives to buy subsystems from their own business divisions rather than from second-tier companies specializing in these subsystems. DOD program managers should monitor these "make-or-buy" decisions to ensure that they are made on the basis of best value to the government.

DOD should give important subsystems the status of full procurements, funding their R&D separately. The value, both military and economic, of military platforms increasingly inheres in their electronic subsystems. These systems are becoming complex, integrated, and expensive. They should be treated as systems in their own right and not merely as subsystems tacked on to the platform.

U.S. Government Policy Should Encourage Robust Trans-Atlantic Defense Industry Linkages

Trans-Atlantic defense linkages reinforce alliance solidarity and, over the long run, will provide efficiencies to all allied militaries arising from the benefits of free trade. Several steps could promote this goal. At the level of the primes, DOD should remove barriers to joint ventures, strategic partnering, and teaming arrangements as well as mergers and acquisitions. DOD should expect and encourage further mergers and acquisitions at the lower tiers. It should support recent reforms in export controls policy favorable to trans-Atlantic linkages, and should initiate further reforms (described in more detail below).

REMAIN THE WORLD'S FASTEST INTEGRATOR OF COMMERCIAL TECHNOLOGY INTO DEFENSE SYSTEMS ("RUNNING FASTEST")

Military advantage in the future will be conferred upon defense establishments that are able to mine the globalized, commercialized technology base the fastest, keeping ahead of competitors who will be able to draw from much of the same base. It is crucial to U.S. military advantage that it be a faster adopter and adapter of technology, since it can no longer hope to be technology's exclusive owner.

Crucial steps to help achieve this would include implementation of the recommendations of Chapter 7 on the "Revolution in Business Affairs" that encourage use of commercial buying practices and commercial systems in defense procurement, because the single most powerful mechanism to make defense a smart buyer of technology is to reduce the artificial barriers that separate defense businesses from commercial businesses. Also critical to success in technology integration are civil service reforms that strengthen the quality of DOD managers who oversee relations with the commercial sector. DOD cannot be successful in these endeavors unless it has well-trained executives.

Increase Front-end R&D Spending

DOD should increase front-end R&D spending — the categories of basic and applied research and exploratory development — as a percentage of overall investment spending (R&D plus procurement). While DOD R&D will not be as large a contributor to the store of technology available to defense as it was during the Cold War, DOD's investments are still important for three reasons. First, commercial investments, while large, focus on relatively near-term and incremental improvements to existing technology. The government still has a role in promoting long-term, high-risk, high-payoff technology. Second, R&D sponsorship is one mechanism by which DOD can attract the interest and involvement of commercial industry in defense problems. Third, by participating in its own R&D programs, DOD retains the technical proficiency and currency needed to be an efficient consumer of commercial technology — to run faster.

Do More to Make R&D Investments by Defense Companies Profitable

Defense companies must be given reasonable financial incentives to ensure that they continue to invest in R&D, both to generate new technology and to be better absorbers of new technology.

Reduce the use of fixed-price R&D contracts. Fixed-price R&D contracts reflect the illusion that the cost of genuine exploration and innovation can be planned in advance. In the past, this fiction was indulged by industry and government because companies could expect to cover their losses from R&D contracts through the long production runs characteristic of the Cold War. Today, however, R&D is too often a losing proposition for defense companies, and they decline to perform it, or perform it poorly. This trend must be reversed, by a reduction in DOD's use of fixed-price R&D contracts.

Increase independent R&D, especially at lower tiers. Since not all good ideas originate in the government, it is important that industry have the option to make investments in innovation that its own scientists and engineers conceive. Such investigator-initiated independent R&D (IR&D) is also a key inducement to technical personnel to remain in the defense industry. DOD should increase its contributions to IR&D, with special attention to the lower tiers of the defense industry, and should refrain from dictating the content of IR&D projects, allowing them to be truly independent.

Resist budget pressures to cut investment in prototypes and technology demonstrations. Budget shortages affecting major acquisitions create pressure to cut funding for such projects. But prototypes and technology demonstrations are critical vehicles for technology development and for retaining systems engineering expertise. Thus DOD should resist budget pressures to cut investments in prototypes and technology demonstrations.

Improve Ties between DOD and the Biotechnology Industry

Biowarfare defense (BWD) technology needs will require stronger ties between DOD and the biotechnology industry. Thus, DOD should support and increase investments by the Defense Advanced Research Projects Agency (DARPA), the Defense Threat Reduction Agency (DTRA), the services, and the military medical system in biotechnology research performed in commercial companies. This is a way of introducing these companies to defense needs and acquainting defense technology managers with a relatively unfamiliar, yet increasingly crucial, industry. DOD should make corresponding adjustments in its treatment of contracting, intellectual property, and indemnification, to align with practices in the biotech industry.

Interagency technical linkages should be strengthened between DOD's BWD efforts and related U.S. government efforts in the National Institutes of Health, the Centers for Disease Control and Prevention, the Food and Drug Administration, and the Department of Agriculture. These agencies have a longer association with the biotech industry, and can help DOD to become more familiar with them.

DOD should establish and fund a new not-for-profit research and development center dedicated to BWD, and associated with a major biomedical research university. In the past, when faced with revolutionary technologies of military significance, the government founded not-for-profit research centers to perform independent scientific and technological work in the public interest. These institutions were able to attract and retain technical talent that the government could not. The Los Alamos and Livermore national laboratories for nuclear weapons, the Aerospace Corporation for space technology, and the MITRE Corporation for information technology are examples of institutions devoted to technical excellence in the service of the government. As the biotech era dawns, an institution devoted to BWD is necessary and appropriate.

The Secretary of Defense should also establish a standing BWD Science Board composed of eminent bioscientists and biotech industry leaders, within the framework of the existing Defense Science Board, to advise the Secretary of Defense on BWD technology.

Information Technology Requires Targeted DOD Action to Keep Pace with Commercial Developments

DOD should require developers of information technology–intensive military-related systems and subsystems to *plan for continuous incremental upgrade, rather than periodic block upgrade,* and this requirement must be incorporated in the system design. DOD should also insist that system design incorporate commercial, open-system architectures. These steps will make it easier for DOD development programs to benefit from the rapid improvements in commercial technology.

DOD should continue to fund high-risk, high-payoff R&D in the information technology field. Notwithstanding its position as a niche player in the overall information technology revolution, DOD has good reason to continue to fund IT R&D. Whereas industry work is frequently focused on near-term developments, DOD needs to encourage fundamental advances. DOD support should include design, production, testing, security, and privacy tools. Investment in these tools will promote DOD's goal of continuing to have an open window into the rapidly changing commercial technology.

DEVELOP AN IMMUNE SYSTEM TO PROTECT SECRETS

A growing amount of important technology is non-defense and non-American, because of increasing commercialization and globalization. Attempting to maintain a hermetic seal around the U.S. defense technology base will therefore not protect security, and could even impede the objective of "running faster." New technology brings with it new categories of threats with which the system of personnel and industrial security must contend. In the face of these changes, current export controls and security systems are increasingly ineffective, as bureaucratic and rule-laden regulatory systems administer simpleminded and outdated hermetic seals. What is needed is a system that measures risk and reacts proportionally to it: an immune system. Some of the recommendations below deal with the basic efficiency of the export controls system, which would be needed even if the world were not changing so rapidly around it. But other recommendations begin the process of continual adaptation that corresponds to the immune system model.

Support the Defense Trade Security Initiative

The aim of the U.S. government's recently adopted Defense Trade Security Initiative is to streamline and rationalize some aspects of export controls administration where the security risks are low.[25] It provides for blanket exemptions of licensing restriction for allied countries that meet specified standards of security controls, flexible one-stop licensing vehicles, and some streamlining (including computerization) of defense-related licensing processes. The new administration should support this Initiative.

Seek Fundamental Change in the Statutory Basis of Export Controls

The new administration should establish a consultative process with the leadership of the new Congress, with the aim of fundamentally altering the statutory basis of U.S. export controls. The new basis should eliminate the statutory and regulatory distinction between munitions and dual-use items, and establish a single, unified licensing system with interagency policy direction.[26] The munitions and dual-use systems share common functions, and harmonizing the two processes, to the extent feasible, is in both the economic and the security interests of the United States. Such efforts would go far in eliminating public and industry confusion due to a welter of export regulations; they would streamline the processes to enhance U.S. competitiveness on the global market, encourage information shar-

---

25. Fact sheets detailing the Defense Trade Security Initiative released by the Bureau of Political-Military Affairs, U.S. Department of State and the Office of the Under Secretary of Defense for Acquisition, Technology, and Logistics, U.S. Department of Defense, Washington, D.C., May 24, 2000, can be found at <secretary.state.gov/www/briefings/statements/2000/ps000524d.html#fs>.

26. While "the end of the Cold War brought about the elimination of parallel export control systems in most nations ... the United States has continued to maintain a robust [dual] system of dual-use and munitions controls." Report of the Commission to Assess the Organization of the Federal Government to Combat the Proliferation of Weapons of Mass Destruction, "Combating Proliferation of Weapons of Mass Destruction," July 14, 1999, p. 41.

ing, and enhance intelligence among the controlling agencies.[27] Meanwhile, agency overhead costs would also be reduced by greater coordination and shared resources.

Centralize Export Controls Licensing, but not Policymaking, in a Single Entity

The new administration should centralize all administrative, training, and technical support to export controls licensing in a single entity. This entity should comprise 90 percent of all U.S. government positions devoted to export controls administration. It should have a full-time administrative director and a well-funded annual training program for its staff. The new licensing entity should be required to develop performance metrics for the export controls regulatory system, to assess timeliness of response to license applications, technical training of the licensing workforce, promotion rates of the licensing workforce compared to their agency peers, the cost to the economy of licenses denied, the reduction of foreign threat through controls, and the costs to the economy and increased threat attributable to different allied export controls practices.

The agency should report these measures regularly to Congress. It is not recommended, however, that the administration attempt to create a central export controls policymaking organization distinct from State, Commerce, and Defense: these agencies would only re-register their legitimate concerns at the cabinet level, wasting time and energy for all. The new central licensing agency should be funded jointly by State, Commerce, and Defense, with the contribution of each agency proportional to its overall budget.

Create a Combined Automated Licensing, Intelligence, and Enforcement Information System and Database

The centralized licensing entity should create a combined State-Commerce-Defense automated licensing, intelligence, and enforcement information system and database. It should be funded in proportion to the total budgets of these agencies, with ample annual funding to maintain and upgrade the system. The combined system should be implemented and managed by the new central licensing organization.

---

27. "Since proliferators purchase both dual-use goods and munitions items, a single system would allow licensing officers to communicate more regarding end-users of concern." Ibid., p. 42.

Develop a Regulatory Policy toward Systems Engineering

The new administration should task the National Security Council working group on export controls to develop a regulatory policy toward systems engineering. Systems engineering represents the lasting American strength in military technology and the attribute most difficult for potential opponents to replicate. It therefore is most deserving of protection through controls. A systems engineering approach should supplement, and to a certain extent supersede, the current lists of "militarily critical" underlying technologies.

Develop a Strategy for Enhanced Use of End-use Controls

The National Security Council working group on export controls should also be tasked to develop a strategy for the enhanced use of end-use controls. End-use controls ensure that items licensed for sale to a civil customer are not diverted to military use. They represent an effective adaptive response if administered properly. Most importantly, end-use controls allow the export controls system to target users rather than entire countries. The strategy should cover both policy and implementation, including funding and personnel to conduct inspections.

Increase Intelligence Support for Export Controls

The new administration should increase funding for intelligence support to the export controls process, including national intelligence, for assessments of security threats both from wider availability of technology and from foreign availability. The immune system concept depends on intelligence that assesses threats and the effectiveness of various responses. Today the intelligence community is too often asked to determine whether export controls rules are being obeyed, rather than illuminating how they can be made more effective.

Seek International Agreement on Export Controls Standards

The Secretary of State should continue to give high diplomatic priority to seeking international agreement on export controls standards and performance metrics for national export controls regulatory systems. When the United States applies controls where others do not, both security and economic objectives are sacrificed.

Increase Support for the Export Controls Systems of Non-allied Nations

The United States should increase its support to non-allied nations for strengthening their export controls systems. States that wish to cooperate with U.S. export controls policy are sometimes frustrated by the absence of effective legal and enforcement mechanisms. They could be assisted through the expansion of such cooperative international programs as the Nunn-Lugar Cooperative Threat Reduction program, the Bureau of Export Administration's Nonproliferation and Export Control Cooperation, and the joint DOD–Customs Service Counterproliferation Program. These initiatives provide expertise, training, and equipment to strengthen the export controls systems of foreign governments in an attempt to head off proliferation of weapons of mass destruction (WMD). However, both are largely limited to the states of the former Soviet Union. Their mandate and scope should be expanded to allow for greater multilateral initiatives that build on current cooperation and program development in other regions of U.S. interest.

Create an Interagency Security Policy Task Force to Develop Policy for New Security Problems Posed by Technological Change

An interagency security policy task force should be created and tasked to develop policy guidance covering the new problems to industrial and personnel security posed by technological change. This guidance should address such issues as problems relating to the increased density of storage media; network security; and the integrity of software, including embedded software, from non-U.S. commercial sources.

Develop a Policy on Risk of Compromise from High Operations Tempo

The new administration should task the Secretary of Defense, with the advice of the Chairman of the Joint Chiefs of Staff, to develop a policy on the risk of compromise of operational security resulting from the high operations tempo increasingly characteristic of U.S. military operations, and the consequent risks of revelation of U.S. capabilities.

Widen Use of Commercial Techniques of Security, Privacy, Technical Monitoring, and Human Resources Management

DOD should apply commercial techniques of security, privacy, technical monitoring, and human resources management to DOD personnel and industrial security. Competitive commercial industries spend a great deal of effort and money on security, and they apply an immune system approach rather than a rule-based bureaucratic system to identify real threats and provide the most effective and least disruptive protection. DOD security managers could benefit from experience gained in industry.

Closing

Technology is a national strength of the United States. Its culture and institutions are well-suited to the rapid creation and adoption of new technology. These national characteristics can continue to infuse national defense if steps are taken to preserve DOD's technological edge in the commercialized, globalized world that is emerging.

7

Advancing the Revolution in Business Affairs

MICHAEL J. LIPPITZ, SEAN O'KEEFE, AND
JOHN P. WHITE

WITH JOHN BROWN

Other chapters in this volume have described new types of threats emerging from a rapidly changing global military and economic environment. In response, they recommend reforms to DOD military organizations, policies, and practices to sustain and expand the nascent "Revolution in Military Affairs" (RMA). This chapter shows how meeting these threats will also depend on implementing management and administrative changes in the parts of the Department of Defense that support military operations. This challenge has come to be known as the "Revolution in Business Affairs" (RBA) because it is a critical counterpart to the RMA. Reforms to DOD's practices for acquiring and managing the delivery of goods and services will enable the continued development of the underlying technologies and practices of the RMA. They ensure that DOD can meet the changing needs of the warfighter efficiently over time.[1]

Among the many ways the RBA supports the RMA, three in particular are worth noting. First, DOD must be responsive to new

---

1. This was emphasized in the 1997 Quadrennial Defense Review (QDR): "Efforts to reengineer the Department's infrastructure and business practices must parallel the work being done to exploit the Revolution in Military Affairs if we are to afford both adequate investment in preparations for the future, especially a more robust modernization program, and capabilities sufficient to support an ambitious shaping and responding strategy throughout the period covered by the Review." Quadrennial Defense Review, Section III, "Defense Strategy," May 1997.

threats more quickly and flexibly than in the past. As explained elsewhere in this volume, future threats are expected to be asymmetric, involve transnational and substate actors, and require operations in difficult venues such as isolated regions or urban locations. The United States will have less time to respond to these emerging threats than in the past. Uncertainty about these threats places a premium on being able to adjust rapidly to surprise. Speed and adaptability are needed not only for operating forces, but also for the organizations that support them with technology development, equipment acquisition, and workforce training. The RBA supports the RMA by encouraging innovation and experimentation among various approaches, operational concepts, structures, and technologies, fusing operating forces and support organizations into a streamlined, unified system for delivering military capabilities.

Second, saving money on operations and support of current forces is an important and politically palatable way to increase investment in technology development and systems acquisitions for future forces. DOD's FY 2001 budget authority for operations and maintenance is $109 billion, more than the $98 billion allocated to acquisition and technology development.[2] Two recent outside commissions established by Congress call for increased spending in acquisition and technology-development accounts.[3] Every dollar shifted from operations and maintenance to modernization due to efficiencies can help DOD realize the full potential of the RMA, without affecting current readiness.

Finally, the RBA can also play an important role in restoring citizens' general confidence in government, both the executive branch and Congress, and in particular their support for investment in improved defense capabilities. DOD has the opportunity to demonstrate that large government institutions can achieve world-class "business" performance. Congress can demonstrate its understanding and support of the use of modern business management methods in the public sector.

Implementing the RBA is a gigantic task, and has been pursued by the DOD since the Quadrennial Defense Review in 1997. The "business affairs" of the DOD embody myriad management and adminis-

---

2. U.S. Department of Defense, 2000 Annual Report to the President, Appendix B-1: "DOD Budget Authority by Appropriation FY 2001."

3. The Commission on Roles and Missions of the Armed Forces (CORM) was established in 1995, and the National Defense Panel in 1997.

trative activities, consuming the majority of the defense budget and of the work of DOD civilian personnel. DOD is not a business and should not be run like one. However, in the past two decades, private industry has made radical changes in business practices and organizational structure, which reflect new business principles that are applicable, with adaptation, to a public-sector organization such as DOD. There are many organizational, infrastructural, and procedural facets to achieving the goals of the RBA, covering areas such as research and development, logistics, test and evaluation, contracting, product support, industrial relations, competition, budgeting, facilities, human resources, and more. This chapter describes ways to move the RBA forward in three particularly important areas: conducting competitive sourcing assessments of functions that are not inherently governmental; establishing a new process to eliminate excess facilities; and initiating value-based systems acquisition practices. In each of these areas, we focus on broad conceptual problems facing DOD and the major implementation barriers.

Key Private-sector Management Improvements and their Applicability to DOD

Just as the Revolution in Military Affairs has been made possible by the marked increase in technological capability of U.S. industry over the last two decades, the Revolution in Business Affairs will be made possible by changes in business organization and management during that same period. The private sector has fundamentally improved the way it conducts its operations. The principles that guided these changes are applicable, with modification, to the management of the DOD.

Since the 1980s, private industry has been focusing on increasing the rates and efficiency of information flow, knowledge generation, and product and process innovation, primarily through the following mechanisms:

- restructuring, in order to facilitate continuous improvement in essential missions and concomitant core competencies, while outsourcing other functions;

- developing alliances with both suppliers and customers to create product value;

- supply-chain management, particularly supplier-excellence programs and paperless, Internet-based procurement;

- flattening organizations and increasing the responsibility of lower-level management and field activities; and

- stressing and rewarding innovation and measured performance, especially metrics related to customer satisfaction.

These changes began in earnest when many American businesses found their market share and profitability in decline, due in large part to strong Japanese competition in the 1980s. In the process of making these changes, customers and suppliers increasingly came to be viewed as strategic partners in product development. Achieving and sustaining quality required focus on core competencies. In many cases, suppliers with expertise in particular domains could better achieve such focus. In non-core areas such as accounting, equipment maintenance, and other support functions, many world-class suppliers existed. As a result, many major companies began to disassemble the vertically integrated organizations built during the 1950s and 1960s. Over time, business competition evolved into competing alliances of firms. By creating such a "constellation," firms can take advantage of their own core competencies while protecting themselves with equally specialized partners.

The growth of constellations of firms meant that innovation was increasingly becoming a decentralized activity. New forms of management — particularly supply-chain management — were necessary. Organizations that had reduced middle-management layers (had "flattened") and distributed product realization activities among many partners began applying advanced information technologies to coordinate better the activities of design teams, managers, and supply-chain players.[4] Many companies developed sophisticated market-monitoring capabilities that permitted them to monitor component development, coordinate subsystem integration, and negotiate better prices.[5] Scarcity of technical and marketing talent compelled some

4. Richard Van Atta, Michael Lippitz, Paul Collopy, Brad Hartfield, and Noah Richmond, *Complex Product Realization 2020: Key Issue Areas,* draft report (Alexandria, Va.: Institute for Defense Analyses, December 15, 1999), p. 1.

5. This is an important activity, as the development of constellations has led to reduced horizontal competition at particular levels.

firms to become better organized to meet the needs of their people, to assure that their employees were of a higher quality and higher motivation than those of their competitors.[6]

Like industry, DOD must cope with new, unfamiliar situations that require rethinking its basic mode of operations. A review of management reform implementation in the United States yields certain fundamental principles that point toward how private-sector innovations can be applied productively to a public-sector organization such as DOD.[7]

FOCUS ON CORE MISSION AND DEVELOPMENT OF CORRESPONDING CORE COMPETENCIES

Achieving continuous quality improvement requires that internal management focus on those skills and knowledge that underlie the organization's competitiveness, while collaborating with partners in order to provide complete solutions. Partnerships allow greater flexibility in responding to a changing environment. More importantly, talented people are attracted to and stay with organizations whose core competencies match their skills.

FOCUS ON DELIVERING CUSTOMER VALUE

Customer focus has changed the way businesses think about their tasks. The most important aspect of customer focus has been the elimination of processes and bureaucracies that do not measurably contribute to customer value. It has also opened feedback channels that are critical to maintaining a company's competitive position.

INCENTIVES BASED ON MEASURED PERFORMANCE

Decentralization increases the need for coordination. Companies have increasingly employed market mechanisms to distribute rewards in order to align incentives deliberately among customer, suppliers, and employees. An emphasis on measured performance helps

---

6. Robert H. Waterman, *What America Does Right: Learning from Companies that Put People First* (New York: W.W. Norton, 1994).

7. The following discussion is a revised and extended version of a similar argument presented in John P. White, Steven J. Kelman, and Michael J. Lippitz, *Reforming the Department of Defense: The Revolution in Business Affairs*, Special Report of the Preventive Defense Project, Vol. 1, No. 4 (February 1999).

in implementing incentive programs, as well as being a requirement for continuous quality improvement.

ACCOUNTABILITY FOR RESULTS

It is people who make changes, not "departments" or "offices." Incentives work only if people are rewarded and penalized based on results that they can reasonably control.

RBA MISSION FOR DOD

Each of these principles is applicable to DOD. Taken together, the ultimate mission statement for the RBA might be summarized as, "an accountable government and contractor workforce with the incentives, skills, tools, and flexibility to achieve the performance necessary to support the warfighter cost-effectively." DOD's recent progress toward that goal is outlined in the next section.

Recent DOD Acquisition and Business Process Reforms

DOD acquisition practices and business processes have been the topic of numerous studies and efforts going back four decades.[8] The most dramatic changes have occurred during the past decade and are continuing today. These changes are based on government-wide legislation and reforms as well as DOD-initiated efforts.

The Government Performance and Results Act of 1993 (GPRA) initiated management reforms throughout government aimed at measuring its performance. GPRA directed federal agencies to measure progress toward outcome goals and submit strategic performance goal plans to the Office of Management and Budget (OMB) at least every three years.

Concurrently, Congress addressed many long-standing administrative and contracting barriers to change. On October 13, 1994, President Clinton signed the Federal Acquisition Streamlining Act of 1994, known as FASA. This law was intended, among other purposes, to make it easier for the government to acquire goods and

---

8. This section draws upon Michael Voth, *MilSpec Reform and Incentives for Commercial Technology Insertion*, December 9, 1997 (unpublished manuscript); *The Road Ahead*, DOD paper released by the Under Secretary of Defense for Acquisition, Technology, and Logistics, June 2, 2000; and the Defense Reform Initiative Website at <http://www.defenselink.mil/dodreform/>.

services from the commercial marketplace. FASA made a wide range of changes in acquisition policy and procurement law, by exempting purchases of commercial products from several statutes, while expanding the definition of a "commercial product." FASA was followed by the Federal Acquisition Reform Act of 1996, or FARA, which made additional statutory changes, such as the elimination of certain cost-accounting standards that had discouraged commercial companies from doing business with the government. FASA and FARA paved the way for reducing government oversight, simplifying contracting procedures, and bringing government contracting closer to commercial practices. The Information Technology Management Reform Act of 1996 (Division E of the Clinger-Cohen Act), made changes to the way DOD acquires information systems, one of the most important areas in which DOD needs to leverage commercial capabilities better.[9]

A number of studies have provided the underpinnings for change within DOD. A 1980 book by Jacques Gansler called for more tightly integrating military and commercial industrial bases as a remedy for the increasing inefficiencies of the defense companies relative to commercial industry.[10] In 1986, the Blue Ribbon Commission on Defense Management, chaired by former Deputy Secretary of Defense David Packard, highlighted the need for DOD to expand its use of commercial products and processes and to eliminate barriers that discouraged application of innovative technology to DOD contracts.[11] In 1992, the Advisory Panel on Streamlining and Codifying Acquisition Laws (known as the Section 800 Panel) published an 1800-page report

---

9. The Clinger-Cohen Act, among other things, requires agencies to include information technology acquisitions in strategic plans and annual budget submissions. It calls for the use of performance measurements in order to encourage information technology investments to be tailored to each agency's particular mission. It seeks to leverage commercial information technology advances by calling for "modular contracting," in which acquisitions are broken into flexible, evolutionary increments.

10. Jacques S. Gansler, *The Defense Industry* (Cambridge, Mass.: MIT Press, 1980).

11. The President's Blue Ribbon Commission on Defense Management (The Packard Commission), *A Quest for Excellence: Final Report to the President and Appendix* (Washington, D.C.: The Packard Commission, June 1986).

that made recommendations in the areas of procurement reform, electronic commerce, and military specification, among others.[12]

William Perry served on the Packard Commission, and he made implementation of its recommendations and those of the Section 800 Panel a high priority when he returned to the Pentagon in 1993 as Deputy Secretary of Defense and, in 1994, became Secretary. Toward that end, on February 24, 1994, he set forth a dramatic vision for simplification of the way the Pentagon buys military systems, in a report titled *Acquisition Reform: A Mandate for Change*. On June 29, 1994, he issued a memorandum titled *Specifications and Standards—A New Way of Doing Business*. The "Perry Memo," as it came to be known, reversed DOD policy by directing the military services to "use performance and commercial specifications and standards instead of military specifications and standards, unless no practical alternative exists to meet the user's needs." It also directed military acquisition programs to reduce their oversight, employing process controls in place of extensive testing and inspection. The memo instructed program managers and acquisition decision-makers at all levels to "challenge requirements ... [because] the problem of unique military systems does not begin with the standards. The problem is rooted in the requirements determination phase of the acquisition cycle."

Other acquisition reform initiatives and directives followed:

- five acquisition reform pilot programs intended to demonstrate that, through the use of commercial products and commercial practices, military items can be acquired more quickly and at reduced cost;

- the Single Process Initiative, under which DOD changed numerous existing contracts simultaneously in contractor facilities, to facilitate the implementation of state-of-the-art manufacturing technologies and more efficient business processes;

- Other Transactions Authority, which allowed flexible contracting procedures for certain prototype projects;

---

12. The Advisory Panel on Streamlining and Codifying Acquisition Laws (known as the Section 800 Panel) was created in response to Section 800 of the National Defense Authorization Act for Fiscal Year 1991, P.L. 105-510.

- Integrated Product and Process Development (IPPD) and Integrated Product Teams (IPTs), mandated throughout DOD by Perry on May 10, 1995;[13]

- Cost as an Independent Variable (CAIV) — i.e., cost targets for programs — mandated for all acquisition programs;

- The Defense Acquisition Deskbook, an automated reference tool that provides easy access to the most current acquisition information; and

- Advanced Concept Technology Demonstrations, which fund the development of prototypes that operational forces can use in simulated realistic combat environments to develop doctrine, operational concepts, tactics, and procedures that will take advantage of new capabilities.

Recent administrations have also initiated broader business process reforms. In 1989, President Bush called for a comprehensive look at the Department's management processes. Under Deputy Secretary of Defense Donald Atwood, an institutional process emerged to consider and act on a range of management initiatives concurrent with the annual budget review. Among the initiatives launched were the consolidation of accounting and finance services, improved spare parts provisioning, and a more comprehensive approach to information management systems. In large measure, the groundwork for implementation of the Clinger-Cohen Act at DOD was laid through these information management initiatives. Similarly, efforts were pursued to develop performance criteria and unit-cost-per-output determination in advance of the Government Performance and Results Act.

The Clinton administration initiated a National Performance Review (NPR) with performance audits that identified problems of or-

---

13. Integrated Product and Process Development (IPPD) is a management technique that brings together representatives from several disciplines in Integrated Product Teams at the very start of a project. The IPPD approach integrates timely input from all team members with varied functional backgrounds, with an emphasis on use of advanced modeling and simulation tools, so that programs are better structured up front and issues arising during development can be more quickly identified and resolved. It also helps various development and marketing activities to be performed concurrently, allowing products to be brought to market more quickly.

ganization and process government-wide. NPR implementation included training government employees in customer-service concepts, and publicizing best practices through "Hammer Awards," some 800 of which have been given. NPR changed its name in 1998 to National Partnership for Reinventing Government with a renewed focus on achieving quality performance by government organizations.

In 1995, the Report of the Commission on Roles and Missions of the Armed Forces (CORM) presented a lengthy analysis of problems with the DOD's support establishment and management practices.[14] It made extensive recommendations in both areas including greatly increasing the use of outsourcing, reengineering DOD support activities, creating a Quadrennial Strategy Review, and restructuring the Planning, Programming and Budgeting System (PPBS). Many of the CORM's recommendations have been, or are in the process of being, implemented.

Recent DOD acquisition, logistics, and management reform efforts have been gathered under the rubric of the Defense Reform Initiative (DRI, released in November 1997), one of the first initiatives of Secretary of Defense William Cohen. The DRI provides a strategic blueprint for adopting business processes in the Department. It has defined a series of initiatives in four areas:

- *Reengineer*: DOD is to adopt modern business practices to achieve world-class standards of performance;

- *Consolidate*: DOD is to streamline organizations to remove redundancy and maximize synergy;

- *Compete*: DOD is to apply market mechanisms to improve quality, reduce costs, and respond to customer needs; and

- *Eliminate*: DOD is to reduce excess support structures to free resources and focus on core competencies.

On June 2, 2000, a report by Under Secretary of Defense Jacques Gansler summarized the key recommendations of recent studies and highlighted planned initiatives.[15] These initiatives are aimed at:

14. The Commission on Roles and Missions of the Armed Forces, *Directions for Defense* (Washington, D.C.: U.S. Government Printing Office [U.S. GPO], May 1995).

15. Jacques Gansler, *The Road Ahead: Accelerating the Transformation of Department of Defense Acquisition and Logistics Processes and Practices* (Washington, D.C.: DOD, June 2, 2000). The studies summarized in this report were un-

- extending military specifications and standards reform to the entire defense system life cycle, not just new acquisitions;

- developing more flexible, long-term acquisition strategies that will create incentives for suppliers to provide innovative products to DOD;

- developing strategic alliances with defense suppliers;

- expanding performance-based acquisition to procurements for services;

- expanding the use of fixed-price versus cost-reimbursed acquisition;

- encouraging consideration of alternative methods to accomplishing missions (that is, managing DOD programs as a portfolio);

- changing DOD acquisition guidance to include consideration of cost, time-phased requirements, and evolutionary acquisition strategies;

- initiating pilot programs aimed at reengineering product support;

- decreasing R&D infrastructure, military bases, and other unneeded DOD facilities;

- moving toward "continuous learning" in the DOD workforce;

- restructuring acquisition career fields to emphasize the skills and leadership competencies necessary to implement the RBA; and

- institutionalizing a continuous "enterprise change" model throughout DOD.

All in all, the need for fundamental reform is well accepted within most of the DOD community and among prime contractors, although there are still pockets of resistance. Much has been accomplished and much is planned to overcome the historical biases and institutional resistance that continues to affect how and from whom DOD acquires good and services, and what it acquires.

---

dertaken in response to congressional direction in Section 912(c) of The National Defense Authorization Act for Fiscal Year 1998.

Recommendations

The remaining sections of this chapter apply the lessons learned and the general principles identified in the previous sections to refine and expand on RBA reforms in three key areas: competitive sourcing, infrastructure reduction, and systems acquisition. *Competitive sourcing* is aimed at evaluating those DOD functions that are not "inherently governmental" in order to determine whether DOD's overall effectiveness would improve if they were performed outside the Department, that is, outsourced. Successful competitive sourcing achieves the numerous benefits discussed in this chapter including additional savings through the elimination of infrastructure, beyond that already justified by reductions in forces. This will add to the Department's current inventory of excess real property that needs to be eliminated. Thus, the need will only increase for an orderly process of *infrastructure reduction*, our second recommendation. Third, we urge a new model for those *systems acquisition* functions remaining within DOD, leading to better performance and lower cost.

COMPETITIVE SOURCING

DOD's core missions — joint military operations and policy development — have not changed. However, as a result of new threats, shifts in national strategy, changing geopolitics, and the globalization of the world economy, some of the specific activities that implement these missions are changing. The new skills must be integrated into the force so that it can respond to a wide range of challenges, old and new. This means redefining DOD's core competencies.

In parallel to the private firm's focus on defining core competencies in the context of its business, the DOD must define core competencies in the context of its public mission. DOD is the sole provider of a fundamental public service: the nation's international security. Thus, most of those who carry out its core missions — such as joint military operations, combat operations, and combat support operations — should be government employees. But many of DOD's functions are neither inherently governmental nor core: their execution does not require special public trust and confidence. Functions such as finance and administration, telecommunications and computer operations, routine logistics, and scheduled equipment maintenance are performed in many public and private organizations. Thus it is clear that people outside the DOD can do them. Deciding exactly which functions should be outsourced will uncover many ambiguities, but there is no doubt that a large number of functions performed by DOD employees could be supplied effectively under contract by private firms. The new administration will need to achieve the correct balance between public and private operations so as to enhance joint military operations while reaping the gains from competitive sourcing.

If done properly, a DOD focus on core competencies and collaborative partnerships carries significant advantages, such as:

- attracting and retaining talented people in both the government and the contractor base;

- encouraging flexibility in staffing over time without political constraints;

- promoting world-class performance and innovation, both internally and in outsourced activities, through an emphasis on both market competition and public and private contracts;

- tapping into key technological advancement in the private sector;

- facilitating modernization by replacing legacy systems with state-of-the-art capabilities; and

- reducing cost.

It has been the policy of the U.S. government since World War II to acquire its armaments and related goods and services from the private sector rather than from government arsenals. It is widely agreed that this has been a wise policy, particularly when it is compared with the experience of some European governments that have gone in the other direction. This policy is enunciated broadly in OMB Circular A-76:

In the process of governing, the government should not compete with its citizens. The competitive enterprise system, characterized by individual freedom and initiative, is the primary source of national economic strength. In recognition of this principle it has been and continues to be the general policy of the government's reliance on commercial sources to supply the products and services the government needs.[16]

---

16. Circular No. A-76, Office of Management and Budget, Executive Office of the President, August 4, 1983 (revised 1999), p. 1.

The privatization of government activity is an attempt to introduce market relationships into the bureaucratic production of public services. In some cases it involves the outright transfer to the private sector of government assets and their attendant responsibilities, such as depots or data centers. Such activities have been widespread in state and local governments in the United States and in many foreign governments. The focus here is on a subset of the privatization activity: outsourcing, or the transfer of a support function previously performed in the government to an outside private service provider who will operate under a contract that includes flexibility as to how it is to meet the government's requirements.

The DOD has had extensive and largely positive experience with the process of competitively assessing whether public functions should be outsourced. The Center for Naval Analysis reported in December 1996 that:

Past A76 competitions within DOD have yielded significant savings ... about 1.5 billion dollars annually or about 30 percent of the baseline cost of performing the functions. The savings seem to result from competition rather than outsourcing per se.[17]

The CNA study identified the characteristics of functions that were associated with high savings: large single-purpose competitions; functions performed primarily by military personnel; research support; real property maintenance functions; services in support of military installations; intermediate maintenance (as opposed to user maintenance or depot maintenance).[18]

In a recent speech, Jacques Gansler, Under Secretary for Defense for Acquisition, Technology, and Logistics, cited some initial results from competitive sourcing of work that is not inherently governmental:

Regardless of who wins (government or industry), empirical data show that performance improves and prices go down from competitive sourcing. In examples of the public-private competition numerous

---

17. R.D. Trunkey, R.P. Trost, C.M. Snyder, *Analysis of DOD's Commercial Activities Program* (Alexandria, Va.: Center for Naval Analyses, December 1996), p. 2. See also William Brent Boning, et al., *Evidence on Savings from DOD A-76 Competitions*, CNA Research Memorandum 98-125 (Alexandria, Va.: Center for Naval Analyses, November 1998).

18. Ibid.

studies have shown that for more than two thousand cases, average savings are twenty percent when the public sector wins and forty percent when the private sector wins. Since to date the winners have been split about evenly, we have an average of thirty-percent savings—with higher performance.[19]

Despite these successes, the number of competitions has been relatively modest, just 2138 under the A76 rules from 1978 to 1994. Most of these competitions involved narrow functions with a small number of employees. For example, the Defense Science Board cites an analysis of 800 such competitions in which less than 10 percent of the activities involved more than 55 employees.[20]

Recently the DOD has expanded its competitive sourcing efforts through the establishment of a strategic sourcing program.[21] The new emphasis is intended to address a broader range of management options including elimination of obsolete practices, consolidation of functions or activities, reengineering and restructuring of organizations and adoption of best business practices. To some extent the new program reflects the DOD's inability to meet its previously stated A-76 job assessment goals for the period 1997–2005.

The Congress has resisted any major increase in the amount of outsourcing in spite of the declared policy in favor of the private sector and the positive results of past competitions.[22] The Defense Science Board analysis cited eight major congressional impediments to outsourcing activities. A 1996 letter from the Deputy Secretary of Defense listed thirteen statutory encumbrances to outsourcing:

---

19. Jacques S. Gansler, "The Defense Industrial Structure in the Twenty-first Century," speech to the American Institute of Aeronautics and Astronautics (AIAA) Acquisition Reform Conference, January 27, 2000.

20. *Report of Defense Science Board Task Force on Outsourcing and Privatization*, the Office of the Under Secretary of Defense for Acquisition, Technology, and Logistics, U.S. Department of Defense, August 1996, pp. 32–33.

21. DOD Interim Guidance, "Strategic Sourcing Program," February 29, 2000.

22. See Chapter 11 by Judith Miller for further discussion of how Congress has substantially constrained the practice of outsourcing by adopting a variety of reporting, timing and other restrictions that have made effective implementation of the policy very difficult.

The numerous statutory requirements of Chapter 146, and related provisions to the Authorization and Appropriation Acts, work together to create an often impenetrable barrier to outsourcing. They impose on the Department requirements to perform detailed studies and analyses that are extraordinarily time consuming, expensive and unrealistic. At the same time they preclude converting to contract if detailed studies cannot be done within a certain time.[23]

The Defense Science Board Study also listed the key problems with the A76 process as:

- complexity in timelines;

- inequitable public-private cost comparisons;

- emphasis on cost, not best value;

- mostly small "stovepipe" functions are affected;

- exemptions and waiver authority not used adequately.[24]

These impediments are reinforced by the general reluctance on the part of the bureaucracy to outsource functions traditionally performed by DOD employees, even if they are not inherently governmental. Evaluations of whether to conduct sourcing competitions are usually made as a part of the "requirements process" and are within the purview of the manpower and support organizations in each service. These organizations have strong incentives to maintain the status quo, because to define many functions as "non-governmental" is to eliminate the need for their organizations to exist. Thus the bureaucracy often gives way to the incentive to identify many functions as "inherently governmental" by using broad and loose definitions.

All of these impediments make it crucial that the senior leadership commit its energy and resources to an expansion of competitive sourcing activities. The results have been modest to date relative to the opportunity. Only a broad, programmatic approach to competitive sourcing will yield the kinds of benefits necessary to make a difference in terms of the overall performance of the Department.

23. Letter from the Deputy Secretary of Defense, John P. White, to the Honorable John McCain, Chairman, Subcommittee on Readiness, Committee on Armed Services, United States Senate, April 22, 1996.

24. *Report of Defense Science Board Task Force on Outsourcing and Privatization*, p. 44.

Overcoming Resistance to Competitive Sourcing

It is our recommendation that the new administration should substantially increase the DOD's competitive sourcing goals to capture its benefits, including the ability to focus on core competencies, take advantage of private sector innovation, and obtain large cost savings. The Quadrennial Defense Review, mandated by law to take place in 2001, should be the vehicle for defining the program and specifying its goals. The Secretary of Defense should issue a new policy statement declaring that the private sector is the preferred provider of goods and services to the Department, and that all services that are not inherently governmental or combat related should be considered competitive candidates. He should make it clear in his guidance to the Quadrennial Defense Review that this is a fundamental paradigm shift in the Department's view of how it will conduct its operations, akin to Secretary Perry's memo of 1994 regarding military specifications.

The Secretary should make a formal request through OMB to the President that he be given wide latitude beyond the strictures of A-76 to pursue a broad, aggressive competitive sourcing program. This new program would complement the DOD's current A-76 program under the Defense Reform Initiative, not supersede it. This relief would allow DOD to adjust study guidelines and timetables, improve cost comparison and value methodologies, and evaluate major functions using the competitive sourcing process.[25] The Secretary should stipulate that public-sector employees whose functions are opened to competition would continue to be allowed to present a public-sector alternative to outsourcing. There is no policy justification for disenfranchising employees or preventing employees from improving their competitive positions and protecting their jobs. Public-private competitions are cumbersome and involve methodological difficulties, but are the foundation of a fair process.

The new administration should also vigorously seek the support of the key political leadership in the Congress, principally on the House and Senate Armed Services Committees and the defense appropriations subcommittees in both houses, for expanded outsourcing. Legislation should be proposed to give the DOD relief from

25. A-76 already allows for waivers and exemptions, but a request for explicit presidential approval is imperative because of the magnitude of the program and its political implications.

past congressional strictures and protect it from imposition of new limitations during the program's execution.

The Department must take the initiative in addressing the personnel issues that will arise from a broad-based competitive sourcing program. It should insist upon early involvement of the unions, provide open and sustained communication with the employees involved, and assure that those affected will receive appropriate retraining, outplacement services, and severance packages. Efforts should also be made to use attrition to reduce any surplus in the civilian workforce. The services should be assured that any uniformed personnel that become available can be reassigned, and that military end-strengths will not be reduced. In addition, there should be written commitments that all cost savings realized by the military departments will remain in those departments to be allocated to other programs. This will eliminate the service argument that the reforms are really disguised budget reductions.

The Secretary should charge the Deputy Secretary of Defense with leading the program, consistent with chairing both the Quadrennial Defense Review and the Defense Management Council. This will assure the direct participation of the Vice-Chairman of the Joint Chiefs of Staff, the Under Secretaries of Defense, the three services' Under Secretaries, and the service Vice Chiefs.

We recognize that making this program an integral part of the QDR puts increased stress on an already overburdened process. But this is critical to assuring that it is a central element of the new administration's strategy.

Candidate Selection Process

The selection of functions to be assessed should be managed at the QDR level, not by the service bureaucracies. A set of selection criteria should be developed, such as:

- the function being outsourced can be reasonably defined;

- outsourcing the particular function would allow for an increase in mission effectiveness;

- risks involved can be well understood, carefully specified, and minimized;

- private firms are providing similar services to private and/or public customers;

- similar private-sector outsourcing demonstrates major innovations, such as effective supply-chain management;

- the number of firms involved is sufficient to assure competition both at the time of outsourcing and thereafter;

- it is principally uniformed military personnel, not civilian employees, that are released from current duties;

- focus on functions where it is hard to attract and keep government employees; and

- DOD can provide the necessary supervision to the contractors to assure that its objectives are met.

Examples of Candidates for Competitive Sourcing
There are numerous candidates inside the Department for competitive sourcing using such criteria. Past studies have identified long lists of such candidates; another such list is not necessary here.[26] Five candidates from a recent DOD study are included here to illustrate the kinds of activities we have in mind.[27]

Long haul (long-distance) communications is a central requirement for the new warfighting strategies. Commercial solutions dominate the market today. The technology is expensive, complex, and moving so rapidly that DOD will find it increasingly difficult to keep up and to attract the necessary skilled people to perform these functions.

Information resource management is concerned with assuring appropriate information capabilities at various levels in the DOD; it is defined more broadly than just "information technology" (but not as broadly as information management, in which DOD decides what information it should have and how it should be used). These information resources reside in a structurally distributed system, so that centralization is not an effective solution, and the technologies involved are, again, expensive, complex, and changing rapidly. In addition, this function has the attractive characteristic that while

---

26. See, for example, Center for Naval Analyses, "Analysis of DOD's Commercial Activities Program"; and "Report of the Defense Science Board Task Force on Outsourcing and Privatization."

27. "Panel on Commercialization of the U.S. Defense Establishment," Peter Dawkins, Chair, Department of Defense, June 1999.

common standards are necessary for interoperability, the services and agencies can be allowed wide latitude in application design.

The Department's non-combat-related efforts in the area of *logistics and supply-chain management* have shown improvement but would benefit from the addition of competitive sourcing. Commercial logistics operations are widespread, highly innovative, subject to measurement, improving rapidly, and often adaptable to the DOD's needs.

The DOD needs a modern, comprehensive, integrated *financial management system*. The defense finance and accounting service (DFAS) has a "migration" plan that is gradually reducing the number of finance and accounting systems and improving other parts of the operation, but the pace is slow and completion is a long way off. Meanwhile, there is a large, sophisticated private industry that provides these kinds of services. Of concern, however, is that DFAS employs a large number of civil servants throughout the United States, an issue that will make this particular change politically difficult.

The *technical skills component* of the training provided by the military services can be done outside the DOD. This training is not uniquely military, but rather parallels skills widely taught in the private sector, such as computer operations and truck driving. Most of the trainers are military personnel, who can be reassigned without the political difficulties inherent in abolishing civilian jobs. The Department has successfully outsourced some of this training already; its resistance to extending that experience further is largely an institutional bias of the services to use uniformed trainers.

Expanded competitive sourcing embodies a major opportunity for the new administration. The groundwork has been laid and it has the appropriate vehicle for implementation in the QDR. This initiative could transform major parts of the DOD and deliver far-reaching benefits.

INFRASTRUCTURE INITIATIVES

Inefficient and unneeded infrastructure is a major RBA problem (and DOD success in outsourcing will increase the excess). In the early to mid-1980s, which witnessed the largest peacetime expenditures for defense in our nation's history, DOD retained infrastructure capacity sufficient to support a military nearly twice the size of the actual force. Since then, the military force structure has declined by over 800,000 active-duty personnel, a reduction of nearly 40 percent compared to

U.S. armed forces levels at the time of the Gulf War. Since 1988, DOD has completed or set in motion a process to close or realign more than 100 military and government-operated bases in the United States. However, this represents less than 20 percent of DOD's infrastructure, facilities, and base operations. The present infrastructure could support a force structure double that of today. While the previous closure and realignment initiatives have saved over $15 billion so far, and will save an estimated $6 billion annually after 2001, these savings could be doubled if the infrastructure were sized to support current forces.

In this section we argue for a renewed commitment to facilities closure initiatives and the establishment of a new process to close excess capacity expeditiously. Such initiatives could be introduced and pursued under existing authority, but we present the arguments, and a strategy, for developing a new process.

Why a Process is Needed

The last wave of base closure initiatives (1988–95) did not even come close to shutting down all redundant facilities. Nonetheless, the effort was a remarkable achievement that made a significant dent in excess capacity and was a testimonial to commendable political courage. Closures and realignments over the past dozen years represent the collective efforts of four separate initiatives to rationalize DOD's support infrastructure. Each of the four efforts required an exhaustive review of the capacity and utility of bases that were candidates for closure and a process to minimize inappropriate political influence over the selection and closure criteria.

In large measure, the carefully monitored closure proceedings were a direct consequence of post–Vietnam era actions, which bore the taint of political motivation rather than national security consid-erations. U.S. military infrastructure had expanded dramatically in the 1950s and through the early 1960s, but as the Vietnam War wound down and military personnel discharges accelerated, the Nixon administration embarked on an effort to close excess facilities. While Congress and the American public welcomed the decision to withdraw from the protracted conflict in Southeast Asia, there was considerably less enthusiasm for terminating activities at home that had contributed to local economic well-being.

At that time, the President had comparatively unfettered authority to "rationalize" the stationing of forces and bases to support them.

Thus, President Nixon decided to close several military bases deemed excess to national security requirements. These happened to be located in congressional districts represented by members of Congress who did not support Nixon's policies. This started a new chapter in the struggle for dominance and control between the executive and legislative branches, and a new element of distrust.

Congress moved decisively to curb the President's authority to close bases or reduce the level of personnel at specific locations. Legislation was enacted in the 1970s to establish guidelines for potential closure. They included requirements for environmental impact statements, community hearings to assess the economic impact of potential adjustments, and extensive reporting prior to any action affecting any installation. In effect, statutory impediments were erected to assure that no base could be closed without congressional approval, which was rarely granted. The process became so onerous that the time and steps required to close a base would inevitably exceed the tenure of any administration, leaving the initiative to be reversed or simply forgotten by successor administrations.

The consequence was to dull the Department's interest in pursuing initiatives affecting local bases and their personnel levels. In time, an entire generation of Pentagon management simply gave up on the prospect of ever reducing the cost of infrastructure or any management initiative that could affect the number of people employed at various military installations. Indeed, through most of the 1970s and 1980s, congressional unwillingness to permit closure without a Herculean effort became a standard Departmental excuse for ever-increasing base-operation budgets and management inefficiencies.

A Process is Born

By the mid-1980s, defense budget growth had peaked and began to decline as the Cold War thawed. Toward the end of the Reagan administration, the Defense Department began paring its funding requests and proposing initiatives to save operation costs. To demonstrate the commitment to fiscal responsibility, but also to illustrate the sacrifice it would entail, Defense Secretary Frank Carlucci invited Congress to repeal the statutory impediments to base closures. While there was hardly a rush to accept the challenge, Carlucci's initiative did have the effect of reintroducing infrastructure costs into the national defense-budget debate. All previous efforts to streamline the closure process had stalled because Congress did not trust the executive branch to be non-partisan in its selection of base-closure candidates. Similarly, the administration considered such initiatives to be a waste of time since, in the end, Congress would protect its members and the bases in their districts anyway.

Concurrent with Secretary Carlucci's proposal, Representative Dick Armey introduced the first legislative framework designed to minimize politics and to expedite base closure and realignment decisions. While not adopted, it was a beginning. Congress had finally wearied of hearing the administration's claim that infrastructure initiatives, the key to any future budget savings, were being blocked by congressional recalcitrance. In 1988, Congress — reasoning that this would minimize political vendettas — authorized a one-time process to convene a bi-partisan commission empowered to select candidates for closure. To neutralize the tendency for logrolling, Congress would retain only the right to accept or reject the entire closure package recommended by the Commission, but could not selectively pass judgment on individual recommendations.

Chaired by the respected former U.S. Senator Abraham Ribicoff, the first Base Closure Commission convened in the spring of 1988. Having started with a blank sheet of paper, just seven months later the Commission delivered its findings. Lacking adequate time and without a framework for selecting closure candidates, the Commission offered up the painfully obvious choices in locations that had widely been identified as redundant or as examples of infrastructure inefficiency. Secretary Carlucci accepted the Commission's recommendations, although they were not all he had hoped for, and the Congress posed no objection.

The 1988 Commission was a historic precedent: a clear indication that the political impasse could be broken. This seminal first effort included a number of important lessons for future consideration. First, it demonstrated the wisdom of a commission set above the political fray, whose members were highly regarded and yet familiar enough with the political arena to know its hazards. Chairman Ribicoff was clearly a bi-partisan, consensus choice, and proved to be the consummate role model. Similarly, the other commissioners were regarded as seasoned political veterans beyond reproach. Selection of a well-regarded legislative Brahmin was a crucial prerequisite, raising the comfort level for Congress as it undertook the extraordinary act of delegating its legislative power.

Second, the shortcomings of its results demonstrated that a baseline was needed. Lacking a framework for rationalizing the massive infrastructure requirements of the Defense Department, members of any commission, however independent, are left to operate from their own instincts, biases, and limited knowledge. That first Commission was thinly staffed and given nothing to start with; on the contrary, it was explicitly directed to begin with a blank sheet of paper, as evidence of its objectivity. In and of itself, this attribute proved inadequate for the preparation of an acceptable, much less a comprehensive, list of excess facilities.

Third, this unprecedented foray into delegated legislative control over the most local of politics (to invoke Speaker Tip O'Neill's famous line) demonstrated that such decisions cannot be well considered during an election year. Even high-minded legislators and independent commissioners are unfairly exposed to wrathful public criticism during campaign periods. Base closures are extremely tough political decisions that cannot be made in a vacuum; their effects on local communities are significant. The choices are difficult at best, and the challenge of making them is exacerbated to the point of impossibility in an election year.

Fourth and finally, this bold initiative demonstrated the virtue of persistence and strategy. Secretary Carlucci had made this initiative a regular part of his stock speech, calling for congressional cooperation in the quest for defense "reform," however it might be defined.

These four factors — politically savvy yet objective commissioners, a force structure baseline from which they could begin work, politically palatable timing, and consistency of objective — proved to be the recipe for dramatic improvements to the process for the next three phases of base closure and infrastructure rationalization initiatives.

Process Improvements with a New Imperative

Fresh from the completion of the 1988 base closure exercise, many in Congress hoped that the base closure demon had been purged. But with the collapse of the Berlin Wall in November 1989 and rapid transformation of the international system, others in Congress clamored for the "peace dividend" that should accrue. Struggling for definition of the "new world order" a scant two months after the

Warsaw Pact collapse, the new Bush administration submitted the FY 1991 budget proposal with the assumption that Congress would agree to a sweeping reduction in defense facilities and infrastructure.

To illustrate that the peace dividend would inevitably have domestic ramifications, the new Secretary of Defense, Dick Cheney, unveiled a laundry list of bases for closure that would be sure not only to reduce the cost of defense infrastructure but also to get the attention of his former colleagues in the Congress. The clear implication was that cutting the defense budget would result in a marked downsizing of defense operations, and Secretary Cheney meant to articulate that consequence early and often. Lacking an expeditious process for consideration of base closure candidates, Cheney's proposal was to follow the cumbersome extant procedures. The requisite announcement of personnel impact was released and the long environmental and community impact assessment was initiated. Meanwhile, prior to the Gulf War, world events kept unfolding, further fueling the presumption that a dramatic reduction in defense spending was not only feasible, but warranted.

However, Cheney's list was challenged, just as any list generated by an administration would be. Congress read partisan intent behind the selection of every candidate base on the list. Regardless, however, Cheney's declared intent was to follow the rules, knowing that this would demonstrate to Congress how painful the process could become. Members of Congress came to realize that fending off each step in the process was likely to occupy a lot of time back in their home districts, while many legislative riders would be required to stave off administrative actions that might disadvantage any of the bases proposed for closure. To the congressional leadership, this had all the makings of legislative chaos.

Given the 1988 precedent of an orderly base-closure process, support began to build for such a solution in lieu of a long-drawn-out campaign of attrition. Congressman Les Aspin, then Chairman of the House Armed Services Committee, had guided the enactment of the previous authority, and knew its strengths and limitations. In late spring 1990, Aspin countered the Cheney initiative with a proposal to initiate a three-stage process: Commissions would convene to consider base closure candidates identified by the DOD and proposed by the administration in 1991, 1993, and 1995. Aspin knew the overall advantages of having the Commission start with a baseline list, and concerned himself with mitigating the attendant disadvantages. To maximize the advantages and diminish the prospect of partisan selection of bases, the Aspin proposal contained several important requirements.

Each of the Department's proposed closures had to comply with eight criteria, and the list of candidates had to contain an assessment of each base, to prove it was "excess." The first four criteria forced an analysis of bases relative to overall force structure requirements: mission requirements and operational readiness; land, facilities and airspace; contingency, mobilization, and future total force requirements; and cost and manpower implications. These four factors required a very specific focus on the mission objectives of the forces and the facilities needed to support those forces. The Air Force utilized these criteria to rank the value of facilities in each of its mission areas, thereby disclosing its decision process and justifying the closure candidates on the basis of their relative value to the rest of the infrastructure. It proved to be a very effective methodology for the other services as well.

The next four criteria assessed the return on investment (ROI) for the costs of closing facilities, and an assessment of impact: cost and savings of closure (with a ROI break-even point within seven years required); economic impact on communities; community infrastructure impact; and environmental impact. This formulation proved invaluable for establishing a cost baseline, useful in assessing conflicting data presented in support of counter-positions. But more importantly, it provided an assessment of the economic development initiatives that would be required to mitigate the impact on communities where bases were to be closed. Protracted efforts to deal with the aftermath of closure decisions were made more productive by these front-end assessments. Failure to do so could have escalated costs far beyond the value of the closure savings the decisions were designed to yield.

Lessons Learned

The Aspin proposal also envisioned a different approach to composing the Commission. Unlike the 1988 approach of appointing political "graybeards," the commissioners were selected based on a formula to assure that the administration and the Congress shared influence. The President and the congressional leadership on each side of the political aisle could nominate a specified number of commissioners. Ultimately, the members of the Commission would be appointed by the President and confirmed by the United States Senate, like other senior presidential appointees. The selection process was clearly designed to minimize political influence, or at least to balance that influence by assuring that all of the players were present at the commission table.

The Aspin proposal introduced some important differences as to how the Commission should conduct its business and how the President and Congress could treat the product of its deliberations. The Commission's primary responsibility was to assure that the Department's list of closure candidates did not deviate from the eight criteria. If the Commission determined that any base proposed was inadequately justified based on even one of the criteria, the Commission was empowered to remove the base from the list. While the Commission could add new candidates for closure, Aspin was confident that it would be unlikely to do so, unless by consensus among the commissioners. His instincts proved to be right.

The Base Closure and Realignment Commission proceedings were to be conducted in public at various locations around the country. The results of the Commission's deliberations would be forwarded to the President, who then had the choice to approve the entire list without modification or reject it as a whole. If the President accepted it, Congress then had the option of rejecting the entire list within a specified period. If it did not, the President's decision could be implemented without further legislative or administration action.

The 1991, 1993, and 1995 Commissions were based on a far more elaborate process than the 1988 variant, but each round of closures was predicated on the same premise: that Congress gained political cover by delegating the authority to close bases. The process had to appear objective in order to be successful. Unfortunately, President Clinton's actions during the 1995 process called that objectivity into question. The Commission's report made decisions about each base that it reviewed that were either specific (for example, "close base A and move its functions to base B"), or offered the administration choices (such as "close base A and either move its functions to base B or outsource them to the private sector"). In his transmittal of the Commission's report to the Congress, President Clinton interpreted its findings concerning two large facilities as allowing him to privatize them rather than relocate the work to other bases. Consequently, those activities remain in operation today, but with a corporate logo over the door instead of the Department's seal. The Congress subsequently allowed the report to become law. However, some members of Congress and other affected constituencies perceived this action as a maneuver to thwart the intent of the base closure process, undermining the perception of fairness.

The special authority for base closure expired in 1995, and thus the rules devised in the 1970s now apply again. While the administration has persistently sought renewal of the expedited closure authority, the Congress has thus far shown no interest in entertaining the request.

Prospects for Future Initiatives

Any future effort to introduce an initiative to rationalize the Department's infrastructure must incorporate the primary ingredients of the previous base closure process:

- the bases to be closed must be demonstrated to be excess capacity, based on an objective analysis of force-structure support requirements;

- cost and impact must be assessed, based on specified criteria;

- assessment of post-closure economic development requirements must be done in advance, during selection of closure candidates;

- the decision-makers must be credible and considered objective;

- Congress must have a limited set of parameters for considering the package;

- the activity must not be conducted in an election year; and

- no subsequent action can be taken to call into question the credibility of the process.

The imperative for future base closure and realignment efforts is evident. The Department continues to support far more infrastructure than the force structure requires. The budget includes at least $6 billion annually to support facilities that are excess to force structure requirements. Both the administration and the Congress acknowledge that the Department's ability to reduce costs will be limited unless facilities can be closed. The persistent stumbling block has always been how those decisions will be reached. The recent history should help guide development of a new framework. However, the recent experience also provides a fresh memory to members of Congress about how hard it is to make decisions to close facilities. Absent extraordinary political courage, the tendency toward political gerry-mandering will predominate. Moreover, the process must be a truly new one, because the previous formula has now been mastered by a broad range of constituencies: as a result, the quality of the result in each successive round of closure and realignment was progressively diminished, as creative tactics were developed to blunt the political consequences of closure decisions.

In a new process, it is imperative that all affected constituencies be afforded a chance to be heard, and that the political accountability for the decisions be diffused as broadly as possible. Indeed, these conditions may be more important for the success of the endeavor than any specific aspect of the process ultimately determined. The activity of formulating the process in partnership with the congressional leadership is likely to achieve both the objectives of inclusiveness and diffusion of decision-making.

Without the next administration's unwavering, consistent commitment to facilities and infrastructure closure, no progress will be achieved. If its objective is merely to berate Congress for thwarting cost-saving objectives and retaining infrastructure for political objectives, no process is necessary. But if the next administration is committed to improving the support infrastructure for the armed forces by eliminating excess capacity, a new process for decision-making must be developed and approved by Congress.

To prompt the development of that future process, the next administration should take a page from former Secretary Cheney's strategy, by introducing a list of base closure candidates and making a commitment to a closure plan that comports with current law. This process is so extensive and public that it is certain to demand an unacceptable amount of time and effort on the part of local and federal officials. Indeed, such an unpleasant assessment drove the previous imperative to devise a more acceptable decision process. The act of negotiating a framework was sufficient to achieve buy-in to the concept, but absent the threat of the initial draconian strategy, the base closure objective would never have been realized. Such an opening strategy should drive the players to the negotiating table in search of a new process paradigm. At the same time, the new administration should draft a legislative proposal in order to accelerate the inevitably difficult negotiations that will follow.

SYSTEMS ACQUISITION

The two previous sections have argued for eliminating functions and infrastructure either that DOD does not need or that it can acquire more efficiently from external suppliers. This section addresses an important part of how DOD should manage its relationship with external suppliers. We outline a concept we call Value Based Acquisition (VBA) and show how VBA, by embodying the incentives, accountability, and customer focus of commercial markets, can improve DOD's systems acquisition.

The Value Based Acquisition (VBA) Concept

DOD acquisition reform efforts described above have cleared away major legal, regulatory, administrative, and bureaucratic barriers to taking advantage of the rapid pace of product improvement and efficiency in commercial markets. In areas where commercial companies perform functions or manufacture products that are nearly equivalent to those needed by DOD, such as housing, health care, and accounting services, DOD has already increased its use of outsourcing and direct purchasing of commercial items. Above, we recommend ways to improve and expand DOD's competitive sourcing activities. However, progress has been limited in cases where DOD acquires clearly noncommercial items such as major systems that are uniquely military in character (e.g., armored vehicles, warships, and fighter planes). There are many in the defense community who believe that DOD must continue to use traditional acquisition methods when acquiring such products. They assert that the development risk associated with complex defense systems, combined with their typically non-competitive production, makes it impossible to apply market mechanisms widely. We disagree. Using Value Based Acquisition, DOD can create market signals that are now lacking in systems acquisition, and in doing so create incentives for contractors that mirror those of commercial producers. VBA allows contractors to profit from finding innovative solutions that meet defense needs.

The VBA concept is already DOD policy. Secretary of Defense William Cohen articulated the fundamental principle in a recent report to Congress: "The Department needs to change its focus from trying to figure what something costs to acquire, to focusing on the value a thing has over its useful life. This change will allow DOD to compete differing solutions and get the best value."[28] This "best value" concept is being promulgated throughout DOD in the form of performance and strategic plans. Office of the Secretary of Defense (OSD) guidance requires that lower-level strategic plans show a clear linkage to DOD's corporate goals, and the military services are beginning to include linkages to performance-based management in their planning and budget documents. But understanding and communicating the relationships among systems, missions, and high-level DOD objectives is still sparse. Even at the level of individual programs, value-based approaches that allow flexible tradeoffs among performance, cost, risk, and schedule have not yet been developed.

VBA has much in common with current efforts within DOD to expand the use of what is called price-based acquisition (PBA). A recent DOD study group defined PBA as follows:

In its purest form, PBA results in a firm-fixed-price (or fixed-price with performance incentives) contract and a fair and reasonable price is established without obtaining supplier cost data.... "Pure" price-based acquisition is at one end of a continuum. At the other end is "pure" cost-based acquisition (CBA) where virtually every aspect of the DOD/supplier relationship demands that the supplier provide DOD with actual or estimated costs.[29]

We believe that VBA, in which both price and performance are traded off, is actually the other end of the continuum from CBA, with PBA as an in-between step. VBA has several advantages over PBA, as we elaborate below. However, in terms of implementation, PBA and VBA face similar philosophical and practical barriers.

Those with philosophical objections to VBA reside principally within the contracting, audit, and legislative communities. They contend that traditional DOD-controlled, cost-plus-fee contracting is still the most sensible way to manage risky, long-term development and production programs in which there is no meaningful competition. They hold that DOD must carefully monitor contractor activities

28. William S. Cohen, *Section 912 Report to Congress*, April 1, 1998.

29. Office of the Under Secretary of Defense for Acquisition, Technology and Logistics, *Report of the Price-Based Acquisition Study Group*, draft of November 15, 1999. This report was submitted to Congress as part of the studies undertaken in response to congressional direction in Section 912(c) of the National Defense Authorization Act for Fiscal Year 1998.

in order to insure adequate performance and to avoid waste, fraud, and abuse. In this environment, there is no practical way to engage in a commercial-style transaction. A fixed-price contract would expose contractors to too much risk, leading to overly conservative designs, while a contract that allowed for variable price or variable performance is unacceptable when spending public funds, as it makes it impossible to allocate budgets in advance and does not hold contractors sufficiently accountable. The public will not tolerate "excessive" profits for companies receiving public money.

The philosophical objections to VBA are sound but shortsighted. To leverage commercial market dynamics, DOD must take a longer-term perspective. In commercial markets, it is "excessive" profits that drive product improvement and process efficiency: commercial companies are motivated to become more efficient precisely because doing so leads directly to increased profitability. But this increased profitability can only be sustained if the improvements continue. In fact, many firms experience recurrent "boom and bust" cycles: extreme profitability is followed by periods of capital reinvestment. It is largely the prospect of "extreme" gains that motivates investment in high-risk innovation. In such an environment, even a monopoly producer must improve in order to prevent competition from being attracted to the market.[30]

In adopting a more "commercial" stance with respect to the defense industry, DOD may indeed pay more in the short run, but it can thus set in motion a dynamic that, over the long run, will lower prices and improve performance. Figure 7-1 depicts these two market scenarios. The commercial market scenario (descending cost and price curves) represents companies succeeding in the marketplace by lowering costs and improving performance. These efficiency gains are passed on to consumers, over time, as lower prices. In the defense market scenario (rising cost and price curves), companies working under cost-plus contracts have exactly the opposite incentive: their profits increase when their costs increase. Over time, rising costs can make the profits earned under such contracts even more "excessive."

30. The speed with which competitors will enter a market depends on the particular barriers to entry. In the case of intellectual property barriers, it can take as long as the expiration of patents. A barrier like high initial capital costs creates incentives to search for alternative technologies and approaches. In any case, no barriers are permanent.

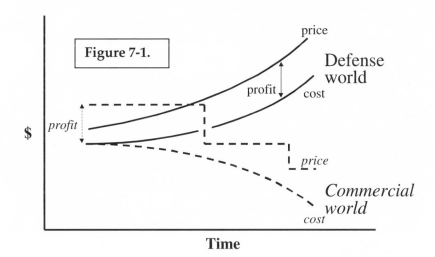

Time

In the figure, the two-sided arrow representing commercial contractor profit in the early years is equal to the arrow representing defense contractor profit in later years.

The important question for DOD is how to engage commercial suppliers in a market environment in which future costs are unknown. Past costs are not a good guide. If DOD set prices for computer or communications equipment based on historical costs, it would pay far too much. Knowledge of past costs can be a good starting point for planning and focusing management effort. But in order to create incentives for the cost-reducing, performance-increasing trends that characterize many commercial technology markets, DOD needs to have relationships with suppliers that are based on value, as suggested by Secretary Cohen.

This brings us to the practical problems with VBA. How can VBA be realized? How does one model and communicate value consistently across different levels of concern? What are the implications for DOD program management? We explore these questions below, beginning at the level of the individual program, and then tracing the implications of VBA for mission-level tradeoffs and for broader DOD and government objectives.

VBA in Practice
The key to VBA at the program level is the development of a value model that embodies key system design features, such as weight,

manufacturing cost, reliability, and the like, as well as key acquisition concerns, such as cost and schedule.[31] Quantification of the elements of value will generally be imperfect and partly subjective. Nonetheless, an explicit value model allows operational benefits — how a particular operational capability affects the ability of the warfighter to accomplish his mission — to be traded rationally and consistently against other important design factors, such as weight, reliability, and manufacturing cost.[32]

Once a quantitative value model has been defined, it can become the basis for contracting. A program office can offer a contract in which price is a function of value. The contract would specify the price that the program would be willing to pay for different levels of performance; that is, it would specify the various combinations of price and performance that would be equally acceptable. Prices would be based on the value model, as well as on market information and historical experience. The contractor would then use the relationship between value and cost to determine a solution that best matched its technical capabilities. Under a value-based contract, a contractor maximizes profit by including only those features whose value to the government exceeds their cost.

To understand how this works, one needs to consider that the development of a complex system can involve hundreds or thousands of designers deep in the contractor's and subcontractors' engineering organizations. These are the people who will make most of the de-

---

31. Our description of weapons-system value modeling is adapted, with permission, from Paul Collopy, "Joint Strike Fighter: Optimal Design through Contract Incentives," *1999 Acquisition Research Symposium Proceedings* (Washington, D.C.: Defense Systems Management College, 1999), pp. 335–346.

32. The advantages offered by a quantitative, value-based approach can be illustrated by an assessment of stealth. The prior method was to estimate, based on cost analyses, the reduction in combat losses due to improved survivability with stealth. The improvement thus calculated was only marginal, because the historical data do not show high loss rates. The reason for that is that squadrons avoid flying missions that put aircraft and crew in great jeopardy; the cost of such missions exceeds the value. The real advantage of stealth, however, as demonstrated in the Gulf War, is that stealthy aircraft can attack high-value targets that would, without the benefits of stealth, be too costly.

tailed design decisions that determine cost and performance. Because the value model captures the relative importance of key system features such as weight, manufacturing cost, reliability, and the like, it can be used as an effective communication tool all the way down the product hierarchy. For example, because the weight of a system is simply the sum of the weights of its components, each component designer can have insight into the overall value of small-scale design decisions. Such information is not communicated in the current system in which rigid specifications as to performance and cost are communicated downward from the top.[33]

VBA also embodies incentives for delivering improved system capability as underlying technologies evolve. The same performance-price relationship that defined payments for initial deliveries implicitly defines payments for upgrades. Whenever making use of a new technology increases value, the contractor is paid for that incremental value based on the original performance-price contract. If that added price is large enough to offset the cost of the upgrade (amortized across some number of units), the contractor improves its profitability by inserting it. Hence the contractor is motivated to design the system to be easy to upgrade so that it can realize increased profit, not only by improving each succeeding production lot, but also by inserting new technology into previously delivered systems.[34]

The ability of DOD to make a transition to use of VBA depends on implementation initiatives that are quite similar to those for price-based acquisition. The *Report of the Price-Based Acquisition Study Group*, submitted to Congress in November 1999, covers several spe-

---

33. What typically happens now in large system design is that Engineer A's part is over the specified weight but under the target cost. His best choice is to change to a lighter-weight, more expensive material that would increase cost by $5,000 and reduce weight by 8 pounds. The design is now satisfactory under the contract specs. Engineer B's part is over cost but under on weight. A cheaper, heavier material increases weight 28 pounds, but reduces cost $2,000, also meeting all specified goals. The net effect of both decisions results in a system that is 20 pounds heavier and costs an additional $3,000. In a value model, the relative value of weight is the same for each designer and is known throughout the supply chain.

34. This type of guidance can improve independent research and development (IR&D) decisions by focusing them better on the warfighter values as reflected in the model.

cific implementation needs, such as managing development risk, remaining knowledgeable about commercial markets, maintaining competition through all system development and production phases (including research and development), performing source selection, financing, handling contract claims and cancellations, training acquisition personnel, and including cost considerations within the DOD requirements process.[35] The Senate Armed Service Committee expressed its approval of that report and urged DOD to implement its recommendations.[36]

Relationship of VBA to Higher-level DOD Reform Goals

We began the discussion of VBA with Secretary of Defense William Cohen's statement: "The Department needs to change its focus from trying to figure what something costs to acquire, to focusing on the value a thing has over its useful life. This change will allow DOD to compete differing solutions and get the best value."[37] A GAO review found that although DOD's FY 2000 Performance Plan states overall performance goals, these goals are not clearly associated with specific missions and with the capabilities of weapon systems designed to help carry out those missions.[38] Using explicit value modeling to describe DOD missions would help DOD accomplish this goal. To build a value model, one must consider in depth how the key attributes of a system relate to the mission goals of the user. The value of the maximum speed of a fighter plane, for instance, is determined by assessing the implications of speed for survivability while attacking a hard target, effectiveness in base defense, fuel costs, and so on, across its most important missions. The value of various missions can be broken down into attributes in the same manner: destroying a hard target, for example, plays a part in winning a campaign, which in

---

35. *Report of the Price-Based Acquisition Study Group.*

36. Senate Armed Services Committee, Report for the Fiscal Year 2001 Defense Authorization bill, states: "Many of the recommendations of [the Price-based Acquisition] report ... show significant promise for the reduction of risk in the acquisition of major systems. The committee urges the Department of Defense to take strong action to implement [its] recommendations."

37. Cohen, *Section 912 Report to Congress.*

38. U.S. General Accounting Office, *Observations on the Department of Defense's Performance Plan for Fiscal Year 2000,* GAO/NSIAD-99-178R, July 20, 1999.

turn plays a part in achieving political objectives. Although such relationships can be difficult to assess and are partly subjective, the basic value modeling structure is the same.

Articulating the structure of values explicitly not only clarifies the key variables in a decision, but can also inspire creativity, by making it possible to separate a problem into its value attributes and then to explore various combinations of those attributes, unconstrained by preconceived ideas. Organizationally, thinking in structured, value-based terms makes it clearer how to separate the pieces of a problem into modular units that can be effectively delegated. A plan for building a subsystem is part of the plan for building a weapon platform; this in turn is part of a plan for waging war. Different groups are involved at these different levels. Value modeling creates a consistent structure that links these different levels and hence can help align organizations around shared goals.

In this way VBA could eventually lead to changes in the high-level process of defining and validating requirements, which are discussed by General Shalikashvili in Chapter 2. We are confident that VBA, properly implemented, would improve communication among program offices, prime contractors, and lower-tier suppliers by moving away from the notion of fixed requirements in favor of more flexible specifications that express the linkage between a system's key performance parameters and its effectiveness in accomplishing its missions. (Architectural requirements such as interface standards and communications protocols will often be an exception: they must be fixed, in order to enhance interoperability for joint capabilities, as described in Chapter 2.) Beyond this, we believe that, if VBA is successful at the individual system level, it could eventually become a language for discussing alternative mission approaches. This would help fulfill DOD's long-standing objective of better matching overall performance goals with specific missions and with the capabilities of weapon systems designed to help carry out those missions.

In the end, the most important goal of VBA is to change the way people think about their tasks. A parallel is found in the commercial world. Success and growth during 1960s and 1970s led to complacency for many companies; consolidated organizations grew in a manner that made corporate managers overly focused on internal matters. Success in the 1980s and 1990s was, by contrast, defined by becoming better organized to meet the needs of customers: more innovative in anticipating customer need, more reliable in meeting customer expectations, and able to deliver a service or product more cheaply.[39] For DOD, a focus on the quality of outcomes as viewed by customers — primarily the U.S. taxpayers and their representatives in Congress, as well as internal customers such as the regional and functional commanders-in-chief — has the potential to change how the entire DOD organization thinks about its tasks, activities, and responsibilities.

Conclusion

Achieving the goals of the Revolution in Business Affairs will require major policy, procedural, organizational, and cultural reforms, as well as significant downsizing. It will engender strong internal resistance. This resistance will have to be addressed with the same seriousness and focus as DOD's national security missions. Success will depend on building alliances with Congress, garnering public support, creating effective long-term programs inside the DOD, gaining the support of DOD's people, and developing new relationships with the relevant parts of the private business sector. It will not be easy but it is necessary. The Revolution in Business Affairs is a critical element of the array of reforms that are required for the DOD to succeed in the ever-changing, highly uncertain, but probably dangerous world of the future.

---

39. Waterman, *What America Does Right*.

8

Ensuring Quality People in Defense

DAVID S.C. CHU AND JOHN P. WHITE

WITH NURITH BERSTEIN AND JOHN BROWN

T he U.S. military and civilian personnel systems represent a remarkable contrast in effectiveness. The overall military system,
based on the foundation of the All Volunteer Force (AVF), has
been a success by nearly every measure. On the other hand, the civil
service system has to be judged a failure in its ability to adjust to
changing requirements and encourage the innovation and continuous
improvement needed by the Department of Defense (DOD).

There have been major efforts to reform each system in recent decades. The military reform that began in the 1970s, which included more
than just the AVF, was a radical departure from a force supported by
conscription. Despite serious early difficulties and a continuing need
for adjustment, it has delivered high-quality people, both officers and
enlisted. In contrast, the somewhat more recent legislative changes of
the civil service rules embodied in the Civil Service Reform Act of 1978
(CSRA), have been largely unsuccessful. The changes that were expected to evolve from the legislation have not materialized.

The successes of military reform offer lessons for new civil service reform proposals. We begin this chapter, therefore, with a brief analysis of
how the military made the All Volunteer Force a success, how it significantly integrated minorities and women, how it improved its professional competence, and how it reshaped itself with the end of the Cold
War. We offer four lessons learned from the military's success. They
should help the military devise policies to meet its new challenges,
which we analyze in detail. We then draw on these lessons to develop
our civil service reform proposal, which follows the AVF review.

Military Personnel: A Case of Successful Management

The history of military personnel management over the last three decades is instructive, both for the problems encountered and the solutions adopted, and how these contributed to the contemporary success of America's armed forces. The same history also reveals some weaknesses, creating challenges for a new administration as it seeks to sustain this success.

A generation ago, the U.S. military emerged from Vietnam a nearly shattered and largely discredited institution. Lieutenant Calley's crimes epitomized the breakdown of the military personnel system: an unprepared officer placed in a position of responsibility with disastrous results. The low quality of military personnel led Congress in 1980 to enact mandatory minimum recruiting quality goals in law: it was a desperate measure, born of intense frustration. The military's ranks were torn by racial tension and even race riots.[1]

A generation later, the military personnel system has produced what is unquestionably one of the finest militaries in history, widely admired at home and abroad.[2] It built a successful All Volunteer Force (an innovation the military at first resisted), achieved a degree of racial and gender integration that is the envy of civil society (despite lingering problems), reached a level of professional competence that leads civilian recruiters to seek its personnel, and reshaped itself successfully when the Cold War ended.[3]

---

1. See, for example, Sheril Mershon and Steven Schlossman, *Foxholes and Color Lines* (Baltimore: Johns Hopkins, 1998), p. 322; and Charles C. Moskos, "Success Story: Blacks in the Military," *Atlantic Monthly*, May 1986.

2. A Gallup poll periodically asks a cross-section of Americans about their confidence in American institutions. The military currently ranks highest, with 64 percent of respondents in June 2000 saying they have "a great deal" or "quite a lot" of confidence, the highest ranking for any American institution. In 1981, the low point for the military in this series of polls, that figure was just 50 percent. See <gallup.ccom/poll/releases/pr000710.asp> (downloaded July 10, 2000).

3. See, for example, Edwin Dorn, "Sustaining the Volunteer Force," in J. Eric Fredland, et al., eds., *Professionals on the Front Line: Two Decades of the All-Volunteer Force* (Washington, D.C.: Brassey's, 1996), p. 20.

THE ALL VOLUNTEER FORCE

The All Volunteer Force (AVF) constituted a major policy experiment. It was born of the Nixon administration's need to deal with the increasing unpopularity of the Vietnam War, specifically the unpopularity of conscription,[4] and the changing demographics of American society: the baby boomers' arrival at draft age meant that there were many more eligible youth than the military needed. At the time, Britain was the only significant military power that used volunteers to staff its ranks, and its military was much smaller.[5] While economists were convinced that, in theory, a volunteer force could work, no one knew in practice exactly how to structure the incentives to guarantee success. The initiative was opposed by most senior military leaders.[6] While the Air Force had long relied on volunteers (as had the Navy and Marine Corps to a lesser extent), these were largely "induced volunteers" fleeing the draft. Moreover, however attractive the concept may have appeared in peacetime, there was grave doubt about its viability in war.[7]

The early years of the AVF were rocky indeed. Statistics on quality trends for Army enlistees provide the standard gauge of success, especially for the Army, since the Army is the largest service and generally viewed as having the least attractive conditions of service. As Table 8-1 indicates, quality levels dropped sharply in the early years

---

4. See Walter Y. Oi, "Historical Perspectives on the All-Volunteer Force," Fredland, et al., *Professionals on the Front Line*, pp. 42–47.

5. *Report of the President's Commission on an All-Volunteer Force* (Gates Commission) (Washington, D.C.: U.S. Government Printing Office [U.S. GPO], 1970), p. 169. In the 1970s, the UK's active military numbered about 300,000, or 0.55 percent of its 56.7 million population. In comparison, the active U.S. military numbered over 2 million, about 0.94 percent of the U.S. population. See, for example, International Institute for Strategic Studies (IISS), *The Military Balance, 1970* (Oxford: Oxford University Press, 1971).

6. At the start of the Reagan administration in 1981, some military leaders urged the Secretary of Defense to return to conscription. For a flavor of how the early AVF was perceived, see John B. Kelley, ed., *The All-Volunteer Force and American Society* (Charlottesville: University Press of Virginia, 1978).

7. The Gates Commission "recommended a stand-by draft which can be put into effect promptly if circumstances a require mobilization of large numbers of men." Gates Commission Report, p. 11.

Table 8-1. Quality Indicators for Active Enlistees without Prior Service (Percent of Total Enlistees)

	FY 1973	FY 1980	FY 1992	FY 1999
High School Diploma Graduate, Army	58%	52%	99%	93%
Upper Aptitude Score (AFQT I–IIIA), All Services	58%	49%	75%	66%
Lower Aptitude Score (AFQT IV), All Services	13%	9%	0.2%	0.9%

NOTES: AFQT = Armed Forces Qualification Test. AFQT I corresponds to the 93rd to 99th percentiles of the distribution, AFQT II, the 65th to 92nd; AFQT IIIA, the 50th to 64th; and AFQT IV, the 10th to 30th percentiles. Individuals scoring below AFQT IV are not permitted to enlist.

SOURCES: <dticaw.dtic.mil/prhome/poprep98/html>; and Secretary of Defense, *Annual Report to the President and the Congress 2000* (Washington, D.C.: U.S. Government Printing Office, 2000), p. 107.

of the AVF, reaching a nadir in the late 1970s, prompting Congress to direct minimum quality goals in law.

Apart from the expected difficulties of implementing a revolutionary personnel concept, the early difficulties of the AVF reflected one significant policy error and one significant technical mistake. The technical mistake was mis-norming the shift to a new Armed Forces Qualification Test (AFQT) in FY 1976, with the result that actual quality was substantially below measured quality.[8] (Policymakers ignored, to their regret, the complaints of sergeants that recruit quality was declining: a lesson for present and future decision-makers.)

---

8. The mis-norming reflected a numerical error at the low end of the scale; it was not discovered until the end of the decade. As a result, the military thought it was accepting 5 percent of its personnel from those with AFQT IV scores (the lowest acceptable ranking), when in fact during 1977–79 over one-quarter of all active recruits with no prior service were AFQT IV. This was far above the statutory ceiling of 20 percent. See Gary R. Nelson, "The Supply and Quality of First-Term Enlistees Under the All Volunteer Force," in William Bowman, et al., eds., *The All-Volunteer Force After a Decade* (Washington, D.C.: Pergamon-Brassey's, 1986), pp. 31–32.

The policy error came about because of the overall federal fiscal strategy of limiting federal pay raises in the face of high inflation, rather than trying to limit the military pay bill. That is, the focus should have been on the labor costs of DOD, which are the product of the number and level of personnel on the payroll, as well as all elements of compensation, not just basic pay. (More on this issue below.)

Congress overrode the executive branch's military pay raise recommendations in 1980.[9] Subsequent Secretaries of Defense have generally paid much closer attention to the military pay raise, although the Office of Management and Budget (OMB) has often sought to limit it for broad budgetary reasons. OMB frequently also insists on equal military and civil service raises, a policy choice for which there may be good political rationale, but little analytic justification. The payoff for a sustained policy of matching competing civilian compensation can be seen in the last two columns of Table 8-1: quality levels in the 1990s have far exceeded the wildest hopes of the 1970s (with the high point reached in 1992, versus the low in 1980), and have been sustained through two conflicts (the Persian Gulf War and Kosovo).[10]

RACIAL INTEGRATION
President Truman's order desegregating the Armed Services marked the start of what is now a fifty-year effort to integrate minorities into the fabric of military society. Racial challenges still confront the military, as evidenced by a recent widely reported survey.[11] But in contrast

9. The FY 1980 Defense Authorization Act provided an 11.7 percent pay raise, substantially more than was recommended by the president. For FY 1981, the Congress voted a military pay increase of 14.3 percent.

10. The actual story is more complex. The success of pay increases in restoring the health of the AVF was also helped by the lag in civilian wage growth for those with just a high school diploma. See James R. Hosek, et al., *A Civilian Wage Index for Defense Manpower*, R-4190-FMP (Santa Monica, Calif.: RAND, 1992); and James R. Hosek, et al., *Military Pay Gaps and Caps*, MR-368-P&R (Santa Monica, Calif.: RAND, 1994).

11. 1997 Armed Forces Equal Opportunity Survey. Overall, 61 percent of respondents said race relations at their installations were good to a "large to very large extent" — but only 39 percent of blacks felt that way (versus 68 percent of whites, 53 percent of Hispanics). When asked to compare social conditions in the military with civil society (e.g., freedom from harassment),

Table 8-2. Minority Active Duty Officers (percent of total in grades, 1987 and 1997)

	1987	1997
Minority Officers in Field Grades (0-4 through 0-6)	7.2%	12.3%
Minority Officers in Flag Grades (0-7 through 0-10)	4.7%	7.0%

SOURCES: Office of the Under Secretary of Defense for Personnel and Readiness, "Career Progression of Minority and Women Officers," Table 2-5, 1998; Office of Workforce Information, "Demographic Data Report: 1998," Table 2.

to civil society, minorities now hold a significant fraction of the military's supervisory positions (0-4 through 0-6, major through colonel in Army, Air Force, and Marine parlance, roughly the equivalent of GS-11 through GS-15), including a growing fraction of the most senior positions (flag rank; see Table 8-2). The number of minorities holding senior positions in the military even compares favorably to DOD's civilian employees (see Figure 8-1), long known for its good record, relative to American society as a whole, in this regard.

This result is not an accident; it reflects steady attention to equal promotion opportunity, and even more important, to preparation for promotion through equal access to training and career-building assignments.

GENDER INTEGRATION

The military services began the significant integration of women only within the last generation, at the direction of the nation's political authorities.[12] Not only have the services been pursuing this objective for a much shorter period of time than racial integration, but in some ways it is a more challenging requirement, reflecting a pervasive re-

an overwhelming majority of respondents in every racial group viewed the military as equal to or better than civilian life. See Defense Manpower Data Center, *Armed Forces Equal Opportunity Survey*, 1997, <http://dicaw.dtic.mil.prhome/eo96exsum.html>.

12. See, for example, Jeanne Holm, *Women in the Military* (Novato, Calif.: Presidio Press, 1992).

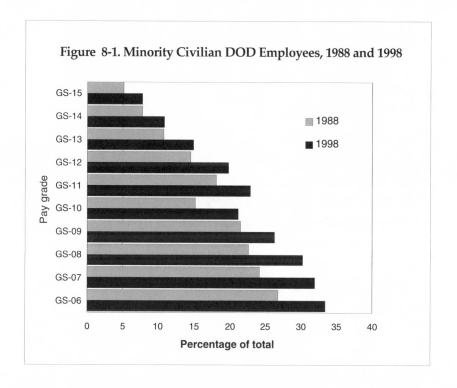

Figure 8-1. Minority Civilian DOD Employees, 1988 and 1998

luctance in American society to see women participate in combat (a reluctance that is sometimes expressed in law). This complicates women's promotion chances, since senior rank disproportionately accrues to those who choose operational careers.

Nonetheless, the progress of women is significant, as measured by the increasing proportion of women — 11.8% in 1997, compared to 6.1% in 1987 — in the field grades (0-4 through 0-6). It lags the record for DOD's civilian employees (see Figure 8-2), but is far ahead of such male-dominated civilian professional fields as orthopedic surgeons (3 percent) and cardiac surgeons (2 percent). Like the progress for racial minorities, this outcome reflects the political commitment and attention of the nation's leaders. It also reflects the fact that military personnel are managed as a system: military leaders gradually opened a wider set of occupational opportunities to women, and ensured they received a share of the early-career opportunities that eventually lead to senior leadership, such as attendance at the military academies and the military's professional schools that are so important to career advancement.

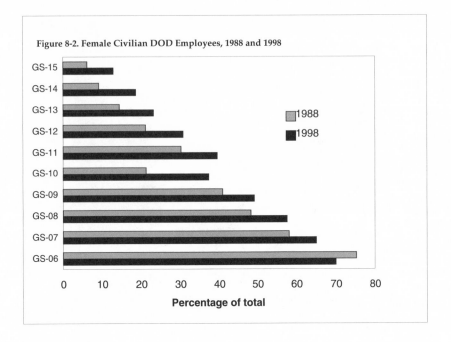

Figure 8-2. Female Civilian DOD Employees, 1988 and 1998

PROFESSIONAL COMPETENCE

Part of the "system management" of military leaders and their development is the emphasis on training. This includes both general training for individuals, such as by the War Colleges and the non-commissioned officer leadership training programs, and specific training including training for particular job skills, including those of officers, of which perhaps one of the most notable is the Navy's nuclear-power training.

Beyond the training that it provides to individuals, the modern American military spends a significant portion of its time in crew and unit training. Indeed, this is viewed as so important to military readiness that military leaders have objected when political authorities have assigned "non-military" missions such as drug interdiction that are perceived as interfering with these preparations.

While the military member may express his or her preferences for individual training, assignments are governed by centrally established policies that seek to prepare individuals for increasingly responsible positions. Thus, training is expressly linked to career progression. For officers and the more senior non-commissioned offi-

Table 8-3. Military Personnel Holding College Degrees (Percent of Total)

	1973	1980	1990	1999
Commissioned Officers	87	95	96	98
Enlisted (4 years)	2	2	2	3
Enlisted (2 years*)	8	8	11	13

SOURCE: Department of Defense, *Selected Manpower Statistics, Fiscal Years 1981 and 1999* (Washington, D.C.: Washington Headquarters Service), Table 2-18 (both years).

* NOTE: Includes all enlisted with two or more years of college, regardless of whether a formal degree was received.

cers (NCOs), that career progression includes service in the "right" variety of line and staff positions to prepare them for senior responsibilities. These are monitored by the central personnel managers of the military services.[13] In effect, military service is a career-long preparation for senior responsibilities, and only those who successfully complete the earlier stages are likely to be competitive.

The military sets entry standards for the start of this competition, by asking that enlistees be high school diploma graduates (or that they be ready to complete their general equivalency diploma [GED] quickly), and in recent decades by effectively requiring that officers have college degrees. (See Table 8-3.) In fact, a growing proportion of enlisted personnel hold college degrees, typically completed while in service, and many officers complete graduate degrees during their military careers. The result is a military whose professional competence is widely admired both at home and abroad. Military personnel, who typically "retire" in their forties, are easily able to secure attractive civilian jobs at the completion of their military careers. The payoff in national security terms is equally impressive: from a strictly military perspective, there is no doubt about the competence of American performance in the Persian Gulf War of 1990–91 and in the recent Kosovo conflict.

13. See Maren Leed, *Keeping the Warfighting Edge: An Empirical Analysis of Army Officers' Tactical Experience over the 1990s*, DB-307-A (Santa Monica, Calif.: RAND, 2000).

FORCE SHAPING

The management of military personnel extends well beyond decisions about recruitment and training. Since the unhappy discovery at the start of World War II that the U.S. military (especially the Army) lacked the youthful, motivated leaders it needed for the successful prosecution of war, the military has made shaping the force a preeminent personnel policy goal.

The shape each service aims to have resembles a pyramid. Most, if not all, personnel enter at junior levels, and progress through posts of increasing difficulty, gaining valuable experience and training. Only the most promising are permitted to move to the next level. The military uses an "up-or-out" promotion system to enforce these choices. Originally applied to officers, the up-or-out philosophy has been extended, in the last generation, to the enlisted force.

The end of the Cold War presented the military services with a significant challenge to their shaping policies, because the entire pyramid had to be trimmed. The last such significant trimming, at the end of the Vietnam War, was widely seen as clumsy and unnecessarily harsh. In the spirit of the AVF, the military services chose to meet this new challenge in an intellectually consistent way: by relying on positive incentives. In effect, the military adopted policies in which it paid people to leave, through both "buyouts" (lump-sum payments and limited annuities for those not yet eligible to retire), and early retirement opportunities.

THE SOURCES OF SUCCESS

The successes of military personnel management over the last generation offer four potential explanations for success and lessons to learn from this experience.

First, in each area a clear, measurable set of objectives was set such as quality standards for enlistees and promotion equity for minorities. Equally important, these objectives were accepted (indeed, sometimes directed) by the political leadership of DOD. The leadership received regular reports on success in meeting these objectives — or the lack thereof — and took action accordingly.

Second, military personnel outcomes were seen to be the product of a system, and attention was focused on management of the system.

Third, quantitative analysis was employed widely and aggressively, to try to understand the relationships between causes and effects. Equally important, policymakers were focused on outcomes, not inputs, and they were willing to use experiments to test, evaluate, and adjust policies.

Fourth, policymakers came to understand early that incentives — bonuses, compensation, promotion opportunity, and the like — rather than "rules and regulations" would be the main instruments to achieve the outcomes they desired. They also understood that rules and regulations might have to be changed or reshaped to produce the incentives they needed.

Critical Challenges for a New Administration in Managing Military Personnel

The management paradigm for military personnel, like any other, also has its weaknesses. Two in particular relate directly to the future challenges confronting the military personnel system.

First, the system is ultimately a market, and market conditions change. However, the mechanisms to monitor those changes are weak and imperfect, leading to an unfortunate lag between changes in conditions and changes in policy. This can be seen in both the failure during the 1970s mis-norming episode to pick up promptly on the sergeants' complaint about enlistee quality, and the more recent lag in linking what appears to be a secular decline in recruiter productivity (resulting in recruiting shortfalls in three of the four services in recent years) with changes in the educational and career aspirations of young Americans (which we discuss further in the next section).

Second, not withstanding its analytic emphasis, the military personnel system retains a healthy respect for tradition. While this can be constructive in restraining the impulse to make sudden, poorly-thought-out changes, it can also inhibit innovation and can even blind decision-makers as to what is actually driving results. An excellent example is the complaint of policymakers about the high rate of marriage and family formation among junior enlisted personnel; many are poorly prepared for these responsibilities, which creates difficulties for the military personnel system. Analysts explain that this outcome is encouraged by retaining a system in which compensation at the junior end of the scale is strongly affected by marital status rather than productivity, one of the surviving traditions of the military compension system.[14]

THREE CHALLENGES FOR A NEW ADMINISTRATION

Three critical military personnel challenges will face a new administration. The first is managing the compensation system well. Military compensation accounts for over a quarter of the defense budget, yet it is widely viewed as manageable only at the margin. It certainly is not regarded as it would be in a business, where attention to keeping the total compensation bill under thoughtful control is one of management's most important responsibilities. Quite the contrary: reflecting both the tradition-bound nature of the structure of military compensation, and the bitter lesson of the 1970s mismanagement of military pay changes, policymakers have allowed a "bidding war" to develop among competing political factions regarding military compensation. This resulted in an inefficient and costly change in the retirement program in 1999, and a disproportionate share of that year's pay increase being awarded on an across-the-board rather than targeted basis.[15] It has likewise led in 2000 to proposals for significant and expensive changes in health benefits for military retirees.

---

14. John Cadigan reports that 23 percent of military males 18–24 are married (16 percent have children), versus 17 percent (13 percent with children) for a similarly educated civilian age cohort (all figures are for 1999). These differences become more pronounced in the mid to late twenties, and approximately 80 percent of military males of age 30 are married, versus approximately 60 percent for civilians. The differences in the percentage with children are even more striking (about 70 percent, versus about 35 percent for an educationally matched cohort at age 30). See John Cadigan, "Demographics of Enlisted Personnel," paper presented at the Western Economic Association, Vancouver, July 2000. For an analysis of how the compensation system might produce these results, see David W. Flueck and Jeffrey S. Zax, "Marriage, Divorce, Income, and Mlitary Marriage Incentives," Discussion Papers in Economics No. 95-4 (Boulder, Colo.: Department of Economics, University of Colorado, 1995).

15. For a discussion of alternative compensation policies, see Beth Asch and James Hosek, *Military Compensation: Trends and Policy Options*, DB-273-OSD (Santa Monica, Calif.: RAND, 1999).

Within a constrained military budget, inefficient compensation changes will rob the country of its ability to modernize the military for the twenty-first century. Thus, managing military compensation more thoughtfully is essential to the military transformation so widely recommended. (It is even more urgently needed for civil service compensation, which we discuss below.)

The second challenge is thinking about "quality of life" from a systems perspective, focused on the ultimate results we wish to achieve, as opposed to the traditionalist perspective that now too often characterizes policy, with its focus on entitlements derived from historical practice. An example is family housing. The military services are struggling to rejuvenate the stock of family housing built over a generation ago, convinced that it is essential to quality of life and thus to successful recruiting and retention. However, recent survey research confirms that military personnel like military housing because it is cheap, not because it is part of a community that creates "quality of life."[16] If so, DOD might be better off getting out of the housing business altogether, perhaps instead encouraging home ownership (the goal of most Americans, reflected in the fact that two-thirds own their own homes). Indeed, military families often complain that they are denied the chance to participate in this element of the American dream. Could such a change be reconciled with the current practice of moving military families frequently? Could we favorably affect recruiting and retention with such a change? This is largely uncharted territory that a new administration must begin mapping.

The third challenge for a new administration in managing human resources, including military personnel, is recognizing, understanding, and responding thoughtfully to the significant demographic changes sweeping through American society. These include the dramatic increase in labor force participation of women, with its implications for the ability to move military families easily, and the consequent effect on career satisfaction and retention. Another is the rapid increase in the share of the population of Hispanic origin, with its implications for the issue of minority representation, especially if, as seems to be the case, there exist differential patterns of behavior

---

16. See Richard Buddin, et al., *An Evaluation of Housing Options for Military Families*, MR-1020-OSD (Santa Monica, Calif.: RAND, 1999).

regarding such issues as the timing of high school completion. If high school completion reflects cultural factors rather than individual traits, the lack of a diploma may not be as negative an indicator as it once was, and the military could reconsider its standard. Indeed, the Army is now experimenting with revised standards in its "GED Plus" program, for just this reason.

Perhaps the most significant demographic change involves the increasing educational aspirations of young Americans. It has been building for some years, but its implications have only recently been widely recognized, and even more recently acted upon. These changing aspirations presumably reflect the greater earnings gains accruing to college graduates in recent years, and the relatively flat earnings trend for those who have only completed high school. The result is a significant shift in the proportion of young Americans attending college. Whereas in 1973 a bit less than half of all young Americans sought to go on to college after finishing high school, that proportion has now reached 66 percent. Put the other way around, only one-third of American youth today look principally to the job market rather than post-secondary education right after graduating from high school.[17] Yet that is the population at which the military enlisted recruiting effort is targeted. It should therefore be no surprise that recruiter productivity in the 1990s seems unable to recover to its 1980s level, despite sizeable additions of resources over the last several years.[18] The market has changed, and military recruiting must change with it.

Such change has begun: both the Army and the Navy have begun programs that allow enlisted personnel to pursue a college degree while in service, and the Army has launched a program to help pay for junior college education before an enlistee comes on active duty ("College First").[19] Only time will tell how successful these efforts will

---

17. See U.S. National Center for Education Statistics, *The Digest of Educational Statistics 1999* (Washington, D.C.: U.S. GPO, May 2000), chap. 3.

18. Investment per recruit has increased 60 percent since 1994.

19. See, for example, "What We are Looking For," remarks delivered by the Honorable Louis Caldera, Secretary of the Army, to the Army University Access Online Industry Day Forum, Reagan International Trade Center, August 2, 2000. Under the College First program, the Army pays a recruit to attend junior college (or two years of college) before entering active duty

be in cracking the "college market" to recruit young people who desire a post-secondary education.

It is likely that the implications of the secular change in college attendance are more profound than first attempts to deal with it recognize. Ultimately, it may require reconsidering what military careers look like, and even perhaps the distinction between officers and enlisted. Such a change is potentially more profound than the transition to an all volunteer force, and one whose management will require great sophistication and wisdom on the part of a new administration.[20]

Recommended Courses of Action

For each of these challenges, we recommend specific courses of action to the new administration.

BASE COMPENSATION ON MILITARY NEEDS

Over the last thirty years, policymakers have overlaid a variety of bonuses on the underlying compensation system, in an effort to secure the recruiting and retention results they need. But they have not changed its underlying character, a "one-size-fits-all" approach whose results are often more affected by the social circumstances of the individual (e.g., housing allowances based on family size) than by the needs of the service, or by any principle that rewards productivity and effectiveness. It is time to consider a targeted compensation system that emphasizes the individual's contribution, and the personnel needs of DOD. Recent decisions to target pay increases on particular grades, rather than simply increasing all pay by the same share, are consistent with this course of action. But the Department has been unwilling to reallocate compensation funds from accounts with low payoff to those that are more critical, as a recent controversy over the

(earlier programs, such as the GI Bill, were only available after at least some service was completed).

20. Retiring Marine Corps General Anthony Zinni, Commander-in-Chief, United States Central Command, has said: "The rank structure is holding [non-commissioned officers] back, despite the fact that their educational attainments ... have far outstripped the structure. This needs to be fixed." Transcript of Robert McCormick Tribune Foundation, U.S. Naval Institute Address, March 2000.

restructuring of housing allowances demonstrates.[21] Nor has the Department been willing to tackle a fundamental overhaul of the system. Such an overhaul might go so far as to make the various allowances that are now strongly influenced by family status, such as housing and subsistence, part of the individual's "salary," and then base salary on the value of the individual to the military, as bonuses now are, rather than on the individual's family situation.

TAKE A SYSTEMS APPROACH TO QUALITY OF LIFE

Direct provision of services such as housing and grocery stores is often the norm in the military's efforts to assure its members' "quality of life." The system originated in the nineteenth century, when markets in areas where the American military was stationed were often inadequate. This history has led to a confusion between means and ends. The means historically was the direct provision of services, but the end is the satisfaction of the military member. Moreover, the environment around most military installations has changed dramatically: in almost no part of the United States are civilian markets now inadequate for the services a military family might want. Quality-of-life policy should focus on assisting families in using those markets, which in some cases may be as simple as putting the money in their pockets and letting them decide how to spend it, rather than acting as if DOD knows what they want. Such policy should take a systems view, in which we constantly remind ourselves that the ultimate objective is attracting and retaining the people DOD needs, and enhancing their productivity. Pursuing such a policy would better focus DOD quality-of-life efforts, which now consist of establishing and running programs, with all the obvious opportunities for bureaucratic growth, rather than concentrating on determining what makes a difference to recruiting and retention, with a concentration on measuring and producing results.

---

21. In the past year, DOD tried to reallocate housing allowance funds from low-cost to high-cost areas, in an effort to deal better with geographic variations in the cost of living, but reversed itself in response to protests from families in low-cost areas (despite "save pay" provisions that maintained allowances for recipients). See Tom Philpott, "Housing Allowance Equity Ends," *The Sun Link*, March 2000.

STRUCTURE PERSONNEL POLICIES CONSISTENT WITH LONG-RUN DEMOGRAPHIC CHANGES

The demographic changes affecting military recruiting and retention are so profound in their implications that it may be time to begin rethinking what a military career looks like. Two changes in particular merit consideration. First, at present the enlisted and officer communities follow essentially separate career paths. Few enlisted people become officers, yet that is where the rewards to a full college education lie. More paths should be opened to allow the most promising enlisted to move to warrant or commissioned status, reflecting their growing educational achievements.

Second, the military services now frequently move personnel among geographic locations, to effect job changes. "Homesteading" — staying in one geographic location for a substantial portion of one's career — is generally frowned upon. This is less so in the case of the Navy, as much of its fleet is concentrated in just two locations, Norfolk and San Diego; to some extent the same is true of the Marine Corps. With more spouses working, frequent moves are obviously a disruptive career pattern, and have long been an issue regarding the stability of schooling for the family's children. As it thinks about its basing structure for the twenty-first century, the DOD should consider how the Navy model might be adapted to the circumstances of the other services. This could have a profound impact on the decisions about base closure and realignment that are expected to confront a new administration.[22]

Civilian Personnel: The Need for Reform

The most fundamental changes in the DOD's human resources system are needed in the policies and practices of the civil service, because they are so out of touch with current and future requirements. No one understands the current deficiency better than the civil servants themselves. In a recent survey of federal executives, they said that:

---

22. For a discussion of how family factors affect service decisions by military personnel, see Gary L. Bowen and Dennis K. Orthner, eds., *The Organization Family* (New York: Praeger, 1989).

the most important leadership attributes in the future will be adaptability and flexibility when faced with change, being accountable for results and visionary and strategic thinking. This is in marked contrast to the practice that government career executives have traditionally obtained their positions through technical expertise. In the future, say respondents, technical expertise is the least important of ten leadership attributes listed in the survey.[23]

The civil service system was fashioned over one hundred years ago to eliminate the so-called spoils system. It was designed as a centralized, rule-based system in order to ensure that personnel selection and promotion were based on merit. It assured continuity from administration to administration through employment security and advancement tied to seniority.

However, the current civil service system has not been consistent with the realities of the federal workplace for some time. Many adjustments to rules and procedures have been made over the years to meet changing needs. As a consequence, the system has become a patchwork, as agencies throughout the government, including the Department of Defense and the intelligence community, have received administrative and legislative relief to accommodate their special personnel needs. Some agencies, including the Federal Aviation Administration and the postal service, have opted out of the civil service system entirely.

The current system is out of touch with the labor market that supplies its people; it inhibits professional development and innovation by its workforce; and it is incapable of responding to the changing needs of the DOD. The system stresses protections in hiring and progression based largely on seniority and experience rather than on performance. This, in turn, puts a particular emphasis on promoting and encouraging people with relatively narrow technical skills rather than those with broad-based management and related experience. It encourages the use of expertise rather than judgment, and rewards specialization rather than broad management skills. These limitations are further compounded by the fact that both internal and external candidates are eligible for jobs but usually are required already to

23. Results of the Governmental Leadership Survey, a 1999 survey of federal executives, by the Price Waterhouse Cooper Endowment for the Business of Government.

have the necessary knowledge, skills, and abilities to be competitive for those jobs. In addition, the civilian's rank inheres in his or her position, rather than in the individual. These factors contirbute to the failure to see personnel outcomes as the product of a system, and therefore focus on the management of the system. In contrast, the military system views enhancements in skill and education as appropriate improvements to members of a certain grade and thus an integral part of their career development.

Recruiting and retention have become more difficult because of the changes in the civilian labor market. One of the great strengths of the American economy is its highly efficient labor market, as evident in the current economic expansion. The traditional post–World War II practice, by which corporations hired people for the full length of their careers, is no longer the norm for new entrants to the workforce. Newer generations of workers have less corporate loyalty, and rely more on their own professional skills and capabilities. The challenge of the work and the environment in which it is performed are increasingly important to professional workers, relative to compensation.[24] As a result, the traditional civil service career has become less attractive to new generations of workers, and the trend will worsen over time.

While there are many highly able and innovative civil servants in the Department of Defense, they often must make much of their progress by figuring out how to get around the various rules and limitations that they confront day by day. The system should be redesigned to encourage professional growth, innovation, and initiative. As the DOD faces numerous requirements for change, it cannot be effective unless it can manage its workforce as a key asset in its overall management system.

The rigidity of the system is a major inhibitor of adjusting to new requirements.

[A] basic fact about the existing civil service system [is that] no one truly understands the system and its complex rules; if no one understands its first principles, then the principles cannot guide the system's operations; and if the system cannot guide its operations, there is little alternative but to resort to an *ad-hocracy* that pushes the government

24. These preferences appear to be particularly prevalent in technical occupations in both the private and public sectors.

and its operations even farther away from the purposes the civil service was created to serve.[25]

Thus major problems can be seen in many specific difficulties with the current system:

- inflexible appointment rules that make it difficult for federal agencies to match their workers to their needs in a timely fashion;

- rigid job classification standards that frustrate various agencies in exercising judgment when evaluating candidates, especially during college recruitment;

- a complex, arcane job-classification system that encourages and rewards narrow technical specialization and thus inhibits innovation;

- formula compensation rules that reward years of service and longevity, and greatly limit the ability of the government to adopt performance-based incentives;

- accountability rules that have led to an unduly cautious "zero defects" mentality (for both military and civilian); and

- rules governing reductions in force that require a chain reaction of five or six separate special personnel actions before an involuntary separation can be obtained, with the consequence that it is those who are most mobile who are the ones most likely to leave.

The current system is not consistent with the original model of civil service reform nor with the 1978 Civil Service Reform Act (CSRA). Rather it is a fractured, balkanized system that makes it difficult to make necessary adjustments to the new reality, as we know all too well: one of us was deeply involved in the passage of the CSRA of 1978, and worked with the current system two decades later as Deputy Secretary. We are in no doubt that the system needs a complete overhaul.

The new administration should reexamine the purposes of the civil service. The traditional image of federal public servants manag-

25. Donald F. Kettl, Patricia W. Ingraham, Ronald P. Sanders, and Constance Homer, *Civil Service Reform: Building a Government that Works* (Washington, D.C.: Brookings Institution Press, 1996), p. 33.

ing programs with direct public contact is but a small part of the total activity. Government does not operate most of its programs, but rather provides funding for others to do so: today over 96 percent of all government funds are passed on in the form of transfer payments to individuals, contracts with companies for goods or services, grants to state and local governments, and the like. The Department of Defense is no exception. The role of the federal civil service is to ensure that the public work that is to be done is done properly, with the proper organizational arrangement and with appropriate management oversight, whether public or private, federal, state, or local. The measure of merit is whether the management of the program meets the needs of the customer. In the DOD, the "customers" are those who conduct joint military operations.

The DOD has to have a workforce that will be a creative force in changing the character of the Department to meet the new challenges discussed elsewhere in this book. Civil servants must be given the incentives and latitude to act as change agents for the DOD. The Department cannot effectively meet its many new challenges until it has overcome the limitations that keep it from shaping the workforce as necessary to effect organizational change.

In other words, execution consistent with the vision requires that the DOD have direct management responsibility for the workforce. The DOD must specify the goals and objectives necessary to create a civil service that meets its needs. The Commission on Roles and Missions of the Armed Forces identified the attributes of a successful DOD in the future:

- responsiveness to requirements over time, sometimes rapidly;

- reliability in delivering predictable, consistent performance;

- cooperation and trust, the *sine qua non* of unified operations;

- innovation in new weapons organization and operational concepts;

- competition directed toward constructive solutions to complex problems; and

- efficiency in the use of resources.[26]

The private sector's organizational innovations that are applicable to the DOD, discussed by Michael J. Lippitz, Sean O'Keefe, and John P. White in Chapter 7, are also of value in this regard:

- focus on core mission and developing corresponding core competencies;

- focus on delivering customer value;

- incentives based on measured performance; and

- accountability for results.

The goal is not civil service reform for its own sake, but the creation of an overall personnel management system that is adaptive to new requirements, responsive in meeting unforeseen needs, integrated with the other management and decision-making processes, and innovative in solving problems. At the same time the system must continue to uphold its fundamental standards of integrity, loyalty, and professionalism, including merit-system principles, prohibitions on certain practices, and restraints on political activities.[27] The quality of the DOD's civilian workforce is at stake, and that quality is one of the pillars of civilian control of the military.

The implementation of a modern human resources management system that meets the needs of the DOD requires that the Department in general and mission managers in particular have extensive authorities as well as obligations. The system must be integrated with other DOD systems and must also be continually adjustable to meet changing needs. It might be possible to create such a capability within the current civil service system, but all experience indicates the contrary. The reform effort of the late 1970s is instructive. The CSRA failed to effect major changes, especially in encouraging initiative by civil servants. Scholars have made the argument that CSRA failed because it was not comprehensive enough, although it repre-

---

26. The Commission on Roles and Missions of the Armed Forces, *Directions for Defense* (Washington, D.C.: U.S. GPO, 1995), p. ES-2.

27. For a discussion of this issue, see the recent study conducted by the National Academy of Public Administration for the Department of the Navy.

sented the broadest and most important set of changes in decades.[28] Recently some experts have called for a major overhaul of the entire system.[29] Such massive reform is highly unlikely, because it is generally seen as having a low priority; it lacks political appeal (it is boring and has a narrow constituency); the congressional committees responsible for it are weak; and it is subject to conflicting interests across the government.

Reform will not be possible without strong leadership from both the executive and legislative branches. There is a compelling case for the new Secretary of Defense and the new House and Senate Armed Services Committees to accept leadership responsibility to bring about a system based in the DOD rather than the Office of Personnel Management, so that DOD has an integrated human resources management system — active and reserve military and civilian — to implement the broader reform agenda. This approach would give civil service reform high priority, because it would be sponsored by one of the new administration's strongest departments; would increase its political appeal, because it would be tied directly to military performance; would shift the legislative responsibility to strong congressional committees; and would allow the reforms to be tailored to real, compelling needs.

We suggest eight criteria for constructing this new DOD-based civil service system. These criteria are consistent with the overarching objectives identified earlier, namely: responsiveness to the larger market environment, upgrading the quality and performance of the DOD's civilian workforce, and allowing management to integrate the personnel system with its other management systems. The new system must:

- be attractive to high-performing, flexible people, both specialists and generalists;

- provide flexibility in careers that allow people to enter the civil service at various levels and more than once in their careers;

- provide civil servants with opportunities for growth and rewarding experiences by providing a system of rotation to build a broad

28. Patricia Ingraham, *The Promise and Paradox of Civil Service Reform* (Pittsburgh: University of Pittsburgh Press, 1992).

29. Kettl, Ingraham, et al., *Civil Service Reform*.

experience base, including experiences in the private sector and career education programs;

- hold civil servants accountable for their performance by providing tough but fair measurements of that performance;

- provide incentives that encourage that work be done where it is most effectively performed for the Department, whether it be in the public sector or the private sector;

- fully integrate the civil service system with the other management systems and guidelines of the Department, including the Planning Programming, and Budgeting System (PPBS), the Government Performance and Results Act (GPRA), Total Force Planning (i.e., both active and reserve forces), and the Federal Acquisition Regulations;

- provide flexibility in the rules and structure of the civil service system so that it can be adjusted as needed to meet new requirements, while at the same time protecting the public interest and the overall integrity of the system; and

- encourage strong leadership by career officials and political appointees in promoting the effectiveness and fairness of the system.

The structure of the new system can be guided in part by the lessons learned from the success of the All Volunteer Force discussed earlier in this chapter: measurable objectives should be established wherever possible; civil service outcomes should be seen as the product of a system, with attention focused on managing the system; quantitative analysis should be employed broadly and aggressively to understand the relationship between causes and effects; and policymakers should focus on the use of incentives as the main instruments for achieving desired outcomes.

Key elements of the National Security Reform Act of 1986 (the Goldwater-Nichols Act) are also instructive guides to creating a new civil service system. The legislation allocates clear lines of authority and responsibility, for example, between the services and the regional commanders-in-chief; provides extensive annual reporting, particularly by the Secretary of Defense and Chairman of the Joint Chiefs of Staff; and stipulates education and experience requirements for promotion to flag and general officer. In other words, it calls for clear lines of authority and responsibility, regular reporting, and perform-ance incentives.

Negative lessons should be heeded as well. One example is found in the joint assignment requirement for eligibility for promotion to flag and general officer. While it has markedly improved the quality of joint-duty officers, particularly the staff of the Joint Chiefs of Staff, the list of specific billets that receive credit for being "joint" has not been systematically upgraded, nor has it had its anomalies removed. As a result, the legitimacy of the joint-billet requirement has been eroded over time. The specification of such requirements must have a built-in mechanism for adjusting to change.

REFORM PROPOSAL

The reforms proposed would require new legislation. First and fore-most, amendments to Title X and Title V of the U.S. Code would be necessary, to transfer the authority for managing the DOD's civilian workforce from the Office of Personnel Management to the Secretary of Defense. This change would permit the Secretary to establish poli-cies to meet changing DOD requirements, as the Defense Science Board called for in its 1999 report:

The Department of Defense should develop civilian force-shaping tools that are appropriate for the twenty-first century. These tools will build on many ongoing initiatives within the Department and must continu-ously evolve in response to changing needs to be effective in the long run. Overall, however, for the Secretary to manage the DOD workforce as it should be — as a total, integrated force — and develop needed force-shaping tools, the Department needs to have appropriate man-agement over the entire civilian workforce.[30]

Developing and passing such legislation requires strong leader-ship from the executive branch and a close working relationship be-tween the Secretary of Defense and the Congress. This working relationship must be on-going, because not every requirement can be anticipated in the initial legislation. The new law should explicitly give the DOD more management latitude to make adjustments over

30. The Defense Science Board Task Force, *Human Resources Strategy* (Wash-ington, D.C.: U.S. Department of Defense, Office of the Under Secretary of Defense for Acquisition, Technology, and Logistics, February 2000), p. 45.

time for continuous improvement. The *quid pro quo* for such latitude would be specific, visible measures of merit and a regular reporting relationship with the Congress regarding the performance of the system.

The legislation would charge the Secretary with managing the civilian workforce. He or she would be required to establish civilian personnel policy rules and procedures for the entire Department of Defense. An early, necessary step would be a thorough, complete audit of the DOD's human resources needs including military, civil servant, and contractor personnel.

It is surprising but true that today we know very little about the overall performance of the civilian workforce. What we do know is principally anecdotal. "The OPM has not kept careful records (of recruitment and retention problems) since the late 1980s, and other data are fragmentary at best."[31] The lack of good and timely government manpower statistics reflects the ineffectiveness of the current workforce management system. Even rudimentary planning is impossible without basic information.

This review would be a major undertaking and would reveal numerous needs or redundancies that are not apparent today. The challenge will be to make it universal, complete, and objective, avoiding the tendency of manpower "requirements" to become inflated through the bureaucratic process of specification.[32]

The Secretary should be required to present to Congress a comprehensive, objective assessment of the implementation of the reforms at the end of the third and fifth years after enactment. These reports would identify progress made to date, plans and timetables for future progress, key measures of effectiveness, and proposed further changes in policy and law.

The Secretary should also be charged with developing a set of performance measures and related standards that would allow the Department, the Congress, and the public to track progress with respect to the implementation and operation of this new system. These metrics would be used in annual reports from the Secretary, beginning in the fourth year after enactment.

---

31. Kettl, Ingraham, et al., *Civil Service Reform*, p. 15.

32. The DOD is completing a new occupational database that should facilitate the review.

The legislation should provide for a permanent independent advisory council, composed of members from the public and private sectors, to monitor the ongoing state of public service in the DOD and to make recommendations for such improvements as they think desirable.[33] The council would be drawn from people with deep experience in the management of large, complex organizations as well as human resources experts and retired civil servants. It should be required to comment on the Secretary's reports to the Congress and to issue its own findings and recommendations, but its principal responsibilities would be assist the DOD, on a regular basis, in its implementation of the legislation.

These general guiding principles of the reform legislation draw upon the lesson learned from the AVF experience, the Goldwater-Nichols legislation, and other proposals made over the years such as those presented by the Volcker Commission in 1989.[34] They emphasize close cooperation with the Congress, broadened authority for the Secretary, regular public reporting, established metrics, managing the system as a system, and continuous improvement. These attributes are important to effecting change, and also to preserving the integrity of a merit-based civil service system.

Other changes are also needed to correct specific deficiencies in the current system, in such areas as hiring flexibility, compensation, performance standards, training, and career flexibility.

HIRING FLEXIBILITY

New legislation should include special hiring authority that would allow the Department flexibility in tailoring its job offerings to meet the demands of the marketplace.[35] There is some urgency to this need, because the DOD's civilian workforce is aging. Due to downsizing, "DOD now has about 75 percent fewer employees in the 20–29 year age group than it did in 1989 [and] nearly 50 percent fewer employees in their 30s, while the number in their 50s has remained con-

33. Report of the National Commission on Public Service (Volcker Commission), *Leadership for America: Rebuilding the Public Service* (1989), p. 95.

34. Volcker Commission, *Leadership for America.*

35. Defense Science Board Task Force, *Human Resources Strategy.*

stant." Moreover, "The median age of this workforce has risen from 41 in 1989 to 46 in 1999."[36]

This means that we need to tailor the key characteristics of these positions to the characteristics and needs of the available workforce. This requires an emphasis on flexible pay; portable pensions (both ways); contracts for limited periods of government service; demonstration projects; and easy entry, exit, and re-entry into the civilian government workforce. The civilian labor-market trend toward increasing the use of contingent workers (temporary, part-time, limited term, or contract) tied to specific projects should also be accommodated.

At the entry level, the Department should be encouraged to expand its programs for recruiting and attracting interns into the federal service. At the upper level, Executive Order 12834 should be rescinded so that post-employment restrictions under the law are reduced from five years to one year, in order to increase the attractiveness of government work to senior professional and technical workers.

COMPENSATION

The Department should be given the authority and the ability to adjust white-collar compensation by region, skill, and experience to compete with civilian job opportunities, given that civilian pay "differs by occupation and by localities characterized by widely differing living costs and labor market pressures."[37]

The legislation should allow other forms of compensation flexibility in response to specific needs. The DSB Task Force on Human Resources noted that:

Specific DOD units have undertaken some interesting and effective pilot programs to modernize human resource management, and demonstrations for science and technology personnel are underway at a number of laboratories, for example, to test new initiatives.... Initiatives being tested in the laboratory experiments include pay and staffing initiatives such as broadbanding, pay for performance, accelerated

---

36. Defense Science Board Task Force, *Human Resources Strategy*, pp. 37, 28.

37. Volcker Commission, *Leadership for America*, Recommendation No. 11.

hiring, modified term appointments, and probation and reduction-in-force modifications.[38]

The Secretary should have the authority to tailor pilot programs and then to make changes based on the lessons learned.

PERFORMANCE STANDARDS

The performance standards that are now used in contracting government goods and services should be adopted for much of the civil service workforce. The new civil service would include an emphasis on management of various organizational forms, because the work would be done within the most efficacious structure, whether public or private. A logical extension of this emphasis is to require similar contractual forms and terms for both public and private activities. Government organizations that provide goods and services should be governed by contracts, just as private firms are. The performance measures should be visible and reportable, in order to improve results and encourage competition through performance comparisons across organizations. Workers' rewards should be tied more effectively to individual and/or group performance measures, which would facilitate comparing the performance of public and private enterprises.

Implementation of such a system will be very difficult, given the traditional reward structure of the civil service and the failure of even the modest changes proposed by the 1978 Civil Service Reform Act. But there is ample experience, successful and otherwise, in the management of such systems in the private sector, state governments, and other nations, including Australia and New Zealand; these lessons should be applied.

TRAINING

The Department has done an inadequate job of providing training and educational opportunities for its career civil-service workforce.

---

38. "Broadbanding" refers to establishing pay bands within occupational groups that are based on recognized career ladders. Effective broadbanding provides managers with more flexibility for progressive compensation within pay bands, based on personnel performance. It also requires them to be more selective in promotion and salary increases. Defense Science Board Task Force, *Human Resources Strategy*, p. 39.

This limitation stems in part from the practice of tying rank to a position, rather than to the person. This should be changed, and the change should be accompanied by a modified up-or-out system for some portions of the workforce (including the Executive Corps proposed below). It would have to be supported by legislative changes in the grade structure, to accommodate personnel progression, and in the retirement system, to assure fair and timely annuities for those who do not continue to progress.

The Department should also implement the DSB recommendation to develop "a comprehensive professional development and career management program for scientific, management, [and] administrative fields." A cornerstone of the program should be the planned expansion of the Defense Leadership and Management Program (DLAMP) to develop managers and leaders with broad-based experience for the future.[39] DLAMP should be complemented by increased civilian participation in university academic programs and the DOD's various professional military education programs. The military schools should be encouraged to expand their curricula to enhance professional capabilities that affect close civil servant–military cooperation. As with the military service programs, the civil service programs should have a competitive aspect with respect to entry, and participants should receive performance evaluations. The programs should be managed systematically to provide a progression of broader and deeper experience as professionals grow in their careers.

CAREER FLEXIBILITY

The new system should embody career flexibility in many different forms. It should stress the ability of civil servants to grow in their careers through a rich variety of experiences, including assignments at various positions throughout the DOD. Promotion at the senior levels would require successful experience in various DOD organizations as well as at least one assignment outside the Department, even outside the government.

---

39. DLAMP participants must obtain successfully: a rotational assignment of at least twelve months, a senior-level course in professional mlitary education, and a minimum of ten advanced graduate-level college courses.

A NEW EXECUTIVE CORPS

Our final proposal would be for new legislation to create an Executive Corps comprising senior civil servants (GS-14 and above) and political appointees.[40] The corps would be the principal civilian instrument for changing the DOD: these are the people the Secretary would rely upon to assist him or her in implementing the reform agenda. The Executive Corps would have its own mission and rules, and the emphases for its members would be on integrity, merit, professionalism, continuity, flexibility, and management skills. The major objectives of the corps would be to:

- embody the key attributes of public service;

- provide policy and professional continuity;

- direct policy implementation;

- conduct professional program management and oversight;

- measure and provide feedback on program performance; and

- assure that program execution is done at the right level with the most appropriate institutions, public or private.

The corps would be staffed competitively through internal promotion and lateral entry. Promotion would be based on merit, and pay would be tied to performance. Rotation, professional education, and professional growth would be prerequisites for expanded responsibilities, promotion, and other indicators of success. Failure to progress would result in early retirement. In other words, it would have the general attributes discussed above for the reformed civil service, but with more rigorous entry requirements, higher standards of performance, and broader obligations for innovation, initiative, and responsiveness.

Conclusion

There will continue to be a great deal of change in the world around us, including changes in the threat, U.S. policy objectives, technology, and geopolitical relationships. We must adjust to a new, evolving world and an uncertain future. The other chapters in this book dis-

---

40. Kettl, Ingraham, et al., *Civil Service Reform.*

cuss change and adjustments that the Department of Defense and the broader national security community should make. Understandably, there will be institutional resistance to the kinds of changes that we are recommending. The resistance will be hard to overcome because the message — that fundamental, dynamic, institutional change is required — is so difficult to accept. This is particularly true in a successful organization such as the DOD.

However, it is not enough to change organizations and operating procedures. The institutional structure in which people operate must also be changed. That requires rethinking the objectives of both the uniformed military and the civil service human resource systems. Improvements to these systems are a critical foundation for the other reforms discussed in this book. The DOD's people are the vehicles for these changes. They must be prepared to work within institutional arrangements that encourage innovation, initiative, and adaptation. The civil service system, like the military personnel system, needs to be integrated into DOD's decision making processes, in order to implement management decisions effectively. Only if such fundamental changes are made will the U.S. defense structure continue to make the best possible use of its most important asset — its people.

9

Managing the Pentagon's International Relations

ELIZABETH SHERWOOD-RANDALL

WITH CHRISTIANA BRIGGS AND ANJA MILLER

A critical leadership challenge for the Department of Defense is the management of its international relations — its ties to allies, partners, international organizations, and non-governmental groups. Just as the phenomenon of globalization, or the world's increasing interconnectedness and interdependence, affects many other aspects of Pentagon management described in this volume, it also influences the interaction of the U.S. military with international militaries and organizations. Paradoxically, although the United States has unparalleled military muscle, it is increasingly inhibited from acting alone. For planning purposes, U.S. civilian and military leaders must assume that most if not all future operations will involve non-U.S. forces and in many cases non-military entities.[1]

I am grateful to General John Shalikashvili (ret.) for the invaluable contributions he made to the conceptualization and substantive development of this chapter. In addition, I would like to thank Coit Blacker, General George Joulwan (ret.), and Victor DeMarines and his MITRE team, which included Charles Arouchon, David Lehman, Charles Sanders, and Peter Tasker, for generously sharing their time, expertise, and wisdom. I would also like to thank Christiana Briggs and Anja Miller for their excellent research. Christiana sleuthed for materials on peacekeeping and humanitarian interventions, while Anja dug for resources on coalition operations; both provided good ideas and feedback. Shane Smith supported the research effort as well with resourcefulness and attention to detail.

1. For the most recent official expression of this requirement by the U.S. military leadership, see Joint Chiefs of Staff, *Joint Vision 2020* (Washington, D.C.: U.S. Government Printing Office, June 2000).

The Pentagon must therefore keep multinational operations in mind as it plans, marshals resources, develops doctrine, and trains for all possible contingencies, including combat, peacekeeping, and humanitarian relief. Yet the international interface is still generally an afterthought for defense planners. The DOD system is not well constituted to deal with the post–Cold War environment's requirement for continuous interaction with other countries and with international and non-governmental bodies, especially during the planning and preparation stages that precede deployment.

This chapter makes recommendations to improve the efficiency and effectiveness of the U.S. military's efforts to engage with other militaries. Such activities range from going into battle alongside the principal NATO allies, to training to keep the peace with former Warsaw Pact members, to conducting multinational disaster-relief operations in conjunction with non-governmental organizations (NGOs). Because of the vastness of the subject, this chapter does not consider all its aspects exhaustively. Rather, it focuses on opportunities for significantly enhancing American security by improving the U.S. military's capacity to cooperate successfully with other countries and organizations in both wartime and peacetime.

To do so, the chapter describes the changes in the international and domestic environment that require the DOD leadership to be innovative in the management of the Pentagon's international relations. It then presents three recent cases that illustrate the range of challenges the U.S. military faces as it seeks to cooperate effectively with other countries and organizations. The first case concentrates on problems with coalition warfare revealed by the NATO operation in Kosovo in 1999. The second case highlights difficulties with peacekeeping as experienced during the UN mission to Sierra Leone in 2000. The third case describes the potential benefits of military-to-military cooperation as exemplified by U.S.-Russian peacekeeping training in the mid-1990s. Each case is followed by analysis and specific recommendations for action.

A Changing Environment Creates New Challenges in the Management of the Pentagon's International Relations

The management of the Pentagon's international relationships requires attention and innovation. Six factors are key to understanding why the status quo is not sufficient:

THE COLD WAR IS OVER, BUT THE U.S. MILITARY IS IN MORE DEMAND TO DO MORE

It is an irony of the post–Cold War world that the U.S. military has not reaped a "peace dividend" from the end of the U.S.-Soviet rivalry. Rather, it has been deployed increasingly frequently and has had to cope with a proliferation of missions that threaten to undermine its combat capability. Undertakings ranging from peace enforcement, such as the NATO-led operation in Bosnia, to humanitarian relief such as in Rwanda, have resulted from the reemergence of civil and ethnic conflicts that had been suppressed during the Cold War, as well as from the perception that the U.S. military is now available to do more because it does not need to prepare to fight the Soviet Union. Indeed, the absence of a major threat permits U.S. policymakers to consider deploying U.S. military forces for purposes only distantly associated with protecting vital national security interests.[2] This has created a new set of requirements for which the U.S. military is just beginning to organize adequately.

MULTINATIONAL OPERATIONS ARE POLITICALLY PREFERABLE, BUT OFTEN MILITARILY INEFFICIENT

U.S. power must walk the fine line between leadership and hegemony. In today's world, unilateral military action by the United States is increasingly unpalatable politically. This is true for a variety of reasons, including the fact that the U.S. public does not want to shoulder the burden of policing the world alone, and the fact that many countries, including America's closest allies, are apprehensive about what they perceive to be overweening U.S. dominance. For the U.S. mili-

---

2. For a further elaboration of this argument, see discussion of "Strategy in the Absence of a Major Threat," in Ashton B. Carter and William J. Perry, *Preventive Defense: A New Security Strategy for America* (Washington, D.C.: Brookings, 1999), pp. 11–14.

tary, however, coalitions often are inefficient mechanisms for waging war. As the technological gap between U.S. forces and other forces increases in the next decade, this reality is likely to become more pronounced.

THE PACE OF TECHNOLOGICAL CHANGE IS CREATING AN EXPANDING CHASM BETWEEN U.S. WARFIGHTING CAPABILITIES AND THOSE OF OTHER MILITARIES

As the U.S. military moves to exploit the advances in technology associated with the information revolution, it will create a distinctive advantage for itself in warfighting capabilities. In *Joint Vision 2020*, the Joint Chiefs of Staff noted that "the continued development and proliferation in information technologies will substantially change the conduct of military operations."[3] Moreover, "DOD will continue to foster both a culture and a capability to develop and exploit [these] new concepts and technologies with the potential to make U.S. military forces qualitatively more effective."[4] However, this enhanced capacity will actually make it harder for the U.S. military to fight alongside other countries in coalitions, and even to operate smoothly with other countries in non-combat contingencies such as peacekeeping. Just when the political imperative for cooperation with other militaries increases, the ability to cooperate will, in the absence of attention to the problem, decline.

PEACEKEEPING AND HUMANITARIAN OPERATIONS WILL CONSUME TOO MANY U.S. MILITARY RESOURCES UNLESS WE BUILD UP THE CAPACITY OF OTHERS TO ORGANIZE AND PERFORM THESE MISSIONS

No other country and no other international organization, public or private, has the capacity to do what the U.S. military can do. As the past decade has proven, the United States will be called upon, if only because of its sheer competence, to solve problems in which it has little direct national security interest. This fosters an environment in

---

3. *Joint Vision 2020*, p. 2.

4. William S. Cohen, *Annual Report to the President and the Congress*, 2000, p. 20. The pursuit of this competitive technological edge, or "offset," has been a centerpiece of American military strategy since the 1970s. For further discussion of the offset concept, see William J. Perry, "Desert Storm and Deterrence," *Foreign Affairs*, Vol. 70, No. 4 (Fall 1991), pp. 66–82.

which other countries have less incentive to become capable and to organize themselves well for individual and collective action. Furthermore, the vociferous and influential anti-UN contingent in the U.S. Congress generates significant friction over giving the UN greater responsibilities. As a result, the United States often appears to be diminishing rather than enhancing the capacity of the UN, and ironically has to expend its military resources to compensate for the UN's limitations.

DOD STILL DOES NOT HAVE STANDING MECHANISMS FOR INTERFACE WITH INTERNATIONAL AND NON-GOVERNMENTAL ORGANIZATIONS

Despite a decade of experience operating in the post–Cold War security environment, the Department of Defense has not yet established or made fully functional the processes required for it to be able to interact on a continuous basis with outside entities. This is the case even with the largest and most well-established international and non-governmental organizations such as the UN and the Red Cross. Because it has historically done its job more efficiently on its own, the U.S. military is not accustomed to depending on others. In addition, the culture of the defense establishment is not naturally an open one; it has traditionally relied on secrecy as a means of bolstering military advantage, and therefore the connections required to maintain ties to the outside can challenge standard operating procedures.

THOUGH OFFICIALLY MANDATED, THE "SHAPING" MISSION IS NEITHER INSTITUTIONALIZED NOR ADEQUATELY FUNDED

In the post–Cold War world, the U.S. military has been ordered to play an increasingly active role in shaping the international environment. This means employing the armed forces as an instrument of American diplomacy, not in the traditional sense of backing up negotiators with the threat of force, but rather in the new sense of using them as leaders in building cooperative relationships with countries that might otherwise be hostile to the United States and its interests. This "peacetime engagement" approach has been embraced by senior civilian defense leaders, and was mandated in the Quadrennial Defense Review in

1997.[5] However, the "shaping" mission has not yet been incorporated thoroughly in the annual military planning process.

The issues highlighted here — coalition warfare, humanitarian and peacekeeping operations, and military-to-military cooperation — can best be understood as dimensions of the Pentagon's international relations, effective management of which will be increasingly important to U.S. military effectiveness. Three cases that vividly illustrate the leadership challenges they entail are presented next. Each case is followed by a set of recommendations for turning existing problems into opportunities for innovation.

Coalition Warfare: The Case of NATO's Kosovo Campaign

NATO faced significant challenges to its effectiveness during Operation ALLIED FORCE, the spring 1999 military action intended to compel Yugoslav President Slobodan Milosovic to cease his harassment of Kosovar Albanians and to create the conditions for their eventual return to the province of Kosovo. This operation showed NATO weaknesses in three critical areas: secure communications; intelligence cycle time and information sharing; and compatible equipment.

The NATO allies lacked secure communications, despite more than half a century of preparation for combat together.[6] They had few secure phone lines, and the major U.S. and NATO secure-messaging systems (SIPRNET and CRONOS) were not interoperable.[7] As a result, all sensitive information, such as the daily Air Tasking Order (ATO), had to be printed out and hand-delivered to allied counterparts. The allies then typed that information into their own secure communications

---

5. Section III on "Defense Strategy" in U.S. Department of Defense, *Quadrennial Defense Review*, 1997, at <www.defenselink.mil/pubs/qdr/sec3.html>.

6. The Pentagon concluded in its after-action report to Congress that: "Problems regarding communications interoperability persisted throughout the campaign." See U.S. Department of Defense, *Report to Congress, Kosovo/Operation Allied Force After-Action Report*, p. 25.

7. Benjamin S. Lambeth, *The Transformation of American Air Power* (Ithaca, N.Y.: Cornell University Press, 2000), p. 213; and James P. Thomas, *The Military Challenges of Transatlantic Coalitions*, Adelphi Paper No. 333 (London: IISS, May 2000), p. 53.

systems to transmit it to their national forces. This same problem had been encountered almost a decade earlier during DESERT STORM, but had not yet been rectified.[8]

The absence of secure and interoperable aircraft communications and radio links was particularly frustrating given NATO's heavy reliance on air power during the Kosovo campaign. U.S. pilots could not use their more sophisticated data-link systems because, with the exception of the British, other major allies did not have a means of connecting to or making use of them. For example, U.S. and British combat aircraft equipped with the joint tactical information distribution system (JTIDS) and "Have Quick" secure radios could not use them because other allied planes did not have similar equipment. Instead, allied personnel had to transmit aircraft positions and target coordinates over open frequencies. The Serbs easily intercepted voice communications signals and frequently moved targets out of the way before they could be hit.[9] Kosovo Liberation Army (KLA) ground forces used commercial cellular telephones to transmit reconnaissance information and target coordinates to NATO commanders. The Serbs could intercept these open communications, so the information was often no longer accurate by the time NATO launched its attacks. After the campaign, U.S. and NATO commanders commented that Yugoslav forces often had advance knowledge of NATO's intended targets.[10]

---

8. Fulghum, "Serb Threat Subsides, But U.S. Still Worries," *Aviation Week & Space Technology*, April 12, 1999, p. 24; John D. Morrocco, "Kosovo Conflict Highlights Limits of Airpower and Capability Gaps," *Aviation Week & Space Technology*, May 17, 1999, p. 31. See also Lt. General Marvin R. Esmond, prepared statement for the House Armed Services Committee, Subcommittee on Military Procurement, October 19, 1999.

9. John D. Morrocco, "Kosovo Reveals NATO Interoperability Woes," *Aviation Week & Space Technology*, August 9, 1999, p. 32; David A. Fulghum and Robert Wall, "Data Link, EW Problems Highlighted by Pentagon," *Aviation Week & Space Technology*, September 6, 1999, pp. 87–88; Lambeth, *The Transformation of American Air Power*, p. 203; Testimony of General John P. Jumper, Commander, U.S. Air Force in Europe, before the House Armed Services Committee, October 26, 1999; and Thomas, *The Military Challenges of Transatlantic Coalitions*, p. 54.

10. See Testimony of General Wesley K. Clark, NATO Supreme Allied Commander, before the U.S. Senate Armed Services Committee, July 1, 1999; see also Jumper testimony, October 26, 1999.

The NATO allies also encountered major problems with their intelligence cycle time — the amount of time needed to obtain, analyze, and transmit information to those making warfighting decisions. There were bottlenecks due to insufficient bandwidth linking the Combined Air Operations Center to operating units, and due to the slow operating speed of the classified NATO internet link. NATO operators expressed frustration over how long it took to move information about enemy air defense threats and targets from sensors to allied forces positioned to engage them. Benjamin Lambeth explains that: "Although the requisite architecture was in place throughout most of the [Kosovo air] campaign ... it lacked a sufficiently high-volume data link with enough channels to get the information where it needed to go quickly."[11] Compounding these problems, the allies used different security classification standards to protect information and did not have interoperable intelligence networks.[12]

Another serious problem with information-sharing arose over the suggestion that some NATO allies deliberately leaked information to the Serbs.[13] This, of course, is more a low-tech than a high-tech problem; it involves human beings, not machines. But it is a problem endemic to coalition operations; the more parties involved, the more likely it is that information will not remain secure. For this reason, the United States deliberately withheld some information from its allies regarding the specifics of sorties for B-2 bombers, F-117 fighters, and Tomahawk missiles. These assets were tasked using a separate ATO, distributed only to U.S. officials, creating some confusion when U.S. assets showed up on NATO radar screens with no advance warning.[14]

Finally, the allies found that despite their years of preparation for war together, they had equipment that was still incompatible and inadequate to the needs of a coalition operation. For example, some allied planes lacked the IFF (identification friend or foe) equipment

11. Lambeth, *The Transformation of American Air Power*, pp. 202–204.

12. *Kosovo/Operation Allied Force After-Action Report*, pp. 49–51.

13. Roberto Suro and Thomas E. Ricks, "Pentagon Acknowledges Leaks of NATO Kosovo Air War Data," *Washington Post*, March 10, 2000, p. A2.

14. John Tirpak, "Short's View of the Air Campaign," *Air Force Magazine*, Vol. 82, No. 9 (September 1999), at <www.afa.org/magazine/watch/0999watch.html>.

that enabled NATO controllers to distinguish between allied and enemy aircraft.[15] Additionally, only U.S., British, Canadian, and French combat aircraft had the ability to deliver laser-guided bombs; no other allied aircraft could participate in the bombing campaign. Thus U.S. aircraft had to carry out about 80 percent of the strike sorties.[16]

The Kosovo campaign pitted the world's greatest military capabilities against one tough but ultimately insignificant adversary. The experience nevertheless revealed significant weaknesses in NATO's collective warfighting capabilities, especially in the domain of command, control, and communications. SACEUR General Wesley Clark commented, "It is sobering to note that over the last decade we witnessed a growing technological gradient rather than a convergence of national capabilities."[17]

THE LESSONS OF KOSOVO

U.S. defense planning for future warfighting must anticipate the high probability that U.S. forces will operate alongside forces from other countries. Coalition operations demonstrate international support for military action, spread burden and risk and, at least theoretically, enhance capability. They are also more palatable domestically; polling data shows that the American people prefer multilateral approaches to unilateral ones. For example, 72 percent of the public think that "in responding to international crises … the United States … should not take action alone if it does not have the support of its allies."[18]

However, coalitions must not only be politically effective; they must also be militarily effective. Reaching agreement to establish a multinational coalition is the first step; making that coalition into a capable fighting force requires many more. There is a wide range of

15. Morrocco, "Kosovo Reveals NATO Interoperability Woes"; and Jumper testimony, October 26, 1999.

16. Lambeth, *The Transformation of American Air Power*, pp. 213–14; and Barton Gellman and William Drozdiak, "Conflict Halts Momentum for Broader Agenda," *Washington Post*, June 6, 1999, p. A21.

17. Wesley K. Clark, "Meeting Future Military Challenges to NATO," *Joint Forces Quarterly*, Spring 1999, p. 44.

18. Polling data in *American Public Opinion and U.S. Foreign Policy 1999* (Chicago: The Chicago Council on Foreign Relations, 1999), pp. 24–25. Interestingly, at the leadership level sentiment is different: only about half of the leaders polled believe in the necessity of allied support.

potential partners, from America's closest NATO allies, to *ad hoc* partners with whom the United States has never deployed before. In *Joint Vision 2010*, the Joint Chiefs concluded: "We must find the most effective methods for integrating and improving interoperability with allied and coalition partners. Although our Armed Forces will maintain decisive unilateral strength, we expect to work in concert with allied and coalition forces in nearly all of our future operations, and increasingly, our procedures, programs, and planning must reflect this reality."[19]

In seeking to conduct militarily effective coalition warfare, the single greatest challenge that the United States faces today is the yawning gap between American military technology and everyone else's technology. The paradox for U.S. defense leaders is that American predominance is creating a potential dysfunction, as domestic and international politics increasingly require the United States to fight in coalitions but U.S. military capabilities make it increasingly harder to do so. The dangers associated with a failure to address this problem are enormous. They have the potential to undermine the cohesion of the Atlantic Alliance and of other U.S. bilateral military alliances, such as those in the Asia-Pacific region.

In the United States, the Revolution in Military Affairs is moving ahead rapidly (although critics say it is not moving rapidly enough, while skeptics believe its potential is exaggerated).[20] It is transforming capabilities in the hardware — the tanks, planes, ships, and munitions — that equips American forces for fighting, and in the software that is revolutionizing command and control for military operations.[21] U.S. allies and coalition partners are not keeping up in either domain.

Although the hardware gap matters, it is not the disparity that will have the greatest impact on allied battle cohesion or coalition capabilities. Rather, the burgeoning information technology gap

19. The Joint Chiefs of Staff, *Joint Vision 2010*, p. 9 <www.dtic.mil/jv2010/jv2010.pdf>.

20. For a critic, see Admiral Bill Owens, *Lifting the Fog of War* (New York: Farrar, Straus and Giroux, 2000); for a skeptic, see Michael O'Hanlon, *Technological Change and the Future of Warfare* (Washington, D.C.: Brookings, 2000).

21. For further discussion of the software revolution, see Chapter 3 by Victor DeMarines.

poses the greatest threat to future coalition operations. David Gompert, Richard Kugler and Martin Libicki argue that:

The use of information technology is far more extensive in U.S. forces than in European forces. The quality of U.S. precision-guided munitions (PGMs) and C4ISR (command, control, communications, computers, intelligence, surveillance, and reconnaissance) has improved greatly since the Gulf War, whereas European forces still remain incapable even of the type [of] operations that U.S. forces conducted in 1991.[22]

It is easy to imagine a scenario in which the U.S. military has dominant battle-space awareness but its fighting partners do not. Using advanced sensors, databases, weapons, and information links, U.S. forces would be able to spot enemy vehicles long before their allies could do so. Acting alone, U.S. forces could launch strikes on those assets. However, allied troops could be maneuvering in the area; they might not receive the information because of poor communications equipment or limited bandwidth, and therefore might be at risk of friendly fire or obstruct U.S. action.[23] At best, U.S. forces would not be as effective as they could be; at worst, they might not be able to operate because of an "intelligence blind spot" caused by the less advanced technology fielded by allied forces.

Most of the work done to date on the emerging technology gap has concentrated on NATO, which is the only multinational coalition with an effective integrated military command structure that has been tested in battle in the past decade. However, in the future the United States may well need to fight alongside other countries, such as its Asia-Pacific region allies, with which it has mutual defense treaties but no standing integrated organizational arrangements. Indeed, the risks of major conflict seem much greater in Asia than they do in the European theater. Thus a parallel effort must be undertaken to address the challenges that U.S. technological innovation poses to waging war in coalition with non-NATO countries with which the United States has a security alliance, such as Australia, Japan, Korea, the Philippines, and Thailand.

22. David C. Gompert, Richard L. Kugler, and Martin C. Libicki, *Mind the Gap: Promoting a Transatlantic Revolution in Military Affairs* (Washington, D.C.: National Defense University Press, 1999), p. 4.

23. Gompert, Kugler, and Libicki, *Mind the Gap*, p. 50.

RECOMMENDATIONS FOR ACTION

Given the likelihood that U.S. forces will deploy with allies and partners in future operations, the Pentagon should make it a first-order defense priority to ensure that fighting in coalitions is a net benefit to the U.S. military.

Establish a Combined Joint Task Force within NATO That Develops a Model for an Enhanced Alliance C3 Capability

It is unrealistic to expect that all of the military forces of the nineteen NATO nations will achieve a high degree of C3 compatibility in the foreseeable future, given the disparities in allies' information technology capabilities as well as in resources available to devote to improvement. Instead, the Alliance should use its Combined Joint Task Force (CJTF) structure to pursue the development of enhanced interoperability for a select group of allied forces. NATO invented the CJTF as a vehicle to be used by "coalitions of the willing," or those countries with the interests, resources, and political will necessary to pursue a given task. This offers a framework for the establishment of a self-selecting CJTF that would build a model force and develop an Alliance standard for C3 compatibility. Interested countries would initially designate specific units to participate; then, as the model was elaborated, participants could work to bring the rest of their forces up to the new standard. Other allies and even non-allied partners might then be motivated to join in the process. DOD could give the U.S. Joint Forces Command the principal role in supporting this effort.

Require the U.S. "System of Systems" Architecture to Accommodate Allied "Plug-Ins"

Although NATO has undertaken a "Defense Capabilities Initiative" to address the growing technology gap, the United States bears the lion's share of the responsibility for ensuring that its new systems are designed and built to allow other countries to "plug in" and connect with them.[24] Furthermore, the bulk of fielded systems are national

24. At NATO's fiftieth birthday celebration in the spring of 1999, Secretary of Defense William Cohen lobbied successfully for NATO to work toward establishing a single, integrated, or at least compatible command and control structure in the future. See William S. Cohen, "The Atlantic Alliance: A View from the Pentagon," *Joint Forces Quarterly*, Spring 1999, p. 33. The resulting Defense Capabilities Initiative (DCI) provides an institutional home at NATO for addressing many of the issues raised in this section of the chapter.

systems rather than NATO systems, so what matters most is what individual national defense establishments procure. Although the technical challenge is great, the politico-economic challenge is greater.[25] In addition to the problem of generating the political momentum for progress, solutions will also depend on whether the United States and its principal European and Asian allies can agree on a fair allocation of costs. For those countries that will not be major players, the United States needs to offer cost-efficient options that provide basic capacity. DOD also needs to give clear policy guidance on requirements and standards to the industrial providers of systems and services.

Set in Advance the Information Security Standards Needed to Enhance Coalition Warfighting Capabilities

In multinational operations, sharing intelligence is a prerequisite for success. Yet information security has been a major obstacle to achieving C3 compatibility. The current system is largely reactive; as a result, questions about whether or not particular information can be released are only asked after an operation is underway. To remedy this, the Secretary of Defense should establish an office reporting to the Under Secretary of Defense for Policy that is charged with establishing policy guidelines to define what kind of information may be released to whom, under what conditions, and over what systems. Through this office, the Pentagon also needs to ensure that U.S. national systems have effective technical interfaces with foreign systems. This means establishing standards and directing industry to build U.S. systems that assume information will need to be released to allies and partners.[26] These two efforts, policy and technical, should

---

For more on the DCI, see Elinor Sloan, "DCI: Responding to the U.S.-led Revolution in Military Affairs," *NATO Review*, Vol. 48 (Spring–Summer 2000), pp. 4–7. For more on the concept of "plugging in" to the U.S. architecture, see Gompert, Kugler, and Libicki, *Mind the Gap*, pp. 47–51.

25. Francis J. Powers, "Multinational Operations C4I Interoperability/The State of Play: Europe Focus," MITRE briefing, May 18, 2000, p. 11; and Charlie Arouchon, "Overview of MITRE's International DoD Programs," MITRE briefing, May 30, 2000.

26. Arouchon, "Overview," p. 19. The Defense Science Board 1999 Summer Study also recommended the establishment of an Integrated Information Infrastructure Executive Office.

proceed simultaneously, so that once the policy is defined, the technology stands ready to implement it.

Encourage the European Security and Defense Identity to Enhance Military Capability and Especially C3 Compatibility among European Nations

Although U.S. policy toward European economic and political integration has been generally positive, America has traditionally been more ambivalent about a distinct European defense identity. In the post–Cold War era, it is clearly in the U.S. interest that Europe organize itself differently with respect to defense. Specifically, the United States should encourage the European Security and Defense Identity (ESDI), but only on the condition that it concentrate explicitly on improving European military capabilities, both individually and collectively. Redundancy in forces and procurement should be reduced, with the savings redirected to spending on research and development as well as on command, control, and communications, two areas in which the Europeans need to do more to keep pace with U.S. technological advances.[27] This would facilitate efforts to build an integrated or at least compatible C3 system for the Alliance.

Encourage Trans-national Defense-Industrial Linkages with NATO Countries and Other Major Military Allies to Enhance Interoperability

If the U.S. goal is to achieve much greater C3 compatibility with allies, then it is not logical to maintain two entirely separate and competitive defense industrial bases. DOD should encourage cross-border defense-industrial linkages with its major military allies in both Europe and Asia.[28]

Build Basic C3 Compatibility with Partners

The Department of Defense should assume that non-allied coalition partners (countries with which the United States does not have explicit security guarantees) will face even greater difficulties operating

---

27. See François Heisbourg, "European defence takes a leap forward," *NATO Review*, Vol. 48 (Spring–Summer 2000), pp. 7–11.

28. For more on trans-national defense-industrial collaboration, see Chapter 6 by Ashton B. Carter. For a variety of additional recommendations on achieving this objective, see also *Making Transatlantic Defense Cooperation Work*, CSIS Report on the Findings and Recommendations of the CSIS Atlantic Partnership Project, Washington, D.C., 2000; and Gompert, Kugler, and Libicki, *Mind the Gap*, pp. 65–78.

alongside U.S. forces in the foreseeable future. With these countries, the United States should concentrate its efforts on improving C3 capabilities. It should identify bare-minimum information compatibility requirements and should provide basic communications packages consistent with anticipated missions. In the case of members of the Partnership for Peace in Europe, NATO and other individual European nations should be contributors to this effort.

Pursue Military-to-Military Cooperation to Improve Operational and Tactical Coordination

The military-to-military cooperation programs that have been established with many countries offer a tremendous resource for preparing to operate together in real-world scenarios. The Pentagon should fully exploit the opportunities they afford to improve operational and tactical coordination with non-allied nations that are likely to participate in coalition operations of the future.

Peacekeeping and Humanitarian Interventions: The Case of the UN Debacle in Sierra Leone

Since the end of the Cold War, peacekeeping missions have proliferated. Most often, the United Nations has taken the lead in putting together these operations. It has done so with good intentions but poor planning and coordination. Although ten of the current fourteen peacekeeping missions (and 26 of the 39 missions that have been completed) were established after 1990, the UN still lacks the organizational infrastructure to lead, manage, and provide resources to these undertakings.[29] A high-level panel convened by the UN Secretary General to study the problems associated with peacekeeping reported recently that: "Without renewed commitment on the part of Member states, significant institutional change and increased financial support, the United Nations will not be capable of executing the critical peacekeeping and peace-building tasks that the Member States assign to it in coming months and years."[30] If proof were needed, proof was found in Sierra Leone during the spring of 2000.

29. Statistics on UN peacekeeping missions undertaken and completed since 1990 at <www.un.org/Depts/dpko>.

30. Lakhdar Brahimi, et al., "Report of the Panel on United Nations Peace Operations," August 17, 2000, A/55/30-S/2000/809, p. viii.

To bring an end to the devastating civil war that had torn apart the small West African country of Sierra Leone, rival factions signed a peace accord in July 1999. Seeking to support that agreement, the UN slowly began to assemble and deploy a peacekeeping force. In February 2000, after some of the initial UN troops were ambushed and forced to hand over their weapons, the UN Security Council voted to double the force sent to police the shaky peace. Although more than 11,000 troops were to have been sent, only some 8,000 arrived. Leading contributors were Nigeria, Ghana, and Guinea, as well as India and Kenya.[31] In May, approximately 500 of the UN peacekeepers were seized by anti-government rebels and held hostage, 200 or so until mid-July. A number of peacekeepers were also reported killed, though no firm figures have been available. Seeking to gain greater control over the situation, the UN worked to expand the force further; as of July 2000, it had swollen to 12,394 troops and observers.

This force had been cobbled together, like most UN peacekeeping forces, with troops that had never had any joint training or operational experience. The Indian commander of the force, General Veejay Jetley, commented that the UN planning was so chaotic that he did not know what troops were coming, from which countries, until they arrived.[32] On the ground, there was inadequate organization to ensure the commander's knowledge of the troops' whereabouts. The UN forces were minimally armed, and therefore lacked the capability to perform the essential function of patrolling Sierra Leone's borders, across which a diamonds-for-arms trade continued to resupply the rebel forces.

The noticeable absence of any Western military in the UN operation underscored the strong U.S. preference to avoid situations that might lead U.S. troops into "another Somalia." However, Sierra Leone put the United States under fire at the UN for "talking the talk" but not "walking the walk" of engagement with Africa. Without U.S. involvement, many believed the mission was doomed from the start. The United Kingdom had also initially refused to participate, al-

31. Robert Holloway, "UN doubles Sierra Leone peacekeeping force," *Daily Mail* (Johannesburg), February 8, 2000 <http://www.mg.co.za/mg/news/2000feb1/8feb-sierra.html>.

32. Jane Perlez, "A Doomed Peace: Missteps and a Weak Plan Marred Effort for Sierra Leone," *New York Times*, May 10, 2000, p. A14.

though Sierra Leone had once been part of its colonial Empire; it only dispatched forces under its own command after the UN peacekeepers had been seized. The British helped keep the peace in Freetown and assisted with training the other peacekeeping troops on the ground, but withdrew the bulk of their contingent within a month. Exasperated by unsuccessful efforts to stabilize the situation, the Clinton administration decided in August 2000 to send several hundred U.S. Special Forces soldiers to train and equip West African troops to join the United Nations force.[33]

As this saga unfolded, a place that most Americans could not identify on a map became a front-page newspaper story, and appeared on the brief segment allotted to international events on the nightly television news. The consistent theme of that coverage was that the United Nations had bungled another peacekeeping mission.[34] Sierra Leone was added to the list of fiascoes associated with the UN's efforts to conduct peacekeeping operations that included Bosnia, Rwanda, and Somalia.

The consequence of the UN debacle in Sierra Leone was a further erosion of U.S. public support for the United Nations and a further weakening of the UN's ability to conduct the operations that no one else wants to undertake. For example, within days of the hostage-taking in Sierra Leone, a key Republican senator used an obscure parliamentary maneuver to block the United States temporarily from paying $356 million that it owed the UN for peacekeeping missions in Congo, East Timor, and Kosovo as well as Sierra Leone.[35] A still more portentous consequence of the UN's failure in Sierra Leone was that the United States, with the requisite military resources to help train peacekeepers for effective action, was ultimately drawn into trying to salvage another mission gone wrong.

---

33. Jane Perlez, "U.S. to Send G.I.'s to Train Africans for Sierra Leone," *New York Times*, August 9, 2000, p. A1.

34. For a succinct and savage example of this view, see Michael Ignatieff, "A Bungling UN Undermines Itself," *New York Times*, May 15, 2000, p. A25.

35. Tim Weiner, "One GOP Senator Blocks Spending on Peacekeepers," *New York Times*, May 20, 2000, p. A1.

THE LESSONS OF SIERRA LEONE

In the post–Cold War era, peacekeeping and humanitarian operations have become a major component of what the U.S. military does on a daily basis. This is in large part because the international security environment has permitted a dramatic shift in focus. Rather than preparing to fight one or possibly two major wars simultaneously, the U.S. military today is asked to undertake activities far beyond the traditional definition of its role. It is spread thin responding to crises in collapsing states, supporting processes of national political reconstruction, protecting civilians from ethnic strife, conducting refugee relief operations, and helping people cope with natural disasters. The Pentagon coined a pointed phrase to describe this new set of missions: "operations other than war" — or OOTW.

In an ideal world, America's civilian defense leadership and military establishment would not devote the preponderance of their attention or energy to addressing these kinds of problems. These are not the major security challenges for which the U.S. military trains to fight; they are problems that absorb much time and effort, but do not present vital threats to U.S. interests. They distract policymakers from spending time on more important issues, and remove U.S. forces from their routine combat training (although U.S. troops do derive some training benefits from these deployments). They also contribute to significant morale problems that cause difficulties with military recruitment and retention.

Yet the United States cannot close its eyes to these crises, nor shield itself from criticism when it fails to act. Indeed, despite the often remote and seemingly obscure relevance of the places that become enflamed, the brutality of these conflicts makes it nearly impossible to ignore them. Furthermore, in most crises, the world looks to the United States for leadership and guidance; without some U.S. involvement, most operations will not happen. The international institutions, such as the UN, that should shoulder some of the burden are only as capable as their members enable them to be. Thus it would not be realistic to recommend that the United States offload these missions completely, though it might be the best thing to do if the Pentagon's sole goal were to maintain the most combat-effective force on the planet.

As these kinds of operations proliferate and impose more on the resources of the U.S. military, it becomes increasingly important that

DOD be able to differentiate among missions to be conducted mainly by U.S. forces and those to be undertaken with or by others. Some will require U.S. leadership; some should be handled principally by other countries or organizations. The range of needs is wide, from situations involving UN Chapter VII peace enforcement, where the initial environment is hostile and skilled combat troops are required, to more traditional peacekeeping, where the presence of foreign troops is largely uncontested. The line is often blurred between peacekeeping and the follow-on tasks of post-peacekeeping policing and civil reconstruction. The latter are huge jobs that have by default fallen to military forces because no one else is able or available to perform the necessary tasks. Humanitarian missions, too, may require military support, especially if a prompt response is necessary to avert greater human suffering.

RECOMMENDATIONS FOR ACTION

Two types of recommendations follow from this analysis. First, the United States should commit to the long-term goal of strengthening other nations and organizations, including the United Nations, in order to reduce its own peacekeeping and humanitarian operations burden. Second, the Department of Defense should organize itself better to facilitate cooperation with the multiple national, international, and non-governmental entities that will most likely be part of any operation in which U.S. involvement is deemed appropriate.

Reduce the U.S. Burden by Strengthening Others

The United States should be selective about how and what it contributes to international peacekeeping and humanitarian efforts so that its participation enhances the role and capacity of others. It should pursue a strategy that helps other countries and organizations to be effective players in peacekeeping, policing, and establishing viable civil institutions. For example, it should be prepared to play a leading role in justifiable missions that involve peace enforcement, a euphemism for creating security where it does not exist that almost inevitably requires combat troops supported by advanced C3, intelligence resources, and strategic lift. In lower-intensity cases, however, countries that emphasize peacekeeping as a principal purpose for their militaries, such as Canada and Denmark, should more often take the lead. There, the United States should seek to limit its involvement to providing assistance in areas of its distinctive competence, such as airlift or intelligence support.

Devote More Political and Financial Capital to Enhancing the United Nations and Other Regional Security Organizations

The only way to achieve the goal of enhanced burden-sharing is to enhance the capabilities of the UN and other international organizations, and this will not happen unless the U.S. leadership makes the case for it. If the United States continues its passive-aggressive relationship with the UN (and other regional bodies such as the Organization for Security and Cooperation in Europe), it is unrealistic to expect that their capacity will be strengthened enough to markedly reduce the burden on the United States. The U.S. Ambassador to the UN presents the argument succinctly with respect to the UN: "Peacekeeping needs three things: More financial resources, more and better-trained military and civilian personnel in the field and a coherent command structure overseas with better central direction out of New York."[36] Two specific actions could demonstrate U.S. willingness to improve the UN's effectiveness. First, the U.S. military advisory presence at the UN should be enhanced by establishing a defense advisor's office similar to that of the U.S. defense advisor at NATO. Second, a UN peace operations training academy should be created with active U.S. support to provide standardized peacekeeping training in such areas as rules of engagement, doctrine, planning, and exercising.[37]

Promote the Establishment of an Effective UN Policing Force

It is highly unlikely that the UN will be authorized by its members to build, train, and maintain its own standing military force. More feasible would be the creation of an international police force under UN auspices. Such a force could be trained and equipped to help maintain law and order after a peacekeeping mission has been completed so that national military forces could go home. To date, U.S. resis-

36. Richard Holbrooke, quoted in Barbara Crossette, "U.S. Ambassador to UN Calls for Changes in Peacekeeping," *New York Times*, June 14, 2000, p. A6.

37. For a variety of complementary ideas that focus on what the UN can do to enhance its capacity to conduct such operations effectively, see Brahimi, "Report of the Panel on United Nations Peace Operations," especially Annex III.

tance to such a force has been one of the main obstacles to its establishment. Given the lessons learned in the former Yugoslavia over the last five years, the United States should recognize that it has a compelling interest in the existence of a competent international policing capability.

A first step and necessary condition in moving toward this goal would be to establish international standards for training and participation in policing roles. The only requirements to qualify for the kind of police force that was deployed in Bosnia were fluency in English, the ability to drive, and eight years of policing experience as defined in the donor country rather than by the UN.[38] Seeking to address the need to build greater transitional policing capability in countries in which peacekeeping missions have been undertaken, President Clinton issued a Presidential Decision Directive in February 2000 to "improve America's ability to strengthen police and judicial institutions in countries where peacekeeping forces are deployed."[39] In addition to fulfilling the goals set forth in this PDD, the United States should work with the UN to define the purposes, capabilities, and requirements of a UN-led policing force.

Prepare from the Start for Interaction with International and Non-Governmental Organizations

In the case of peacekeeping and humanitarian operations, the Pentagon should organize itself to interact regularly and efficiently with multiple non-DOD and non-state organizations that are increasingly involved in providing services in such contingencies. Despite the growing role that these missions play in the daily life of the U.S. military, the United States has resisted making organizational adjustments to reflect this new reality. This is true both internally — within the U.S. government — and externally, in the nodes established to deal with international and non-governmental organizations and institutions.

---

38. Larry Wentz, contributing editor, *Lessons from Bosnia: The IFOR Experience* (Washington, D.C.: National Defense University, 1997), p. 143.

39. See Clinton Statement on New Presidential Decision Directive, February 24, 2000, at <www.fas.org/irp/offdocs/pdd/pdd-71-2.htm>; and "The Clinton Administration White Paper on Peace Operations," February 24, 2000, at <www.fas.org/irp/offdocs/pdd/pdd-71-4.htm>.

The U.S. government does not have an efficient interagency coordination process for managing these kinds of operations internally. Despite several attempts to provide direction and order to U.S. involvement, much of the U.S. process is still *ad hoc*. Three Presidential Decision Directives since 1994 have addressed the complex of problems associated with such operations. However, the general consensus is that these PDDs have yet to be fully implemented.[40] The Pentagon should not wait for the rest of the government to organize itself perfectly before it builds the bridges necessary to mission success. Rather, it should take steps immediately to improve its links to international organizations and NGOs in order to enhance operational effectiveness, all the while participating fully in whatever interagency management system is available.

With respect to sustaining external ties to non-state entities, DOD does little planning and has limited organizational capacity for work at the strategic level. What does happen occurs on a case-by-case basis, or in the field at the operational or tactical level. The Pentagon has some liaison arrangements with the UN, but no formal links with any NGOs, nor any mechanism for establishing or maintaining them. For example, there were an estimated 530 NGOs in Bosnia when the NATO-led IFOR forces deployed in the peacekeeping operation that began in December 1995.[41] Yet in preparing for the operation, U.S. military planners did not have any mechanism for exploiting the "on the ground" experience or expertise of these NGOs. Furthermore, because the United States did not have an overall strategy for work-

---

40. PDD 25, signed on May 3, 1994, represented an early Clinton administration initiative to reform U.S. and UN involvement in multilateral peace operations. PDD 56, signed on May 29, 1997, concentrated on managing complex contingency operations. PDD 77, signed on February 24, 2000, was intended to improve U.S. ability to strengthen police and judicial institutions in countries where peacekeeping forces are deployed. Some critics believe that the very use of PDDs for this purpose reveals the extent to which these issues are being treated as ancillary, at best, to the planning process. See, for example, Chris Seiple, "Window Into an Age of Windows: The U.S. Military and the NGOs," *Marine Corps Gazette* (Quantico, Va.), April 1999, pp. 63–71.

41. Wentz, *Lessons From Bosnia*, p. 135. For more on this case and on the failure to develop adequate liaison with the NGO community, see ibid., pp. 419–420.

ing with these groups, the military was largely reactive in providing support to the humanitarian aspects of the operation.[42]

To plan and train from the start for U.S. military interaction with international and non-governmental organizations, DOD needs to identify points of contact, on the Joint Staff and at regional commands, with the relevant players. Such standing cooperative liaison arrangements would mean that, where appropriate, these entities would be included throughout the conceptualization and planning of humanitarian and peacekeeping missions and, crucially, would participate in exercises. Initial efforts are underway in the field; for example, the Third Fleet conducted a novel humanitarian assistance exercise in June 2000 involving UN agencies, the American Red Cross, and other non-governmental organizations.[43] Another organizational innovation that could be replicated as needed is the establishment of Civil Military Operations Centers, or CMOCs, which were used to coordinate more effectively with NGOs and other assistance providers when U.S. forces were deployed in Somalia, Rwanda, Haiti, and Bosnia.[44] In the case of the United Nations, a senior U.S. military advisory presence along the lines of the U.S. defense advisor to NATO would not only enhance the UN's operational capabilities but also contribute to greater coordination between the Pentagon and international efforts.

Finally, the recommendations offered above for improving upon the U.S. capacity to operate effectively with *ad hoc* partners in warfighting apply in the peacekeeping and humanitarian relief context as well. The United States should identify bare-minimum information compatibility requirements, provide basic communications packages consistent with anticipated missions, and pursue military-to-military cooperation to improve operational and tactical coordination.

---

42. Wentz, *Lessons From Bosnia*, p. 429.

43. Bryan Bender, "U.S. Forces Seek Closer Links with UN on Disaster Assistance," *Jane's Defense Weekly*, June 28, 2000, p. 9.

44. Antonia Handler Chayes and Abram Chayes, *Planning for Intervention: International Cooperation in Conflict Management* (The Hague: Kluwer Law International, 1999), p. 69.

Military-to-Military Cooperation Programs: The Case of Russian Participation in Bosnian Peacekeeping

Although initial military-to-military contacts were established during the late Soviet period, cooperative relations between the U.S. Department of Defense and the Russian Ministry of Defense were only institutionalized by a Memorandum of Understanding in September 1993. From the U.S. perspective, the goal of this initiative was to do nothing less than revolutionize the relationship between the American and Russian defense establishments, which had been mortal enemies for nearly fifty years.[45]

The military-to-military contacts program proposed by the United States was designed to break down the barriers to communication and reduce the high levels of suspicion and hostility that had characterized relations between the superpowers' armed forces throughout the Cold War. It therefore contained opportunities for senior defense and military leaders to meet regularly, and for soldiers to get to know one another and pursue joint training experiences appropriate to the challenges both countries would face in the future. As the cornerstone of this new program, the United States proposed to Russia the initiation of a series of peacekeeping exercises. This was deemed to be a relatively non-controversial first step, as peacekeeping did not involve combat training and therefore would raise fewer barriers on both sides.

U.S. and Russian planners worked together for nearly a year to develop a landmark manual entitled *Russian–United States Guide for Tactics, Techniques and Procedures of Peacekeeping Forces During the Conduct of Exercises*, which was the first-ever jointly developed document on how U.S. and Russian forces would conduct a peacekeeping operation together. Published in both English and Russian, it served as the basis for the unprecedented "Peacekeeper-94" exercise that took place at Totskoye, Russia, in September 1994. This event, and the planning process that led up to it, laid the groundwork for future cooperation that would culminate in U.S. and Russian forces deploying together in

---

45. For a more detailed account of the role of military-to-military cooperation in revolutionizing relations with the former Soviet states, see Elizabeth D. Sherwood, "Revolution and Evolution in Russia, Ukraine and Eurasia," *Defense '95* (Department of Defense), No. 6, pp. 20–27.

Bosnia to support implementation of the Dayton peace accords. In October–November 1995, the United States hosted a follow-on joint exercise in Fort Riley, Kansas. This occasion also provided Secretary of Defense William Perry and his Russian counterpart, Minister of Defense Pavel Grachev, with an opportunity to work out the details of the real-world military operation that was taking shape to address the crisis in the Balkans.[46]

In February 1996, Russian airborne forces deployed alongside the U.S. First Armored Division in Bosnia. The overall operation was led by General George Joulwan, Supreme Allied Commander Europe; the Russian brigade was subordinated to Joulwan in his capacity as a U.S. general. This was the first time since the Second World War that U.S. and Russian troops had jointly pursued a shared military objective. More than four years later, U.S. and Russian forces continue to patrol the enforcement of the Bosnian peace agreement together. Furthermore, building on this historic precedent, Russian forces also participate in the NATO-led Kosovo peacekeeping effort established in 1999.

THE LESSONS OF MILITARY-TO-MILITARY COOPERATION WITH RUSSIA

During the Cold War, U.S. military forces undertook cooperative programs with other militaries for two principal reasons: first, to increase American combat capabilities; and second, to improve the capabilities of multinational coalition forces. With the end of the Cold War, Pentagon civilian leaders envisioned an additional role for America's military forces. The logic of the case they made was that the United States should engage former enemies through military-to-military cooperation in order to transform relationships from confrontation to cooperation. Thus a third more explicitly "political-military" rationale was articulated for military-to-military programs. They would be used as an instrument of U.S. diplomacy, both to diminish the prospects of future conflict and to develop the capacity to operate together to advance common interests.

Three broad policy initiatives were undertaken in the mid-1990s that made this objective a reality. The first was the Nunn-Lugar Co-

46. For a detailed discussion of the events that led up to Russian participation in IFOR, see Carter and Perry, *Preventive Defense*, pp. 23–46.

operative Threat Reduction Program, which provided U.S. funding and technical support in the four former Soviet nuclear states to assist with reducing their weapons of mass destruction. Working in collaboration with Russia, Ukraine, Kazakhstan, and Belarus, the United States organized an unprecedented effort to dismantle and destroy weapons delivery systems, and to provide for safe storage of the fissile material in nuclear warheads. The second initiative was an expanded military-to-military cooperation program, initially funded through the Nunn-Lugar appropriation, that developed bilateral defense relationships with all the countries of the former Soviet Union. In a parallel undertaking that progressed more slowly, DOD also sought to reestablish military ties with China, which had been cut off in 1989 after Tiananmen Square. The third endeavor was a major U.S. push to develop NATO's Partnership for Peace (PFP) program as a vehicle through which former Warsaw Pact members could establish tangible security ties with the West. In each of these three efforts, the logic and goals were similar: to reduce suspicion and establish relationships among counterparts, especially at the leadership level; to sustain a dialogue about security concerns; to reduce possibilities of misunderstanding and inadvertent action in a crisis; and to pursue prospects for both policy and operational cooperation reflecting the real-world interests of both sides.

These efforts called upon the U.S. military to stretch itself to fulfill a new mission. Indeed, the initial use of the military for such "diplomatic" purposes preceded the formal mission definition. It was not until 1997 that the military's leading role in transforming the international security environment was codified. In "A New National Security Strategy for a New Century," the so-called "shaping" role was officially established: "Our military promotes regional stability in numerous ways.... With countries that are neither staunch friends nor known foes, military cooperation often serves as a positive means of engagement, building security relationships today in an effort to keep these countries from becoming adversaries tomorrow." In addition, the U.S. strategy statement asserted that the armed forces are "a role model for militaries in emerging democracies around the world. Through modest military-to-military activities and increasing links between the U.S. military and the military establishments of Partnership for Peace nations, for instance, we are helping to transform military institutions in central and eastern Europe."[47]

Although the political value of the "shaping" role is increasingly clear, it is a controversial military goal because there is no direct combat-proficiency payback. Given the numerous new missions that the U.S. military has been assigned — missions that often seem far removed from its warfighting responsibilities — this is sometimes seen as yet another distraction that consumes resources and diminishes combat readiness. Furthermore, it has been difficult to translate the new mandate into specific military requirements. "Shaping" programs are not integrated into the annual training cycle developed by the Joint Staff and the Services, and the funding is still piecemeal and *ad hoc*, coming from sources such as CINC Initiative Funds, rather than being funded in a coherent and systematic fashion.

RECOMMENDATIONS FOR ACTION

A challenge for the Office of the Secretary of Defense, working closely with the Joint Chiefs of Staff, is to ensure that these new programs are understood to be an important dimension of deterrence — as important as fielding the most capable troops, or the most advanced weapons systems.

Institutionalize and Use Military-to-military Cooperation to Prepare for Future Coalition, Peacekeeping, and Humanitarian Action

Because of its relative novelty as a defense tool, the "shaping" mission has not yet been thoroughly institutionalized within the Department of Defense, the Joint Staff, the CINCs, and the services. It continues to require a high degree of intervention by the civilian policy leadership to ensure its implementation. Over time, military-to-military events should become part of the formal defense resource allocation process so that they are treated like other regularly scheduled rotations for U.S. forces. To ensure consistent and adequate levels of funding, they should be incorporated into the Planning,

---

47. "A New National Security Strategy for a New Century," The White House, Washington, D.C., May 1997, p. 10. See also Secretary of Defense William S. Cohen's prepared statement to the Senate Armed Services Committee, February 3, 1998, entitled "New Defense Strategy: Shape, Respond, Prepare."

Programming, and Budgeting System, the complex Pentagon exercise that results in the formulation of the annual DOD budget.[48] Yet some flexibility must also be preserved to ensure that out-of-cycle opportunities for improving critical military-to-military relationships can be exploited.

Military-to-military cooperation is, literally, defense by other means. Consistent with this understanding, these programs need to be used fully and effectively to prepare for real-world contingencies. This means that they should focus increasingly on meaningful military training across the spectrum of anticipated operations. With reference to the issues raised in the previous discussion of coalition warfare, a specific focus of U.S. military-to-military cooperation programs, especially with countries that belong to the Partnership for Peace program, should be to enhance command, control, and communications compatibility. Exercises should place special emphasis on the C3 dimension of operating together.

Use the Cooperative Threat Reduction Program to Full Effect

The highly successful Cooperative Threat Reduction (CTR) program, which has until now concentrated on reductions in former Soviet nuclear weapons and their delivery systems, should develop a fissile materials storage and disposition program of comparable effectiveness. The efforts of the national nuclear laboratories, in particular those at Livermore and Los Alamos, have laid the groundwork for concrete progress to be made at key Russian facilities. To achieve results on the scale intended, such important programs require steady funding and sustained involvement by the U.S. government, with DOD and the Department of Energy fully coordinating their efforts. DOD should also continue to pursue fissile material and weapons export control initiatives in the former Soviet states that have vulnerable borders.

In addition, the CTR program should be utilized to reduce the chemical and biological weapons stockpile on the territory of the former Soviet Union. Funding constraints have impeded program development in both of these important areas. A renewed effort

---

48. For more on the defense resource allocation process, see Executive Level Text in *Resource Allocation*, Vol. 1: *The Formal Process*, 3d ed. (Newport, R.I.: Naval War College, March 1999).

should be made to persuade Congress that these initiatives merit significant and sustained support.

Make the Most of DOD's Newly Established Regional Centers

The Pentagon's five relatively new regional security studies centers should be fully utilized as instruments of military engagement by DOD's civilian and military leadership. The centers include the Africa Center for Strategic Studies, the Asia-Pacific Center for Security Studies, the Center for Hemispheric Defense Studies, the Marshall Center for European Security Studies, and the Near East–South Asia Center for Strategic Studies. Although each has its own distinct identity, they share common purposes: to foster communication and build relationships among future U.S. and regional security leaders, both military and civilian; to create an environment in which cooperative approaches to regional security problems can be safely explored; and to seek innovative solutions to challenges that might otherwise result in conflict.

Ensure that the Partnership for Peace Remains a Vital Institution in Eurasia and Explore Similar Arrangements Elsewhere

NATO's Partnership for Peace, created in 1994 as a means of building bridges between NATO nations and former Warsaw Pact states, should be utilized fully to foster security cooperation across Eurasia. For countries most active in the program, such as Ukraine, the United States and NATO should seek to make membership in PFP as similar to membership in NATO as possible. The United States should also consider developing similar security cooperation mechanisms for regions that lack institutions to facilitate bilateral and multilateral military-to-military engagement, such as in Asia, where the need is likely to be greatest.

Managing Global Roles and Relationships

The U.S. Defense Department must manage far broader roles and far more complex international relationships for the U.S. military than ever before. Both demand innovative leadership, imaginative policies, and inventive organization, a number of suggestions for which are spelled out in this chapter. To ensure effective coalition capabilities in the future, the Pentagon must develop a coherent and sustainable plan for connecting America's likely partners to the U.S.

military information architecture of the future. To enhance overall international capacity but reduce the U.S. burden in conducting peacekeeping and humanitarian missions, DOD must strengthen other participants and at the same time cooperate more efficiently with them. To fulfill the ambitious goals of the "shaping" mission, it must pursue innovative military-to-military cooperation programs that advance U.S. national security goals and are fully integrated into the defense resource allocation process. Taken together, these recommendations comprise a blueprint for managing critical aspects of the Pentagon's global ties in the first decade of the new century.

10

Strengthening the National Security Interagency Process

JOHN DEUTCH, ARNOLD KANTER, AND
BRENT SCOWCROFT

WITH CHRISTOPHER HORNBARGER

Today we manage our national security affairs according to the National Security Act of 1947.[1] This Act, created from the lessons of World War II, moved the country toward a unified defense establishment, established the Central Intelligence Agency (CIA), and created the National Security Council (NSC) as the framework for an interagency process. This system has served U.S. interests well. It has proven sufficiently flexible to meet successfully the twin challenges of the postwar period: winning the Cold War, while avoiding war with the Soviet Union. In this essay we suggest changes — more evolutionary than revolutionary — that will improve our ability to manage national security in the face of an international environment that differs in key respects from that of the past.

The primary motivation for the establishment of the National Security Council after World War II was the recognition that the nation's foreign policy interests could not be pursued exclusively through the efforts of executive departments acting separately. The importance of joint air, sea, and land operations led to the creation of the Department of Defense to integrate the efforts of the military

---

1. The enabling legislation consists of the original National Security Act of 1947; the 1949 Amendment to the Act, which created the CIA; the 1958 Defense Reorganization Act; and the 1986 Goldwater-Nichols Act. The United States Information Agency (USIA) was established by the United States Information and Educational Exchange Act of 1948 and the Mutual Educational and Cultural Exchange Act of 1961.

services. Military and diplomatic efforts with both allies and adversaries required coordination between the Departments of State and Defense. Civilian leaders and military commanders had different intelligence requirements that needed to be reconciled. For all these reasons, the President needed a process and a staff to coordinate the efforts of the various agencies on key national security issues.

The principal concern was the Soviet Union, and the procedures that were put into place were tailored largely to deal with the Cold War. As a result, the NSC focused primarily on international politics and on defense and arms control issues and not, for example, on economic security issues. The National Security Act and related legislation, as well as subsequent presidential directives, created sharp distinctions between domestic and foreign activity, and especially between national security and domestic law enforcement. These distinctions reflected deeply rooted public concern about government involvement in domestic matters. Congress wanted to be sure that the CIA did not become a domestic secret police, and that the United States Information Agency (USIA) did not direct propaganda at the American people. With the demise of the NSC's Operations Coordination Board at the end of the Eisenhower administration, the NSC staff focused on policymaking and became less involved in program management and implementation. The Departments of State and Defense, with support from the intelligence community and other agencies, were the primary means by which policy decisions were implemented and programs were executed.

The New Threats

The principal threats of the Cold War may largely have disappeared, but new threats, in new forms, have taken their place. The Soviet Union, with its geopolitical ambition and capability for major conventional conflict, no longer exists. But Russia still has a formidable nuclear arsenal, which is one central reason why its progress toward democracy, a market economy, and responsible international behavior is a major U.S. concern. Similarly, the path that China takes will have a decisive influence on the political, economic, and security climate in Asia. The progress we make in engaging China will determine whether we will live with a degree of stability, or instead enter a dangerous age of regional instability. These are problems that William

Perry and Ashton Carter term our "A-list" concerns, because they have the potential for disastrous conflict.[2] These are traditional concerns, and if these were the only serious issues we faced, the existing NSC machinery would certainly suffice.

However, an entirely new range of interrelated threats has also appeared,[3] including the proliferation of weapons of mass destruction and their means of delivery,[4] the potential for "catastrophic" terrorism,[5] and conflict with "rogue" nations such as Iran, Iraq, Libya, and North Korea.[6] There is an increase in the related threats of globally organized crime, including drugs, money-laundering, and computer intrusion, especially against our vulnerable information infrastructure. In addition, there is a growing number of peacekeeping crises, where U.S. and allied forces may intervene in a country to stop atrocities and restore peace between warring ethnic factions. Post–Cold War examples include Haiti, Bosnia, Kosovo, Rwanda, and East Timor.

These new threats are often accompanied by complex linkages between economic and security issues. For example, we use export controls and sanctions to make it harder for nations or sub-national groups to acquire dual-use technology, deadly weapons (or critical

2. Ashton B. Carter and William J. Perry, *Preventive Defense: A New Security Strategy for America* (Washington, D.C.: Brookings Institution Press, 1999). Perry and Carter also place proliferation of weapons of mass destruction in the "A" category.

3. A good summary is found in Ashton B. Carter, "Adapting U.S. Defense to Future Needs," *Survival,* Winter 1999–2000, p. 101.

4. See Report of the Commission to Assess the Organization of the Federal Government to Combat the Proliferation of Weapons of Mass Destruction, pursuant to P.L. 293, 104th Congress, Washington, D.C., July 1999.

5. Ashton B. Carter, John Deutch, and Philip Zelikow, "Catastrophic Terrorism," *Foreign Affairs,* Vol. 77, No. 6 (November–December 1998), pp. 80–96, at p. 80.

6. Unclassified National Intelligence Estimate, "Foreign missile developments and the ballistic missile threat to the United States through 2015," National Intelligence Council, September 1999; and the Report of the Commission to Assess the Ballistic Missile Threat to the United States (the Rumsfeld Commission), 1998.

components), and the means to deliver them.[7] Our allies often disagree with us as to the appropriate balance between the commercial
benefits from exporting dual-use technology and protecting security.
(Export controls are addressed in Chapter 6.) There is disagreement
about how or whether to make commercial encryption available for
secure electronic commerce. We have sometimes found it difficult to
pursue economic policies that advance our security interests, for example in promoting pipelines from the Caspian Sea through Turkey.
We face a difficult balancing act in trying to make international economic assistance to Russia contingent on internal reforms, without
applying so much pressure that Russian internal order collapses, increasing the likelihood that dangerous technology and weapons of
mass destruction will find their way around the world.

These new threats present challenges for the interagency process
and NSC structure because a number of distinctions upon which the
original system was built can no longer be assumed:

- there is no longer a clear distinction between peace and war, hot
  or cold; an example is a peacetime intrusion into another country's information network and communication system to collect
  intelligence that gives the ability to disrupt and attack;

- there is no longer a clear distinction between foreign and domestic
  matters; an example is combating terrorist groups, which have no
  national identity and may operate both in the United States and
  abroad, and may include members who are U.S. citizens;

- there is no longer a clear distinction between "domestic" law enforcement and "national security"; an example is collecting
  information for a law-enforcement purpose that may have significant national security implications, such as a suspected illegal
  technology transfer;

- effective action can no longer be anything other than dependent
  on coalition response; while coalitions were important during the
  Cold War, they are now an indispensable feature of virtually every
  peacekeeping operation;

---

7. "Dual-use technology" refers to technology with both military and commercial applications, such as fermenters that can be used to make either beer
or biological warfare agents.

- effective outcomes are now dependent on integration of economic and military measures; an example is the linkage of economic assistance to Russia to improved security of the Russian stockpile of weapons of mass destruction.

The emergence of these new threats, with new characteristics and the changes in world geopolitics they reflect, compel us to ask whether we should alter our national security structure and process to deal effectively with them.

Challenges to the Present NSC Structure

There is no possibility, of course, of constructing a perfect organizational structure, and any new structure would, like the one in place, be a compromise. There may well be more than one acceptable alternative, reflecting differing trade-offs among competing objectives, and we must be able to assess each as to how it might perform.

Many will argue that formal organizational structure is not important, provided one has good leadership: a President and a senior foreign policy team who possess judgment and experience. But leadership, essential as it is, is not sufficient to manage our complex foreign policy enterprise. Those who have participated in the policy formulation process or have managed security programs will attest to the importance that organization plays in facilitating or impeding the conduct of foreign affairs. Presidential leadership, if it is backed by good organization, can be much more effective in pursuing our country's interests than if the President is burdened with an inappropriate organizational structure. As President Eisenhower noted: "Good organization doesn't guarantee success, but bad organization guarantees failure."

It is useful to think of the conduct of government affairs as occurring in three phases: information gathering, decision-making, and implementation. Organization is critical at every stage, but especially in information gathering, i.e., intelligence, and in the implementation of policy and program decisions. Organization is an important determinant in ensuring that relevant information (from both open and clandestine sources) is collected, analyzed, and distributed to the President and senior policymakers in a timely way.

Organization is also vital to policy and program implementation, particularly when implementation takes several years and requires the expenditure of significant budget dollars. In such circumstances, one key to success is to ensure clear responsibility and authority for resource allocation decisions. Examples where authority is currently unclear include the Cooperative Threat Reduction efforts with Russia, programs to combat proliferation of weapons of mass destruction, and anti-drug programs. If a well-planned enabling organization is not in place, the success of such programs, to say nothing of the time and cost needed to achieve stated objectives, is in doubt.

Effectively dealing with situations arising from the new threats will challenge the existing organizational structure in four major ways. First, the high national priority given to defeating the new threats may conflict with traditional priorities of agencies. They may stumble where there are conflicting and overlapping agency responsibilities, which are especially severe between law enforcement and security, and between domestic and foreign jurisdictions. Second, success often requires coordinated action by several agencies, accompanied by flexible resource allocation. There are substantial organizational, political, and even legal barriers to this happening in a timely manner. A vivid case in point has been peacekeeping, where it has proven difficult to program the economic and civil-assistance resources that are the indispensable complements to military operations. Third, interagency plans supported by multi-year budget commitments are not in place to address critical threats, such as infrastructure protection or homeland defense against weapons of mass destruction.[8] Fourth, fragmentation of responsibilities for collecting, analyzing, and distributing intelligence means that policymakers do not always receive adequate and timely information about these new threats. Thus, we are ill prepared to deal with these threats — information warfare, use of chemical and biological weapons, infrastructure vulnerability, and peacekeeping — and their likely consequences.

A particularly important shortcoming is the absence of program and budget planning required to harmonize the efforts of various agencies involved in such matters as infrastructure protection, preventing and responding to catastrophic terrorism, and counter-

8. Some steps have been taken. Presidential Decision Directive 62 and PDD 63 issued on May 22, 1998, established a National Coordinator for Security, Infrastructure Protection, and Counter-terrorism, but this official has limited authority and responsibility to address the required cross-agency multi-year program planning.

proliferation. The current process and organization are not capable of carrying out common multi-year program planning for critical inter-agency efforts. The budget is aligned to agencies and traditional line items, and there is little cross-agency analysis or evaluation by the Office of Management and Budget (OMB) of spending on programs that rely on a variety of agencies to address these new threats. Where we need to acquire a new capability — for example, to contain the consequences of possible chemical or biological attack — there is no mechanism to achieve a multi-agency acquisition plan and manage the needed technical effort.

The NSC has had to devote increasing attention to economic in-struments of national security: trade sanctions, export controls, Cooperative Threat Reduction, and economic assistance to Russia. However, the NSC has historically not had the expertise adequate to address these economic security issues.

In sum, the strength of the existing NSC system is in reaching policy decisions involving the traditional national security agencies. The weaknesses of the system are that it does not do a good job of transcending the outmoded boundaries between "foreign" and "do-mestic" agencies, and that it does not do a good job of planning, budgeting, or coordinating programs that require integrated, sus-tained effort by several agencies. These shortcomings do not necessarily argue for a wholesale overhaul of the system: in several cases, simply establishing clearer responsibility, especially in the in-teragency context, for taking and implementing decisions would make a big difference. But reliably dealing with such challenges pre-sented by the new threats almost surely will require some changes in the current organizational structure.

Some Different Models

Reorganizing the national security system is not a new idea. Both ge-neric alternative models and numerous specific proposals have been put forward. Many recent studies and commissions have recognized the need for stronger integration of national security matters. For ex-ample, the U.S. Commission on National Security in the Twenty-first Century, in its Phase II *Report on Seeking a National Strategy*, states:

All this means that the integrating function of U.S. policy making processes will be challenged as never before. Traditional national security agencies (State, Defense, CIA, NSC staff) will need to work together in new ways, and economic agencies (Treasury, Commerce, U.S. Trade Representative) will need to work more closely with the traditional national security community. In addition, other players — especially Justice and Transportation — will need to be integrated more fully into national security processes. Merely improving the interagency process around present structures may not suffice.[9]

The Phase II Commission report does not make recommendations; Phase III will address changes to the U.S. national security structure and processes to enhance the U.S. government's capability to deal with the new threats. However, several other recent proposals make specific recommendations. One such proposal recommends replacing the NSC staff with a National Security Directorate headed by a new, Senate-confirmed presidential assistant, in place of the National Security Advisor.[10] We believe that, among other problems, this proposal places too much responsibility for executing programs in the White House.

The Commission to Combat Proliferation proposed creation of a new deputy national security advisor for combating proliferation.[11] (As will be seen below, our proposal broadens the responsibility of a new deputy to the entire range of new threats.) Former National Security Advisor Anthony Lake advocates creating a new post of Assistant to the President, parallel in authority to the National Security Advisor, with authority direct from the President to address the new threats.[12] All of these proposals seek to give the President greater control over the planning of activities that require concerted action by several executive branch agencies.

Several other conceptual approaches for dealing with the perceived shortcomings of the current system deserve consideration:

9. The U.S. Commission on National Security in the Twenty-first Century, Gary Hart and Warren Rudman, co-chairmen, Phase II, *Report on Seeking a National Strategy*, April 15, 2000, p. 14.

10. Stephen A. Cambone, *A New Structure for National Security Policy Planning* (Washington, D.C.: The CSIS Press, 1998).

11. Commission to Assess the Organization of the Federal Government to Combat the Proliferation of Weapons of Mass Destruction.

12. Anthony Lake, *Six Nightmares: Real Threats in a Dangerous World and How America Can Meet Them* (Boston: Little Brown, forthcoming 2000).

greater centralization, a region-centered structure, and a Department of Homeland Defense.

GREATER CENTRALIZATION

One proposed model is more centralized management, achieved either by formation of a "super department" or a "super NSC staff." The purpose of the centralization would be to provide stronger direction, better integrated planning, and perhaps implementation across departments. In this regard, it is interesting to note that while all the postwar reforms have successively increased centralization of national security matters, particularly in the DOD, the U.S. system is still less centralized than those of other countries.

Other proposals over the years have included creating a second vice president for foreign affairs or a super cabinet agency.[13] One approach would greatly strengthen the authority and scope of the Secretary of Defense to include responsibility for execution of critical programs appropriate to the characteristics of the new threats — including their *domestic* dimensions — programs which now flounder because of the absence of an adequate interagency process. The title of Secretary of Defense might thus be changed to Secretary for National Security.

A REGIONAL STRUCTURE

One of the biggest shortcomings in the present structure is the separation between foreign economic and security concerns. Examples where difficulties arise include economic and security assistance, especially to Russia and other states of the former Soviet Union, and export controls. A regional structure would permit a better integration of foreign economic and security interests. It would also help integrate the instruments that are needed to meet today's peacekeeping challenges, such as in Bosnia and Kosovo.

How might a regional organization be structured? Regional Under Secretaries, "double-hatted" in the Departments of State and Defense, would be designated as responsible for U.S. foreign economic and security policy in a specific geographical region. These individuals would have the authority to integrate instruments and resources that

---

13. U.S. Senate, Committee on Government Operations, "Staff Report of the Subcommittee on National Policy Machinery," in Senator Henry M. Jackson, ed., *The National Security Council: Jackson Subcommittee Papers on Policy-Making at the Presidential Level* (New York: Praeger, 1965).

would be provided by the same executive branch departments that now exist. This approach would have the flexibility to maintain stable geographic responsibility or to establish a limited authority to coordinate a crisis region; for example, the President might appoint a Special Coordinator for Balkan Peacekeeping Affairs.

What regions might make sense? A division that parallels the unified military commands would be a good starting point: Western Hemisphere (including SOUTHCOM and the Atlantic region covered by Joint Forces Command); Europe and Africa (EUCOM); Asia (PACCOM); and the Middle East (CENTCOM). Variants with a greater or lesser degree of centralization are also possible; for example, responsibility for Europe and Africa might be separated.

A more radical approach would be to abolish the functionally organized executive departments — State, Defense — in favor of regional departments that contain the diplomatic, economic, and military instruments needed to advance U.S. interests. There is historical precedent for such an approach: in the nineteenth century, the British Empire organized itself along regional lines. A Colonial Office, an India Office, and a Foreign Office each had responsibility for diplomatic, economic and, when necessary, military matters in its area.

A DEPARTMENT OF HOMELAND PROTECTION

An even more radical approach to the problem of conflicting national security and law enforcement objectives would be to create a new agency or executive branch department that would include all functions relating to domestic security that involved foreign threats. This agency would become part of the national security structure, like the Departments of State and Defense and the intelligence community, and its secretary would be a member of the NSC. The Department of Justice would give up its responsibilities for managing domestic security activities and focus exclusively on assuring the protection of the rights of U.S. citizens, prosecuting internal security cases referred to it, and ensuring respect for legal procedures.

The Department of Homeland Protection might include the following agencies:

- the FBI, from Justice;
- the Drug Enforcement Administration, from Justice;
- the Immigration and Naturalization Service, from Justice;

- the Bureau of Alcohol, Tobacco, and Firearms, from Treasury;

- the Customs Bureau, from Treasury;

- the Coast Guard, from Transportation;

- the National Guard, from Defense; and

- the Federal Emergency Management Administration.

The new agency would be granted sufficient resources and expertise to address certain new trans-national threats: infrastructure protection, including information systems; biological and chemical warfare defense; and counter-terrorism, both domestic and foreign. The scope of responsibility would be similar to that encompassed by the ministry of interior in many countries.

As part of this approach, the ambiguity about the legal authority that DOD has to use U.S. military force within the United States to defend against certain kinds of threats, the so-called *posse comitatus* issue, would have to be resolved.

EVALUATING THE MODELS

Each of these alternatives has advantages and disadvantages compared to the current arrangement. The centralization model that would replace the Secretary of Defense with a more powerful "Secretary for National Security" has the advantage of building upon the DOD's proven capacity to plan and implement complex programs. Not only would this proposal improve the effectiveness of these programs over time, but it could do so efficiently, and in a manner that would maintain congressional oversight.

The disadvantages are that DOD has little or no experience with many aspects of the new missions it would assume, such as managing the consequences of a domestic disaster. Second, even though assigning "homeless" missions to the explicit authority of one department could improve implementation, DOD might view these missions as diluting its military focus, and relegate them to a secondary status. Third, the Secretary of Defense already has a complex management job; expanding the scope even more could make the job impossible, and undermine the increased management effectiveness that centralization would presumably provide. Lastly, giving DOD a greater role in domestic security could be seen as a threat to civil liberties: the safeguards established by the Posse Comitatus Act would likely need revision and, at a minimum, significant procedural safeguards would have to be established. The DOD, however, is the only existing executive branch agency that could carry out the broader responsibilities envisioned.

The second model — moving to a regional organization — would put the focus on where the problems are, rather than on what tools are required to solve them. In this sense, the model is analogous to the DOD's unified combat commands, widely regarded as having increased the effectiveness of the military's joint warfighting capability. A regional organization would "bake in" a functionally integrated approach, fostering greater coordination of diplomatic, military, and economic responses as needed. Its potential benefits notwithstanding, however, one overwhelming disadvantage of the approach is that it is the biggest discontinuity from the present way of doing business; a transition would be difficult, perhaps impossible.

The third model — establishing a Department of Homeland Protection — has the virtue of directly addressing one of the vexing characteristics of the new threats: the increasingly imprecise distinction between national security and law enforcement. The advantage of this approach is that it would place in one new agency all of the functions that bear on internal security, thus providing the best long-term opportunity for dealing with threats posed by catastrophic terrorism and cyber attacks. (However, establishing a Department of Homeland Protection does not resolve the parallel issue of relations between the CIA and FBI outside the United States.) This proposal would remove from the Department of Justice and other executive branch agencies the security functions that are not part of their central mission. In particular, it would permit the Justice Department to focus on perhaps its most important responsibility: ensuring that the rights of individual U.S. citizens are not infringed. This model, however, like the DOD centralization model, has the strong disadvantage that Americans are very suspicious of reorganization proposals that have the potential to change the balance between individual freedoms, such as privacy, and the surveillance and police power of the state. It is therefore unlikely that Congress would be willing to create an agency along the lines envisaged in this approach.

What Should be Done?

In light of the major disadvantages of more radical approaches, as well as the absence of a compelling case that such far-reaching measures are needed to address the problem, we propose a relatively modest change in the present NSC structure. The President should give the NSC greater authority and capacity to carry out planning and coordination — but not implementation — of interagency programs. This is close to the present way of doing business, and that in itself is a considerable advantage. The principal disadvantage of this approach — like several of the alternatives discussed above — is that the arrangement does not closely conform to the organizational principle that policy instruments should be aligned as closely as possible to the main national security threats and objectives. It is a weaker form of centralization and might prove insufficient to achieve the needed interagency program effectiveness. A second potential disadvantage of this approach is that even the modest expansion of NSC responsibilities might argue for greater legislative oversight of the NSC than has historically been the case, or else inappropriately shield program planning and coordination functions that have historically been subject to legislative oversight.

Our suggestions build on the existing strengths and flexibility of the NSC. They continue the historical trend of adapting the NSC process to enable the President to manage and coordinate interagency efforts better. The common thread is that successful response requires the concerted action of many agencies, both traditional security agencies including State, Defense, and Intelligence, and what have heretofore usually been considered "domestic" agencies: Justice, Treasury, Health and Human Services, and Commerce. Accordingly, changes to the process should focus on integrating the traditional "domestic" agencies into the NSC process, and improving interagency action by establishing clearer authority and responsibility for "interagency" issues.

BALANCE NATIONAL SECURITY AND LAW ENFORCEMENT BETTER

First, the President should establish a new interagency process to manage better the tension between national security and law enforcement responsibilities. The Clinton administration assigned responsibility for responding to terrorism and for infrastructure protection to the Department of Justice (DOJ). There were several reasons for this assignment: many of the threatening activities are U.S. crimes; there is the historical reluctance to have DOD or the military involved in law-enforcement activities in the United States; and the DOD's plate is already quite full.

Responsibility for terrorism and infrastructure protection can remain with the DOJ, but our recommendation is that the Attorney General, in carrying out these responsibilities, give greater weight to national security. Specifically, national security concerns should take precedence over law enforcement concerns with regard to threats to the homeland. In addition, the DOJ effort should be part of the NSC process, and the NSC should be the mechanism for coordinating the government efforts at combating terrorism, infrastructure protection, and domestic consequence management.

The Department of Justice has limited capacity for program management. The DOD is much better able than the DOJ to plan and execute programs that require significant acquisition activity. This suggests that some of the program-management responsibility that has been given to the Department of Justice over the past decade — for example, for information infrastructure protection — should be shifted to the Department of Defense. The FBI should remain significantly involved in these matters but in the first instance as part of the national security process.

The intelligence collection activity of the FBI's National Security Division should be responsive to collection priorities established by the Director of Central Intelligence (DCI); the dissemination of intelligence from FBI sources should be the responsibility of the DCI. Any adjustment of responsibility should not affect the Attorney General's responsibility to ensure that intelligence activities are carried out in a legal manner, and that these activities do not infringe on the rights of American citizens.

INCREASE THE AUTHORITY OF THE DCI

Second, the President should give the Director of Central Intelligence greater authority to accomplish his or her responsibilities effectively. The intelligence community must give the earliest possible warning of imminent threats of terrorism, acquisition or possible use of weapons of mass destruction, and other trans-national threats. To accomplish this, the intelligence community must have an integrated approach to the collection, processing, exploitation, and distribution of both clandestine and open information. With the explosion of information technologies, the intelligence community faces a shift from its historic priority on technical collection to a priority on processing, validating, analyzing, and communicating information of value to policymakers. (A broader look at these intelligence issues is included in Chapter 4.)

Up to now, the intelligence community has dealt with the new threats by forming Intelligence Community Centers that bring together representatives from all the intelligence agencies. Existing Centers address terrorism, proliferation, and narcotics and crime. However, the Centers have had limited success, because the Director of Central Intelligence lacks the authority to require participation by intelligence agencies in the Center activities and to set collection priorities for all intelligence agencies on these subjects.

The Director of Central Intelligence needs authority in three specific areas. First, the DCI must ensure an integrated collection plan across all disciplines — imagery (space and air), signals, measurements and signature, and human intelligence collection (from both domestic and foreign agencies) — that addresses each element of the new threats. This information should provide the basis for dissemination of community-wide intelligence assessments and warning.

Second, the DCI must have authority to create a community-wide acquisition plan to ensure the development of new technology and the acquisition of new systems for collection and exploitation of information. The expanded NSC process recommended below should approve this integrated plan. Because of DOD's strong program management capability, much of the responsibility for program implementation should be delegated to the DOD. Third, the DCI should have the authority to develop, with the support of the DOD and the FBI, and subject to presidential approval and subsequent congressional notification, plans for covert action to prevent or respond to the new threats. These plans should include peacetime information operations.

In order to carry out these responsibilities, the DCI would need to have greater authority over those aspects of the intelligence budget that deal with the new threats.[14] For these matters, the DCI's authority should be greatly strengthened for planning, resource allocation, tasking collection, and intelligence production. This would entail a limited shift of responsibility from the Secretary of Defense to the DCI. The shift in responsibility is limited because it applies only to intelligence activities bearing on the new threats and not on intelligence activities that are more immediately relevant to warfighting. It also should be emphasized that this recommendation is not intended to change the relationship between the Secretary of Defense and the DCI in support to military operations. Nevertheless, there will inevitably be some blurred areas, such as protection of deployed forces in peacetime, that would require stronger DOD involvement in intelligence planning. Furthermore, while the DCI's authority for *planning* intelligence activities to address the new threats would be expanded, responsibility for program *execution* would remain with the existing agencies such as the Central Intelligence Agency, the National Security Agency, the Defense Intelligence Agency, and the National Imagery and Mapping Agency. The 1996 Aspin/Brown Commission saw the need for — but did not recommend — such centralization.[15]

Many "national" users of intelligence (consumers of intelligence from agencies other than Defense, e.g., State and the NSC staff) would probably favor a move in this direction. This centralization of responsibility under the DCI for intelligence related to the new threats should also be an opportunity to provide more timely and responsive intelligence to the regional military commands (the "CINCs"), since it would give military commands access to information previously difficult for them to obtain. Indeed, if improved support to military operations is not assured, any shift is likely to be strongly opposed by the Pentagon and the cognizant congressional committees.

14. The intelligence budget includes the National Foreign Intelligence Program (NFIP), the General Defense Intelligence Program (GDIP), and Tactical Intelligence and Related Activities (TIARA).

15. The Commission on the Roles and Capabilities of the U.S. Intelligence Community (the Aspin/Brown Commission), *Preparing for the Twenty-first Century: An Appraisal of U.S. Intelligence*, Washington, D.C., March 1996.

STRENGTHEN NSC'S INTERAGENCY ROLE, IN PARTNERSHIP WITH OMB, AGAINST NEW THREATS

Third, the President should strengthen the ability of the NSC to plan, direct, and coordinate interagency programs that build capability for meeting the new range of threats. This activity will involve several agencies — including the Office of Management and Budget (OMB) and "domestic" agencies that do not routinely participate in the NSC process — and often a multi-year effort will be required. The heart of our recommendation is to assign responsibility for the preparation of necessary interagency plans to the NSC, with the active support of OMB. This will be new for the NSC, at least since the 1950s, when the NSC under President Eisenhower had an Operations Coordination Board (OCB). Our proposal differs from the OCB in two important respects: the focus on programs that require coordinated interagency resource allocation, and the partnership with OMB.

To supervise and coordinate this expanded planning and programming function, we propose the creation of a new position at the level of Deputy National Security Advisor. This individual would have the responsibility and authority to run a process that sets interagency program priorities, supported by a small dedicated staff.[16] The multi-year plans would include program outcome, schedule, and cost, thus permitting better presidential control and congressional oversight of these programs so critical to our future national security.

An important part of our proposal is to task the Office of Management and Budget (OMB) to work with this new Deputy National Security Advisor to translate the multi-year program plans into agency budgets. OMB would also be responsible for monitoring agency compliance during the annual budget cycle.

Thus, OMB would be asked to do something quite different from what it does today. Today, OMB's principal resource allocation activities have an "agency" focus: providing budget "targets" to agencies, reviewing agency budget requests, and recommending to the President what should be approved. For the security issues that require multi-agency efforts, we envision a process in which the NSC takes

16. The Clinton administration has taken tentative steps in this direction. A Presidential Directive has created a National Coordinator for Security, Infrastructure Protection, and Counter-terrorism, but the position does not explicitly include responsibility or authority to establish interagency program priorities.

the lead in coordinating the development of multi-agency programs, and OMB has the responsibility for developing the interagency budgets required to implement these programs and for ensuring that the agencies implement the presidentially-approved interagency program. Consideration should also be given to creating a new budget category for these multi-agency programs, similar to the category that covers the atomic energy defense activities of the Departments of Defense and Energy. This would help focus attention on these critical interagency efforts and facilitate oversight by both OMB and Congress.

The new NSC responsibility we propose for integration of agency efforts would not replace the work of the departments: execution of approved programs and operations would remain with the executive branch agencies. Separating responsibility for planning and coordination — to be placed with the NSC and OMB — from the responsibility for program execution, which remains with the agencies, is a compromise, because it would split authority and responsibility for overall outcome. We believe such a compromise is justified, although less than ideal, for two reasons. First, the Executive Office of the President is notoriously poor at program execution and has an overall mission that is incompatible with the kind of congressional oversight appropriate to program implementation.[17] Second, program management competence resides in the agencies. Nevertheless we recognize that this split in accountability between program planning and program outcomes is undesirable.

The new interagency system that we recommend to deal with the new threats would also be capable of addressing what has been a vexing problem with regard to coordinating interagency efforts in peacekeeping. The recommended partnership between the NSC and OMB could more effectively ensure that needed resources were programmed for agencies other than DOD that participate in peacekeeping activity, including State, the Agency for International Development, and the Immigration and Naturalization Service. As the examples of Haiti, Bosnia, Kosovo, and Somalia indicate, a successful peacekeeping effort requires more than military presence; it

---

17. John Tower, Edmund Muskie, and Brent Scowcroft, *Report of the President's Special Review Board* (The Tower Commission Report), Washington, D.C., February 26, 1987.

also requires some assistance for police, economic assistance, health care, and other matters.

Conclusion

We have focused on changes in the executive branch that will improve our nation's ability to address the new threats. Success will also require that Congress make some corresponding changes to its procedures. For example, Congress traditionally prefers to give money to the DOD rather than to the Department of State or domestic agencies. This means that it is often difficult to obtain funding for an integrated program involving both defense and civilian agency efforts. More fundamentally, congressional oversight is currently organized largely along agency lines. Authorizing committees do not review programs that cut across the responsibilities of several agencies, absent exceptional circumstances. While the appropriations committees have both the power and the practice of taking action to assure that agency efforts conform to congressional guidelines, these actions tend to be *ad hoc* or retroactive responses to perceived shortfalls, rather than the result of assessment of success in achieving planned results. If Congress is not prepared to consider the multi-agency program plans prepared by the new Deputy National Security Advisor as coherent, integrated proposals, then surely these plans will not have the force to drive agency programs.

We hope that this chapter and these recommendations stimulate thought and discussion about what changes the United States should make to better protect the republic and the interests of our citizens in a changing international environment.

11

Implementing Change

JUDITH A. MILLER

The premise of this book is that significant organizational change is necessary, both inside the Department of Defense and across departmental boundaries. If the new national security team agrees, how should it go about making these changes? Those who have studied the process of institutional change assert that time horizons matter: smaller incremental steps toward change can be carried out in several years, but fundamental change more realistically requires on the order of five years — *not* counting any legislative authorizations that might be necessary. Even for a new administration looking forward to a potential two terms in office, those timelines could be chilling. But assuming the administration can crystallize quickly behind a change agenda,[1] and can seize the opportunity for a bipartisan dialogue and partnership with the 107th Congress, we believe many of the changes outlined in prior chapters can be made promptly by executive branch decision, and can be made to stick by follow-on legislation. To put these points in context, this chapter first briefly outlines prior significant legislative and administrative efforts to achieve fundamental change for the national security establishment, and then turns to this book's specific recommendations for change.

The information and help provided by Alice Maroni, Harvey Nathan, Deborah Lee James, Paul Koffsky, Karen Yannello, Eliana Davidson, and John Casciotti are gratefully acknowledged.

1. I do not suggest that the proposals for change presented here need be swallowed whole. The point of this chapter is to suggest how the new administration and the new Congress could go about implementing whatever portion of these changes they adopt as their own.

Prior Defense Reform Efforts

A brief review of how structural change within the national security establishment has been achieved in the past reveals legislative and administrative changes of considerable significance, typically occurring virtually simultaneously. For example, the national security structure we live with today was first laid out legislatively by the National Security Act of 1947.[2] It reflected the lessons of World War II, and positioned the United States for the Cold War to follow, in a number of fundamental ways. It created a Secretary of Defense; provided for Departments of the Army, Navy, and Air Force within the National Military Establishment; established the National Security Council; and created a Director of Central Intelligence. But even before its enactment, a Joint Chiefs of Staff (JCS) directive approved by President Truman formally spelled out JCS authority with respect to the unified commands. This was a significant mandate *not* spoken to by the 1947 Act, but it was then folded into the follow-on "Key West Agreement" of 1948, which in turn helped implement much of the 1947 Act for the National Military Establishment.[3]

The departmental structure resulting from this first effort at organizational change had unfortunate similarities to the Articles of Confederation with which this country started in 1781. Although the military departments were part of the National Military Establishment, they were each cabinet-level departments that at best acted as a loose federation of equals, with uncertain ties to the Secretary of Defense.

At the urging of Secretary of Defense James Forrestal and the Eberstadt Task Force Report to the Hoover Commission, the National Military Establishment was replaced by the Department of Defense pursuant to the National Security Act Amendments of 1949.[4] As a result, the military departments no longer had cabinet-level authority, and instead became part of the Department of Defense. The position of Chairman of the Joint Chiefs of Staff was also officially created by

---

2. P.L. No. 80-253, 61 Stat. 495 (1947) (codified as amended at 50 U.S.C. § 401).

3. U.S. Department of Defense, *Functions of the Armed Forces and the Joint Chiefs of Staff* (March 11–14, 1948).

4. P.L. No. 81-216, 63 Stat. 578 (1949) (codified as amended in various sections of 5 and 10 U.S.C.).

this statute, but given the authority only to preside as a non-voting member of the Joint Chiefs of Staff.[5]

At the beginning of the Eisenhower administration, the new President used his reorganization authority under Title V of the U.S. Code to submit his 1953 Reorganization Plan to Congress for approval.[6] It took further steps to strengthen the Secretary of Defense and his staff, and the role of the Chairman. The Key West agreement was thereafter revised, and Department of Defense Directive 5158.1 was issued to carry out other presidential recommendations, for example, that the JCS duties of the Chiefs were to be their principal duties.[7]

In 1958, in the aftermath of Sputnik, and at the urging of President Eisenhower, Congress passed additional reform legislation: the Department of Defense Reorganization Act of 1958.[8] It was this Act that defined the authority of the Secretary of Defense over the Department of Defense as "direction, authority and control," even with respect to the military departments.[9] It also gave the Secretary broad discretion to reorganize the Department. The military departments were taken out of the chain of command; unified and specified combatant commands were established by statute. Again, the broad outlines of the Act were implemented in detail through Secretary of Defense directives.

Although the cumulative effect of the 1947, 1949, and 1958 Acts (and the 1953 Reorganization Plan) was to increase the authority of the Secretary of Defense over the Department, to lay a strong foundation for joint commands, and to decrease the relative role of the military departments, at best these were trend lines. In many respects the Department remained an uneasy coalition of competing power centers; the Chairman of the Joint Chiefs of Staff, the Joint Staff, and the unified commands were especially perceived as being left with the short end of the stick.

In theory, many of the problems on the joint side of the Department could have been fixed by directives from the Secretary of

5. 63 Stat. at 581-83.

6. 5 U.S.C. § 903; Reorganization Plan No. 6 of 1953, 5 U.S.C. app. 1.

7. U.S. Department of Defense, Directive 5158.1 (July 26, 1954).

8. Department of Defense Reorganization Act of 1958, P.L. No. 85-599, 72 Stat. 514 (1958) (codified as amended at 50 U.S.C. § 401).

9. 72 Stat. at 514.

Defense; e.g., giving more clout to the Chairman of the Joint Chiefs of Staff and the combatant commands, or insisting that the military departments proffer better officers for service on the Joint Staff. For those who knew the Department of Defense *before* the Goldwater-Nichols Department of Defense Reorganization Act of 1986, however, the idea that lasting results could have been accomplished by Secretary of Defense fiat — or even presidential direction — is preposterous.[10] Even a decade and a half after the passage of Goldwater-Nichols, many of its ambitious goals are yet to be achieved. To pick just one example, the Commanders-in-Chief (CINCs) of the Unified Commands (the four-star heads of the major joint commands) were empowered by the legislation — but *not* authorized by JCS directive — to exercise logistic and administrative authority broadly during peacetime.[11] The military departments in particular opposed Goldwater-Nichols before enactment, and each now even more zealously, if possible, protects its "organize, train and equip" role that the Act preserved. But what Goldwater-Nichols did was empower and legitimate change that the Secretary of Defense might legally have carried out in large part on his own. The Act itself was a statement of a bipartisan consensus in Congress that reform was needed, and an implicit promise to the reform-minded at the Department of Defense that Congress would not chip away at the basic outlines of the Act at the behest of one or more disappointed losers.

Time for Goldwater-Nichols II?

Do we need a Goldwater-Nichols II? And should it extend beyond the Department of Defense? The empowerment of institutional reform that the Goldwater-Nichols Act provided cannot, fourteen years later, be denied. The Joint Staff has been transformed from a relatively sleepy backwater to an effective, efficient — and some would argue too single-minded — staff supporting the Chairman of the Joint Chiefs of Staff. The Chairman and the Vice Chairman have clearly played, day in and day out, an institutionally effective policy and leadership role — at the National Security Council, in the Joint Re-

---

10. The Goldwater-Nichols Department of Defense Reorganization Act of 1986, P.L. No. 99-433, 100 Stat. 992 (1986) (10 U.S.C. §§ 111 et seq.).

11. 100 Stat. at 1013 (codified at 10 U.S.C. § 164).

quirements Oversight Council (JROC), and in assisting the Secretary of Defense and the President in operations and in budget delibera-tions — that they simply were not staffed to play before Goldwater-Nichols. DESERT STORM — and our operations in Haiti, Bosnia, Kosovo, and Iraq — have been just the visible pay-off of these reforms on the operational side. But the underlying theme of this book is that Gold-water-Nichols was just the beginning. It permitted the re-tooling of DOD's missions and power centers that made DESERT STORM, and subsequent missions up to and including Kosovo, successful.[12] But Goldwater-Nichols — like the National Security Act of 1947 itself — was written and originally implemented with the Cold War in mind. The Soviet Union transformed itself only in 1989. The Department, and the country, have been rethinking DOD's organization and mis-sion ever since. It may, in fact, be past time for a concerted restatement of organizational principles that will take us well into the new century.

Does that mean that an enormous redrafting of statutory provi-sions is called for? Or that management change within the Secretary of Defense's existing powers must wait for a new legislative frame-work? I would argue emphatically not. The most striking driving force and enabler in Goldwater-Nichols, to my eye, were the specific personnel changes mandating joint-duty positions, establishing Joint Specialty Officers, and making promotion to flag rank dependent on joint experience — all backed up by the strengthening of the Chair-man's role that permitted him to achieve their successful implementation.[13] This change could *not* have effectively been carried out by Secretary of Defense mandate — a mandate that could vary from Secretary to Secretary, let alone from administration to admini-stration. Such a fundamental shift in promotion and staffing policy could only be implemented through legislation. But while these shifts in joint-duty requirements were a fundamental underpinning of the Goldwater-Nichols reforms, none of Goldwater-Nichols' sponsors would have spent years in study and support of that Act if all it ac-

12. The U.S. experience in Somalia makes it clear, however, that the Gold-water-Nichols reforms were a necessary but not sufficient basis for success. See, e.g., Mark Bowden, *Black Hawk Down: A Story of Modern War* (Boston: Atlantic Monthly Press, 1999) for a further description of what went wrong in Somalia.

13. 100 Stat. at 1025-34 (codified at 10 U.S.C. §§ 601, 612, 619, 661–668).

complished was some tinkering around the edges of the personnel system.

What made Goldwater-Nichols a continuing engine for reform within DOD was — to use a hackneyed phrase — the "vision" expressed in the Act's statement of purpose that allowed those bent on reform in the Department to claim the Goldwater-Nichols mantle. "Goldwater-Nichols II" could ultimately perform a similar function today, if Congress and the executive branch put aside their differences and jointly push to achieve needed change. As outlined in prior chapters, the stakes are genuinely high: we could end up with the "wrong" defense for the twenty-first century, and we would be paying too many billions even for that. But this effort to achieve change will come to naught without sustained leadership, trust, and political will at *both* ends of Pennsylvania Avenue. If the branches work against each other, there will be no lack of partisans with entrenched views to exploit their differences.

But to recognize the obvious — that some changes either cannot be achieved without legislation or need to be propelled by a legislative mandate — does not gainsay the other lesson that leaps from a brief review of the significant structural changes that have occurred in the past fifty-plus years: that the administration can do much on its own *if* the Congress is with it. To point to just one example from the historical sketch laid out above, unified combatant commands were not officially established by statute until 1958.[14] They were not empowered to make fundamental command decisions in peacetime with respect to their components until Goldwater-Nichols. And yet they had been used in World War II, were defined by presidential directive in 1946, and were further bolstered by the Key West agreements of 1948. In other words, the President's authority as Commander-in-Chief and the Secretary of Defense's "direction, authority and control" can achieve a lot, if Congress ultimately embraces their decisions.

It perhaps also goes without saying that if the Congress is hostile to the changes being implemented, it can do much to hinder or stop their execution. A classic example is in the area of competitive privatization. While Congress, in 1988, declared a policy to rely on the

---

14. P.L. No. 85-599.

private sector for supplies and services if it is cost-effective to do so,[15] it substantially constrained that policy in practice by adopting a variety of reporting, timing, and other restrictions that made effective implementation of the policy almost impossible.[16] Because the Armed Services Committees of the House and the Senate continue (generally to the Department of Defense's great good fortune) routinely to produce a substantial Authorization Act each year, they can also quickly take action to stop or endlessly complicate a change not to their liking. This means that if the new administration decides to push for change — and to maximize its chance for success, to implement what it can administratively — it needs at least the tacit and preferably the enthusiastic support of the responsible committees.

Ideally, the new administration and the new Congress will jointly embrace a change agenda for national security. To help that partnership along, the executive branch should think explicitly about what the Congress would gain if it adopted some or all of the suggestions for change laid out in Chapters 1 through 10 of this book. Apart from satisfaction in helping to maintain the American military's edge over all comers, they can be effective participants by insisting on reports on implementation efforts and by effectively monitoring the results. The defense authorizing committees in particular, by virtue of their long tradition of effective annual legislative activity, may be especially suited to help lead Capitol Hill's efforts generally to grapple with the overlapping and cross-cutting inter-agency challenges that many of this book's recommendations present.[17] And working on the "big picture" might also re-establish a certain balance between the

---

15. 10 U.S.C. § 2462.

16. These constraints are found at 10 U.S.C. §§ 2305(a)(1), 2461, 2464-2467, 2469, 2470, 4532; Department of Defense Appropriations Act of 1996, P.L. No. 104-61, §§ 8020, 8037, 8050, 109 Stat. 636, 656, 659, 661-62 (1995); National Defense Authorization Act for Fiscal Year 1987, P.L. No. 99-661, § 317, 100 Stat. 3816, 3855 (1986).

17. For example, the Senate Armed Services Committee already has a functioning subcommittee on "Emerging Threats and Capabilities." The Nunn-Lugar Cooperative Threat Reduction Act of 1993 (Title XII of the National Defense Authorization Act for Fiscal Year 1994), Pub. L. No. 103-160, 107 Stat. 1777 (codified, as amended, at 22 U.S.C. §§ 5951-58), is another, earlier example of bipartisan cooperation by authorizers that crossed traditional jurisdictional lines.

authorizers on one hand and the appropriators on the other, who by definition appropriate on an annual time-line, and recently, often before the authorizers have even completed their work.

Implementing Defense Reform

The recommendations in this book vary greatly in sweep and in detail, from the revolutionary, clearly requiring legislation, such as civilian personnel reform, to the fundamental but almost prosaically counter-revolutionary, such as returning independent research and development (IR&D) funds to the cutting-edge research role they had twenty to thirty years ago, requiring a mix of legislative and regulatory change.[18] One approach to categorizing these rather lumpy proposals is whether — or how far — they can be implemented without the need for legislation. Another approach is to look at whether the current appropriations process will permit an otherwise achievable administratively or legislatively authorized reform to be carried through.

It is clearly beyond the reach of this chapter, or this book, to offer a tutorial on the executive branch's budget process or the committee structure and appropriations process of the Congress. Yet their interactions often seem to defeat reform even when many on both sides of the aisle seem genuinely determined to achieve it. Although this section's focus is largely on what the new administration can do on its own and what it needs to defer to authorizing legislation, it also tries to keep a wary eye on where the money is, and how those bent on reform could play more successfully in the budget arena.

If the new administration agreed in whole or in part with this book's recommendations, what could it do starting on the day the President is sworn in? In the joint world, it could implement virtually all of the recommendations of Chapter 2 and Chapter 3. That is, the Secretary of Defense could direct, pursuant to 10 U.S.C. § 162, that the Chairman of the Joint Chiefs of Staff (CJCS) publish an annual roadmap setting out joint architectures, integration needs, and capability shortfalls. The Secretary could make the CINC Joint Forces Command (CINCJFCOM) an advisor to the JROC and the Defense Advisory Board (DAB), and could recommend to the President that the next

18. See 10 U.S.C. § 2372; 48 Code of Federal Regulations (CFR) § 231.205-18 (1999).

CINCJFCOM have had prior service as a CINC or Service Chief or Vice Chief. The President could set out in the Unified Command Plan (UCP) the CINCJFCOM's responsibilities as an action agent for jointness, future capabilities, and joint experimentation.[19] The Secretary could direct the comptroller to assure proper resources for these missions at the beginning of the Program Objective Memorandum (POM) cycle. Since TRANSCOM and the Defense Logistics Agency (and the other agencies identified in Chapter 2 for consolidation as part of a unified logistics command) are not functions vested by law, the Secretary could direct their consolidation.[20] The Secretary could instruct the comptroller to work out the undoubtedly complicated resource issues that would flow from combining a unified functional command sponsored by the Air Force with several other defense agencies. The Secretary could allocate resources to standing joint logistical commands, and could cause the Office of the Secretary of Defense to publish logistics-deployment guidelines pursuant to recommendations of the Chairman of the JCS. To lock in a minimal legislative baseline for these changes, the Secretary could direct the General Counsel to include in the Department's authorization proposal legislative provisions making the CJCS's roadmap a statutorily required report, defining the experience requirements for the CINCJFCOM position, and making the CINCJFCOM a statutory member of the JROC.

Similarly, the command and control, information technology, and information assurance recommendations in Chapter 3 could also be authorized in large part by Secretary of Defense directive. Simply recognizing command and control (C2) as a readiness issue — and thus to be measured and reported on in the Senior Readiness Oversight Council (SROC) and the Joint Requirements Oversight Council — can be done by Secretary of Defense Memorandum. The Unified Command Plan can assign responsibility for command and control to Joint Forces Command. That responsibility was first given to the CJCS in 1962, and he could of course continue to have oversight re-

---

19. See 10 U.S.C. § 161, which provides that the Chairman periodically, and not less than every two years, review the missions, responsibilities, and force structure of each combatant command, and recommend changes to the President through the Secretary of Defense.

20. See 10 U.S.C. § 125(a); 10 U.S.C. § 191.

sponsibilities pursuant to 10 U.S.C. § 162. Either through the Unified Command Plan or by Secretary of Defense directive, CINCJFCOM could be directed to establish a Joint Task Force command and control system, an "expercise" office, and a Joint Command and Control Blueprint office. The UCP can separate responsibility for computer network attack (leaving it with CINCSPACE), from computer network defense. The Secretary of Defense can put computer network defense into the hands of the Department's Chief Information Officer (CIO), and direct that the National Security Agency (NSA) take on a supporting role on computer network defense.

This is nevertheless an area where saying it can be done significantly understates the difficulty of the task. First, the cumulative effect of the changes proposed in Chapters 2 and 3 is to shift power from the services to the joint world and from civilian decisionmakers, such as the Assistant Secretary of Defense for Command, Control, Communications, and Intelligence (ASD C3I), to the combatant command chain. Moreover, these shifts somehow have to work against a DOD internal funding system largely laid out and defended by the military departments, not the joint commands.

The way these cross-cutting funding problems have been handled in the past leaves much to be desired. The CINCs are constantly perceived as having wish lists unconstrained by budgeting realities and articulated far too late to the OSD to have a prayer of being included in the Secretary of Defense's guidance to the services that, each winter, kicks off the budget cycle for the following year. So if these organizational shifts in responsibility are to stick, the Secretary must be ready to tell the comptroller by February that the sponsoring services (Navy for JFCOM [formerly ACOM], Air Force for SPACECOM) must include some particular number of dollars in their submissions for these joint priorities. Somehow working with their sponsoring services, the CINCs need to be staffed in order to play in this broader budgeting environment.[21]

Of course, even if the funding process can be worked inside the Pentagon, the information technology revolution that it would enable also does not fit neatly into the traditional congressional appropria-

---

21. With respect to changes in CINC and other headquarters staffs, the Secretary must also keep an eye on 10 U.S.C. § 130a's limitations on management headquarters personnel.

tions process. The pace of change in this world simply outstrips by years the traditional appropriations process used for major defense procurements. A process that may work for a ten or twenty-year major procurement cycle for platforms like fighter planes or aircraft carriers — although perhaps not optimized even for them — does not seem to work at all in the nimble information-technology world. Ideally there, you want a pot of money against which you can draw to execute an architecture that may evolve every three months and where the very purpose is to have systems that stay cutting-edge instead of being bought to last twenty years. Industry is reinventing itself in this area apparently on a daily basis — shifting suppliers and ideas apace — and it does so by recognizing that it will have to budget some amount for information technology, without being able to specify its precise contours in advance. Appropriators tend to take a dim view of this approach. The Navy has nevertheless apparently managed in the FY 2001 appropriation and authorization process, after considerable struggle, to achieve initial approval of a multi-year contracting-for-services approach to the Navy/Marine Corps Intranet program, by funding it largely through operations and maintenance (O&M).[22] Perhaps in this one special area, the appropriators will find a way to accommodate themselves to an after-the-fact oversight role, but it is important to recognize how much this cuts against the grain. In another context — DESERT STORM — with 100,000 soldiers on the ground, the administration's request for an adequate pot of money up front to cover their costs was turned down by the appropriators for lack of specificity, twice forcing DOD to resort to the Food and Forage Act.[23] This is obviously not an appropriate fix for information technology or command and control issues.

Assuming that congressional oversight and funding complexities can somehow be resolved, there are also other difficulties: civilian oversight issues must be untangled, and the responsibilities under

22. Reports in various defense-related publications have made it clear that the source of funds and the program itself have been challenged both inside the Navy and by Congress. See, e.g., John Robinson, "Incoming CNO Warns Navy Intranet Effort Can't Bankrupt Readiness," *Defense Daily*, June 29, 2000, p. 2; "Senators Want to Further Restrict Navy Intranet," *Inside the Pentagon*, June 29, 2000, p. 10. See also H.R. 4205, 106th Cong. § 332 (2000), S. 2539, 106th Cong. § 810 (2000).

23. 41 U.S.C. § 11.

the Clinger-Cohen Act of the Chief Information Officer and ASD C3I in the command, control, and information technology areas must be worked through.[24] This chapter does not resolve these issues. If the Secretary of Defense and Deputy Secretary of Defense hit the ground committed to this reform agenda, they will also have to be committed to working out these issues with the relevant stakeholders. With issues as cross-cutting as these, that means the Deputy Secretary of Defense must be prepared to head an *ad hoc* task force of affected players, backed up by a working group that drafts implementing directives. To make this work, timelines have to be set and stuck to by the Deputy Secretary of Defense, without waiting for the new senior political team to make it through the confirmation process. Conceivably this effort could be merged (if not submerged) into the Quadrennial Defense Review, which the Deputy Secretary of Defense will chair and which will unfold on the same timeline. The Director of Central Intelligence (DCI) will also want to take part on at least some of these issues.

The main recommendation of Chapter 4 is to fold all the technical intelligence agencies — the NSA, the National Reconnaissance Organization (NRO), the National Imagery and Mapping Agency (NIMA), and the Central Masint Office — into one. This cannot be accomplished without legislation, because NIMA is a creature of statute, and thus apparently beyond the Secretary of Defense's otherwise broad reorganization authority, while NSA and NRO are so protective of their respective charters that it is inconceivable that they could be merged without congressional approval and oversight.[25] If the experience with NIMA is any guide, the Secretary cannot simply put forward a legislative proposal and wait to see how the Congress responds. To pursue this proposal, a transition team needs to be designated and given responsibility for working the myriad details of this change with the affected agencies, the national intelligence com-

24. The Clinger-Cohen Act of 1996 (also known as the Federal Acquisition Reform Act of 1996 and the Information Technology Management Reform Act of 1996), P.L. No. 104-106, 110 Stat. 642 (1996) (codified in numerous titles); Chief Information Officer responsibilities: 40 U.S.C. § 1425, 10 U.S.C. § 2223; ASD C3I responsibilities: 10 U.S.C. § 138.

25. NSA's charter is National Security Council, Intelligence Directive No. 9 (October 24, 1952). NRO's charter is U.S. Department of Defense, Directive 5105.23 (June 14, 1962).

munity, and the Congress, with particular emphasis on the Intelligence Committees, and with concern for the defense authorizing committees as well.

By contrast, the National Assessment Center proposal in Chapter 4 appears capable of implementation by the DCI — perhaps with a Presidential Decision Directive outlining its mission to the rest of the national security community.

Several recommendations in Chapter 5 for countering asymmetrical threats will clearly require congressional action in the form of legislative authorization and supporting appropriations: to establish a university-affiliated, government-owned laboratory for biowarfare defense technology; and to organize a government-funded but private National Information Assurance Institute.[26] The biowarfare defense technology laboratory, if modeled as suggested on the Department of Energy's nuclear laboratories, needs to include provisions for oversight mechanisms endorsed by Congress from the beginning. It would also have to be designed with an eye to the Biological Weapons Convention Protocol, currently being negotiated, that will deal with implementation of the Convention through on-site inspections. Other recommendations, such as creating a Deputy National Security Advisor for such cross-cutting issues as catastrophic terrorism and counter-proliferation (addressed at greater length in my discussion of Chapter 10's recommendations), and adopting strong programs to develop and deploy security technology and techniques like the "two-man rule," are clearly steps that could begin to be implemented immediately by the executive branch.

Chapter 6 on America's technological edge can largely be implemented through DOD decision-making. The Department can encourage second and third-tier consolidation of defense industry; support teaming, joint ventures, and export reform; improve education within the acquisition community; and grapple with whether and how to intrude into make/buy decisions. This is a far-reaching but nevertheless bread-and-butter docket for the incoming Under

26. The experience of the Financial Services Information Sharing and Analysis Center to date may also be relevant to this proposed public-private partnership effort. That center brings together a secure database, analytic tools, and information gathering and distribution facilities to share information on security threats, vulnerabilities, incidents, and solutions among its members in the banking, securities, and insurance industries.

Secretary of Defense for Acquisition, Technology, and Logistics (USD AT&L). But some legislative changes that go back to a prior way of doing business appear to be called for in the areas of IR&D;[27] improved cash flows to defense industry;[28] and the ability to establish a Federally Funded Research and Development Center (FFRDC) in the area of biological warfare defense.[29] A statutorily required report on the defense technology base by the Secretary of Defense would highlight and enable the Congress as well as the executive branch to track the overall capability of the defense industry.

Chapter 6 also calls for dealing with antitrust law and export control policies. Antitrust laws have a substantial constituency, along with resident bodies of expertise at the Federal Trade Commission and the Department of Justice (DOJ), and are reformed even less often than DOD.[30] Export control policies have been the subject of major congressional focus and investigations in the last few years (even though substantial administrative steps have been undertaken to streamline the process through the Defense Trade Security Initiative).[31] A major commitment of resources within the administration and on the Hill would be required to make further changes in these two areas. The proposal for an export agency funded by State, Defense, and Commerce would require legislation to overcome the explicit fiscal-law rule that effectively forbids the mixing of departmental appropriations.[32]

The implementing strategy for the Revolution in Business Affairs is largely laid out in Chapter 7: use existing base closing authorities as leverage to inspire a renewed effort to enact BRAC-like legislation; repeal the many legislative impediments to privatizing and outsourcing; and again grapple with A-76 reform within the execu-

27. 10 U.S.C. § 2372.

28. 31 U.S.C. § 3903.

29. 10 U.S.C. § 2367.

30. See, e.g., Sherman Anti-Trust Act, 15 U.S.C. §§ 1 to 7, Robinson-Patman Act, 52 Stat. 446, 15 U.S.C. § 13.

31. See, e.g., 65 Fed. Reg. 45,282 (2000).

32. Treasury and General Government Appropriations Act, 2000, 106 P.L. No. 106-58, § 610, 113 Stat. 430.

tive branch.[33] In order to overcome internal resistance to competitive sourcing, the Secretary of Defense should issue specific policy guidance to the Quadrennial Defense Review, declaring that the private sector is the preferred provider of goods and services. The acquisition reform proposals of Chapter 7 build on the last eight years and do not require legislative action.

It is apparent from the scope of Chapter 8 on human resources management that the multiple recommendations for reform require legislation.[34] They also require a full-bore commitment to change from the entire Department. The payoff here is in some ways the highest: the ability to renew and protect the talented base on which the entire Department rests. But change requires the Secretary of Defense to get buy-in from the President up front, and a presidential direction to the Office of Management and Budget to permit enabling legislation to be submitted on the civilian side. On the military side, the Joint Chiefs of Staff must commit to the idea that unless the Army, Navy, Air Force, and Marine Corps take a more targeted approach to compensation and skill sets, none of them will be able to cope with and compete against the dot-coms for talent.

Much of Chapter 9 on managing the Pentagon's international relations can be implemented through the Presidential Decision Directive (PDD) process. But support from Congress will be necessary for an augmented role at the UN, for support of a UN military police force, and to further burden-sharing through military-to-military training and cooperation.[35] Funding for military-to-military contacts and contacts with non-governmental organizations would need to be regularized in the budget cycle at DOD and on Capitol Hill as well, not just thought of as CINC-initiative funds or viewed as an after-thought in the budget process.

With respect to the interagency mission of dealing with new threats, Chapter 10 recognizes the structure put in place at the NSC by President Clinton, but goes considerably further. It calls for creat-

33. Existing base closing authority is at 10 U.S.C. §§2341, 2687. See Defense Base Closure and Realignment Act of 1990 (part A of Title XXIX of P.L. 101-510) for an example of prior "BRAC" legislation. Impediments to privatization and outsourcing are cited at note 16 above.

34. 5 U.S.C. § 1101 et seq.

35. 10 U.S.C. § 168.

ing a Deputy National Security Advisor with real clout, by enabling him to be a player who can direct agency investment and program priorities in his interagency areas of responsibility, backed by OMB enforcement. This much can be accomplished by the President directing it. A budget process that tries to suggest priorities months after DOD has almost finished its budget cycle will not work here any more than in the joint arena described above, which means NSC and OMB must come to the table with their priorities, preferably by February of each year, to assure that at least at DOD the services take these numbers into account.

But this is obviously not just a DOD problem. As was seen this year, appropriators for the various departments with a current role in the anti-terrorism mission drastically under-funded the requests: for DOJ training of first responders; for Terrorism Task Force Offices; and to protect government computers from hackers.[36] Two years ago a modest effort by DOD to get needed authority for the Department — much desired by DOJ, the State Department, and the NSC, as well as DOD — to provide certain non-reimbursable support to civil authorities for combating terrorism in the United States and overseas at the request of the Attorney General or the Secretary of State, resulted in an even more modest temporary provision that required such support, limited to $10 million, to be reimbursable, absent a Secretary of Defense waiver "in extraordinary circumstances."[37] Congressional staff members have noted that one problem was that these cross-cutting budget requests were not made until May: that is, a good three months too late. But there also appears to be a recognition that multiple committees of jurisdiction cannot develop an integrated view of what is needed, and may see other more traditional programs within their respective oversight agencies as having priority.

The new administration can do more to present its requests in a timely way, and the recommendations of this book, including consideration of a new budget category for these multi-agency programs, will help assure that fix. But this is an area where Congress may also

---

36. Stephen A. Holmes, "Antiterrorism Spending Falls Short, Administration Says," *New York Times*, July 30, 2000, p. A18.

37. Military Assistance to Civil Authorities to Respond to Act or Threat of Terrorism, P.L. No. 106-65, § 1023, 113 Stat. 747 (10 U.S.C. § 382 note).

need to do more: to consider, for example, a special appropriations subcommittee drawn from the regular appropriations subcommittees of the affected agencies to deal with an integrated anti-terrorism budget. On the authorizer's side, an openness to joint meetings or an *ad hoc* conference-type committee drawn from each of the committees of jurisdiction might be an unorthodox but effective measure for dealing with this problem. We have not, however, suggested special select committees, because over time they tend to become permanent, and to multiply even further the jurisdictional barriers to action in the Congress.

Other recommendations in Chapter 10 — to assign the job of information infrastructure protection to DOD; to give national security precedence over law enforcement with regard to threats to the homeland; and to increase the DCI's authority over the intelligence collected and disseminated by the FBI's National Security Division and over the intelligence budget for new threats — may be harder still. While the more "radical" models were rejected in Chapter 10, many of its proposals contain elements that can be challenged on similar grounds. It is not, moreover, at all clear that a change in FBI culture can be achieved simply because a DCI directs it, as numerous Attorneys General might attest from their own experience, and despite their apparent authority. A different approach might be to amend Federal Rules of Criminal Procedure 6, to make grand-jury material shareable within the government for national security reasons. An Infrastructure Protection Institute legislatively authorized under DOD auspices, as proposed in Chapter 3, might be a gentler means of having DOD play effectively in the information infrastructure arena. But by directly proposing the reshuffling of significant agency authorities, these proposals could certainly form the basis for a renewed and spirited discussion within the executive branch and on Capitol Hill.

Conclusion

The preceding section of this chapter has taken a "nuts and bolts" approach to the question of how to go about implementing the recommendations of this book, recommendation by recommendation, laying out a menu of choices for the new administration and the new Congress to implement or not. This approach appeals because, almost by definition, organizational reform across a host of tangentially related subject areas resists a catchy "campaign" phrase to rally to. But the lack of a slogan or theme does not mean that these efforts at change need go forward in isolation from each other. A broad effort to implement change across the national security establishment, packaged more or less as laid out in this book, could instead be presented to the Congress and the executive branch officials charged with implementing it as an integrated set of initiatives to ready defense for the twenty-first century. To "sell" the legislative and administrative package as another "Goldwater-Nichols" leap forward will require commitment from the President and from the military and civilian leadership at DOD, combined with a willingness to make the case inside the Pentagon and on Capitol Hill. A similar commitment from the leadership in Congress is just as important, perhaps using the device of joint hearings to underline a congressional readiness to take on these issues in a bipartisan spirit of cooperation with the President's new team. While full-throated endorsement by Congress of many of these initiatives is not a prerequisite for their implementation, broad congressional support for the package of initiatives outlined here, whether by way of supportive hearings or legislation, is clearly desirable — and indeed essential if lasting change is to be achieved.

About the Core Group and the Authors

DENIS A. BOVIN

Denis A. Bovin is a member of the Defense Organization and Management core group of the Preventive Defense Project. As Vice Chairman, Investment Banking, and Senior Managing Director of Bear Stearns & Co., he is a member of the management team that directs all of Bear Stearns' worldwide Investment Banking activities. Mr. Bovin previously spent more than two decades at Salomon Brothers Inc., where he headed the firm's Investment Banking Corporate Coverage and Capital Markets Divisions, and led the firm's Communications and Technology Group. He holds a BS degree from the Massachusetts Institute of Technology and an MBA degree from the Harvard Business School. He serves as a member of the MIT Executive Committee, and was elected a Life Member of the MIT Corporation. He is also an Executive Committee Member of the *Intrepid* Air, Sea and Space Museum, and a member of the Council on Foreign Relations, the National Policy Association's Committee on New American Realities, the Board of Directors and the Policy Committee of Business Executives for National Security, Inc. (BENS), the Investment Association of New York, the New York Society of Security Analysts, and of the Boards of Directors of Bear Stearns & Co. and of IDT Corporation, an international telecommunications and internet carrier. Mr. Bovin also serves as a member of the Defense Science Board, and in 1995 he was awarded the Department of Defense Medal for Distinguished Public Service, the highest honor that can be conferred on a civilian. He has also been honored with the *USS Intrepid* Salute Award and with awards from MIT, including its highest honor for alumni.

ASHTON B. CARTER

Ash Carter is Ford Foundation Professor of Science and International Affairs at Harvard University's John F. Kennedy School of Government, and he is Co-Director, with William J. Perry, of the Preventive

Defense Project. He served as Assistant Secretary of Defense for International Security Policy from 1993 to 1996, with responsibility for national security policy concerning the states of the former Soviet Union (including their nuclear weapons and other weapons of mass destruction), arms control, countering proliferation worldwide, and oversight of the U.S. nuclear arsenal and missile defense programs. He also chaired NATO's High Level Group. He was twice awarded the Department of Defense Distinguished Service medal, the highest award given by the Pentagon. He continues to serve DOD as an adviser to the Secretary of Defense and as a member of DOD's Defense Policy Board and its Defense Science Board, as well as its Threat Reduction Advisory Council. In addition, he serves in an official capacity as Senior Adviser to the North Korea Policy Review, chaired by William J. Perry.

Dr. Carter has also served as director of the Center for Science and International Affairs in the Kennedy School of Government at Harvard University and chairman of the editorial board of *International Security*. He holds bachelor's degrees in physics and in medieval history from Yale University and a doctorate in theoretical physics from Oxford University, where he was a Rhodes Scholar. His most recent book is *Preventive Defense: A New Security Strategy for America* (with William J. Perry). He is a Senior Partner of Global Technology Partners, LLC, and a consultant to Goldman Sachs and the MITRE Corporation on international affairs and technology matters. He is a member of the Advisory Board of MIT Lincoln Laboratories, a member of the Draper Laboratory Corporation, and a member of the Board of Directors of Mitretek Systems, Inc. He is also a member of the Council on Foreign Relations and the National Committee on U.S.-China Relations, and a fellow of the American Academy of Arts and Sciences.

DAVID S.C. CHU

David Chu is a member of the Defense Organization and Management core group of the Preventive Defense Project. He is the Vice President responsible for RAND's Army Research Division and Director of its Arroyo Center, and is also a member of the Army Science Board. He previously served as Director of RAND's Washington Office and Associate Chairman of RAND's Research Staff. He has also served in the Department of Defense as Assistant Secretary and Director for Program Analysis and Evaluation (1981–93); and as the Assistant Director of the Congressional Budget Office for National Security and International Affairs (1978–81). An economist with RAND from 1970 to 1978, he served in the U.S. Army from 1968 to 1970. He holds a BA in Economics and Mathematics and a Ph.D. in Economics from Yale University. He has been awarded the Department of Defense Medal for Distinguished Public Service with Silver Palm and the National Public Service Award of the National Academy of Public Administration, of which he is a Fellow, and on whose Board he serves as Chairman.

VICTOR A. DEMARINES

Victor A. DeMarines, a member of the Defense Organization and Management core group of the Preventive Defense Project, is the former President and Chief Executive Officer of the MITRE Corporation, having retired in 2000. He is a member of the MITRE Board of Trustees, and serves on the executive committee. He is a member of the board of the Massachusetts Business Roundtable. He previously served MITRE as Executive Vice President, Senior Vice President, and General Manager of MITRE's Center for Integrated Intelligence Systems, and in various technical management positions. In 1972–73 he participated in the President's Executive Interchange program, in the position of staff analyst in the Department of Transportation's Office of Research and Development Policy, and was awarded the Secretary of Transportation's Meritorious Service Award. Before joining MITRE, Mr. DeMarines was a lieutenant in the Air Force and worked as a design engineer with G.L. Martin Company. Named 1996 Businessperson of the Year by the Massachusetts North Suburban Chamber of Commerce, Mr. DeMarines speaks and writes frequently on technical issues, holds patents on local area network techniques, and has served on numerous study groups within the national security arena. He holds a master of science degree in electrical engineering from Northeastern University and a bachelor of science degree in aeronautical engineering from Pennsylvania State University.

JOHN M. DEUTCH

John M. Deutch, a member of the Defense Organization and Management core group of the Preventive Defense Project, is an Institute Professor at the Massachusetts Institute of Technology. He served as

Director of Central Intelligence from May 1995 to December 1996, as Deputy Secretary of Defense (1994–95), and as Under Secretary of Defense for Acquisition and Technology (1993–94). He previously served as Director of Energy Research (1977–79), Acting Assistant Secretary for Energy Technology (1979), and Under Secretary (1979–80) in the U.S. Department of Energy. In addition, he has served on the President's Nuclear Safety Oversight Committee (1980–81); the President's Commission on Strategic Forces (1983); the White House Science Council (1985–89); the President's Intelligence Advisory Board (1990–93); the President's Commission on Aviation Safety and Security (1996); the President's Commission on Reducing and Protecting Government Secrecy (1996); and as Chairman of the President's Commission to Assess the Organization of the Federal Government to Combat the Proliferation of Weapons of Mass Destruction.

Dr. Deutch is currently a member of the President's Committee of Advisors on Science and Technology. He holds a BA in history and economics from Amherst College and a BA in Chemical Engineering and Ph.D. in Chemistry from MIT. He has been awarded honorary doctorates from Amherst, University of Lowell, and Northeastern University. A member of the MIT faculty since 1970, Dr. Deutch has served as Chairman of the Department of Chemistry, Dean of Science, and Provost. He has published over 120 technical publications in physical chemistry, as well as numerous publications on technology, international security, and public policy issues.

JANE HARMAN

Jane Harman is a member of the Defense Organization and Management core group of the Preventive Defense Project. From 1992 to 1998, she represented California's 36th district in Congress, where she served on the National Security, Science, and Intelligence Committees. She is currently seeking to regain the congressional seat she left in 1998 to run for Governor of California. A graduate of Los Angeles public schools, Harman holds a BA from Smith College and a JD from Harvard Law School. She has served as Chief Counsel and Staff Director of the U.S. Senate Subcommittee on Constitutional Rights, Deputy Secretary to the Cabinet for President Jimmy Carter, Special Counsel to the Department of Defense, attorney, and businesswoman. Harman was appointed Regents' Professor by UCLA in

1999, where she taught public policy and international relations. A 1998 recipient of the Department of Defense Medal for Distinguished Public Service, Harman served on the congressionally mandated Commission on Terrorism, which issued its report in May 2000.

ROBERT J. HERMANN

Robert J. Hermann is a Visiting Scholar at the Kennedy School of Government at Harvard University, and an Affiliate of the Preventive Defense Project. Dr. Hermann is a member of the President's Foreign Intelligence Advisory Board, a member of the Defense Science Board, and a member of the National Academy of Engineering, as well as Chairman of the Board of Directors for Draper Laboratory and Chairman of the Board of Directors of the American National Standards Institute. He is also a Senior Partner, Global Technology Partners, LLC. He holds BS, MS, and Ph.D. degrees in electrical engineering from Iowa State University.

ARNOLD KANTER

Arnold Kanter, a member of the Defense Organization and Management core group of the Preventive Defense Project, is a Principal and founding member of The Scowcroft Group, an international business consulting firm. He also is a Senior Fellow at The Forum for International Policy and at RAND. From October 1991 until January 1993 he served as Under Secretary of State for Political Affairs. As the State Department's third-ranking official, he functioned as its "chief operating officer" with responsibility for the day-to-day management of U.S. foreign policy. He served on the White House staff from 1989 to 1991 as Special Assistant to the President for National Security Affairs, and in a variety of capacities in the State Department from 1977 to 1985. Mr. Kanter has also been a member of the senior staff at RAND, where he served first as Associate Director of the International Security and Defense Program, and then as Director of the National Security Strategies Program. He has been a member of the research staff at the Brookings Institution, and a member of the faculty at Ohio State University and at the University of Michigan. Mr. Kanter serves on the Defense Policy Board, the boards of the Atlantic Council and the Stimson Center, and on the International Advisory Committee of CMS Energy, a global energy company. He is also a member of the Council on Foreign Relations, the Aspen Strategy

Group, and the International Institute of Strategic Studies. He holds an undergraduate degree from the University of Michigan and master's and doctoral degrees from Yale University.

MICHAEL J. LIPPITZ

Michael J. Lippitz is a member of the Defense Organization and Management core group of the Preventive Defense Project. He consults and lectures on technology strategy and industrial management for clients including the Office of the Director of Defense Research and Engineering in the U.S. Department of Defense, the Institute for Defense Analyses, and Stanford University. He served from 1994 to 1997 as Special Assistant for Strategic Technology Planning in DOD's Office of International and Commercial Programs. He previously worked at Lawrence Livermore National Laboratory, Rockwell International, and Hewlett-Packard. He holds a bachelor's degree in electrical engineering *magna cum laude* from Brown University and a master's degree and Ph.D. in Engineering–Economic Systems and Operations Research from Stanford.

JUDITH A. MILLER

Judith A. Miller, a member of the Defense Organization and Management core group of the Preventive Defense Project, is a partner at Williams & Connolly LLP, where she advises on a wide range of business and governmental issues. As the General Counsel of the Department of Defense from 1994 to 1999, she had responsibility for advising the Secretary and Deputy Secretary and their senior leadership team on the host of legal and policy issues that came before the Department, including mergers and acquisitions, international affairs and intelligence matters, operations law, acquisition and business reform, major procurements, significant litigation and investigations, globalization, computer security, and alternate dispute resolution, as well as personnel, fiscal, environmental, and health policy issues. In January 1997, Secretary Perry awarded her the Department of Defense Medal for Distinguished Public Service. Secretary Cohen awarded her the Bronze Palm to that medal in 1999. She is a recipient of the Department of the Army's Decoration for Distinguished Public Service and has also been an honoree of the Marine Corps.

Ms. Miller's practice at Williams & Connolly has included civil and criminal litigation and investigations related to defense procurement, healthcare, and financial institutions; and complex torts. She is the Co-Chair of the Federal Practice Task Force of the American Bar Association, a Fellow of the American Bar Foundation, and a member of the ABA Standing Committee on Law and National Security as well as the American Law Institute. She is a member of the bars of the Supreme Court of the United States, six federal circuits, the D.C. Court of Appeals, and the United States Court of Appeals for the Armed Forces. She was appointed to the Civil Justice Reform Act Advisory Group for the United States District Court for the District of Columbia, and its follow-on implementation committee. Prior to joining Williams & Connolly, Ms. Miller clerked for Judge Harold Leventhal, U.S. Court of Appeals for the D.C. Circuit, and Associate Justice Potter Stewart, Supreme Court of the United States. She was an Assistant to the Secretary and Deputy Secretary of Defense in the Office of the Special Assistant from 1977 to 1979. Ms. Miller also served in 1994 as a member of the Advisory Board on the Investigative Capability of the Department of Defense. Ms. Miller graduated from Beloit College *summa cum laude* and holds a law degree from the Yale Law School.

SEAN O'KEEFE

Sean O'Keefe, a member of the Defense Organization and Management core group of the Preventive Defense Project, is the Louis A. Bantle Professor of Business and Government Policy, and Director, National Security Studies, at the Syracuse University Maxwell School of Citizenship and Public Affairs. He served as Secretary of the Navy and as Comptroller and Chief Financial Officer of the Department of Defense in the Bush administration, after eight years on the staff of the U.S. Senate Committee on Appropriations, where he served as Staff Director of the Defense Appropriations Subcommittee. He entered public service in 1978 as a Presidential Management Intern. In 1993, President Bush and Secretary of Defense Cheney honored him with the Distinguished Public Service Award, and he was the 1999 faculty recipient of the Syracuse University Chancellor's Award for Public Service. He currently serves as chairman of the Secretary of the Navy's Task Force on Personnel. He holds a BA from Loyola University and an MPA from the Maxwell School.

WILLIAM J. PERRY

William J. Perry is the Michael and Barbara Berberian Professor at Stanford University, with a joint appointment in the School of Engineering and the Institute for International Studies. He is a Fellow at the Hoover Institute, and Co-Director, with Ashton B. Carter, of the Preventive Defense Project. He was professor (half time) at Stanford University from 1988 until 1993, while he was the Co-Director of the Center for International Security and Arms Control (now known as the Center for International Security and Cooperation). Dr. Perry was the nineteenth Secretary of Defense for the United States, serving from February 1994 to January 1997. He has also served as Deputy Secretary of Defense (1993–94) and as Under Secretary of Defense for Research and Engineering (1977–81).

His business activities have included serving as a laboratory director for General Telephone and Electronics, founding and serving as the president of ESL, Inc., serving as Executive Vice-President of Hambrecht & Quist, Inc., and founding and serving as chairman of Technology Strategies & Alliances. He serves on the boards of Cylink and several emerging high-technology companies. He is the chairman of Global Technology Partners. Dr. Perry holds BS and MS degrees from Stanford University and a Ph.D. from Penn State, all in mathematics. He is a member of the National Academy of Engineering and a fellow of the American Academy of Arts and Sciences. He has been honored with the Presidential Medal of Freedom, the Department of Defense Distinguished Service Medal, and Outstanding Civilian Service medals from the Army, the Air Force, the Navy, the Defense Intelligence Agency, NASA, and the Coast Guard.

BRENT SCOWCROFT

Lieutenant General Brent Scowcroft, USAF (ret.), a member of the Defense Organization and Management core group of the Preventive Defense Project, served as Assistant to the President for National Security Affairs for Presidents Bush and Ford. A retired U.S. Air Force Lieutenant General, General Scowcroft served in numerous national security posts in the Pentagon and the White House prior to his appointments as Assistant to the President for National Security Affairs. He also held a number of teaching positions at West Point and the Air Force Academy, specializing in political science. He holds a BS degree from West Point and MA and Ph.D. degrees from Columbia University. General Scowcroft serves as a Director on the boards of Devon Energy, Pennzoil-Quaker State, and Qualcomm corporations. He is also on the Board of Advisors of ExpertDriven, Inc.

JOHN M. SHALIKASHVILI

General John Shalikashvili (ret.) is a Visiting Professor with the Institute for International Studies at Stanford University, and is a Senior Advisor to the Preventive Defense Project. Additionally, he is a member of the board of directors of Boeing, L-3 Communications, Plug Power, United Defense, and the Frank Russell Trust Company, as well as a senior consultant to a number of corporations. He also serves on the boards of various non-profit corporations. General Shalikashvili was appointed the thirteenth Chairman of the Joint Chiefs of Staff by President Clinton, and served in that position from October 1993 until September 1997. In this assignment he was the principal military advisor to the President, the Secretary of Defense, and the National Security Council. He previously served as NATO's Supreme Allied Commander, Europe, and as Commander-in-Chief of the United States European Command. He holds a bachelor's degree in mechanical engineering from Bradley University and a master's degree in international affairs from George Washington University.

ELIZABETH SHERWOOD-RANDALL

Elizabeth Sherwood-Randall is a Senior Advisor to the Preventive Defense Project, and a Senior Research Scholar at Stanford University's Center for International Security and Cooperation. She served from 1994 to 1996 as Deputy Assistant Secretary of Defense for Russia, Ukraine, and Eurasia, with responsibility for national security policy toward the newly independent states of the former Soviet Union. In this capacity, she was honored with the Department of Defense Distinguished Service Medal. She continues to serve the Pentagon as a consultant to the Office of the Secretary of Defense and as a member of the Regional Centers' Board of Visitors. She also advises Lawrence Livermore National Laboratory on its nonproliferation and arms control initiatives in the former Soviet Union. Prior to her government service, Dr. Sherwood-Randall was co-founder and Associate Director of the Strengthening Democratic Institutions Project at Harvard University. She has also served as Chief Foreign Affairs and Defense Policy Advisor to Senator Joseph R. Biden, Jr., and has been a Guest

312 | KEEPING THE EDGE

Scholar in Foreign Policy Studies at the Brookings Institution. She has authored numerous publications, including *Allies in Crisis: Meeting Global Challenges to Western Security*. She holds a bachelor's degree from Harvard-Radcliffe Colleges and a doctorate in international relations from Oxford University, where she was a Rhodes Scholar.

JOHN M. STEWART

John M. Stewart is a member of the Defense Organization and Management core group of the Preventive Defense Project. Since 1961, he has been a director of McKinsey & Company, Inc., a management consulting firm, where his work focuses on international competition, research and development, and factory operations in the pharmaceutical, electronics, aerospace, telecommunications, and auto industries. He has been a member of the Defense Science Board, the National Council on Economic Education, the Manufacturing Studies Board of the National Research Council, the New York State Temporary Committee on Management and Productivity in the Public Sector, the Economic Policy Council of the United Nations Association of the United States, and the Yale University Council. He is a trustee of the Hospital for Joint Diseases, the Woods Hole Oceanographic Institution, and the Mt. Sinai/NYU Medical Center. He has previously been a member of the U.S. National Commission on Productivity (1972–74), and served in the U.S. Navy from 1953 to 1955 in the Atlantic and the Mediterranean. He holds a BS from Yale University and an MBA from Harvard Business School.

JOHN P. WHITE

John White is presently on the faculty of the John F. Kennedy School of Government, Harvard University, and is an Affiliate of the Preventive Defense Project. He served as U.S. Deputy Secretary of Defense from 1995 to 1997, Deputy Director of the Office of Management and Budget from 1978 to 1981, Assistant Secretary of Defense, Manpower, Reserve Affairs and Logistics from 1977 to 1978, and as a lieutenant in the U.S. Marine Corps (1959–61). He has twice been awarded the Department of Defense Medal for Distinguished Public Service. Prior to his most recent government service, Dr. White was the Director of the Center for Business and Government at Harvard University and the chairman of the Commission on Roles and Missions of the Armed Forces. His extensive private-sector experience includes service as Chairman and CEO of Interactive Systems Corporation from 1981 to 1988 and, following its sale to the Eastman Kodak Company in 1988, as General Manager of the Integration and Systems Products Division and as a Vice President of Kodak until 1992. In nine years with the RAND Corporation, he was the Senior Vice President for National Security Research Programs and a member of the Board of Trustees. Dr. White is currently Managing Partner of Global Technology Partners, LLC. He is also a Senior Fellow at the RAND Corporation and a member of the Council on Foreign Relations. He serves as a director of Wang Government Services, IRG International, Inc., and the Institute for Defense Analyses, as well as the Concord Coalition and the Center for Excellence in Government. He is also a member of the Global Advisory Committee of Mitsubishi Electric, Tokyo, Japan. Dr. White holds a BS degree from Cornell University and an MA and Ph.D. in economics from the Maxwell Graduate School, Syracuse University.

HERBERT S. WINOKUR, JR.

Herbert S. Winokur, Jr., a member of the Defense Organization and Management core group of the Preventive Defense Project, is Chairman and Chief Executive Officer of Capricorn Holdings, Inc., a private investment company, and Managing General Partner of Capricorn Investors, L.P., Capricorn Investors II, L.P., and Capricorn Investors III, L.P., private investment partnerships concentrating on investments in restructure situations. He has also been Senior Executive Vice President and Director of Penn Central Corporation. Mr. Winokur holds a Ph.D. in Decision and Control Theory, and AB *cum laude* and AM, all from Harvard University. Mr. Winokur serves on various boards of directors, including those of Enron Corporation and Azurix Corp., and is a member of the Harvard Corporation and a director of Harvard Management Company, which oversees the Harvard University endowment. He is a former director of UCLA Medical Center, a former Trustee of Greenwich Academy, and a former Co-Chair of the New-York Historical Society. He is a member of the Council on Foreign Relations and of the Woodrow Wilson International Center for Scholars Council, where he chaired the search committee for the Center's current Director. Mr. Winokur also serves on the Board of Second Stage Theatre.

Assisting the Primary Authors

DAVID AIDEKMAN, a graduate of Harvard's John F. Kennedy School of Government, works on national security issues in Washington, D.C.

NURITH BERSTEIN is a Project Administrator and Research Associate at the RAND Corporation working primarily in the areas of national and international security and defense.

CHRISTIANA BRIGGS is a graduate student in the National Security Studies Program at MIT and is a graduate intern at the National Security Council.

JOHN BROWN joined the Marine Corps after graduating from Harvard in 1995, and served as a lieutenant in the artillery before returning to Harvard to study at the Kennedy School of Government and the Harvard Business School.

COMMANDER PHIL EHR was a National Security Affairs Fellow at Stanford's Hoover Institution, and is now assigned to the Headquarters of the Commander-in-Chief, U. S. Naval Forces Europe; a graduate of the University of the State of New York and the Naval War College, he holds a graduate degree from Troy State University.

CAPTAIN CHRISTOPHER HORNBARGER is a Strategic Analyst for Headquarters, Department of the Army, and was previously an Army fellow at the Kennedy School of Government, Harvard University.

DAVID LEHMAN is Vice President and Chief Technology Officer of the MITRE Corporation.

MARCEL LETTRE, an Associate with Booz-Allen & Hamilton and a Research Affiliate with the Preventive Defense Project, previously served on the staff of the Commission to Assess the Organization of the Federal Government to Combat the Proliferation of Weapons of Mass Destruction.

THOMAS LONGSTRETH is Deputy Under Secretary of Defense for Readiness, and has also been Principal Deputy Assistant Secretary of Defense for Strategy and Requirements and a strategic planner on the Joint Staff.

ANJA MILLER is a recent *cum laude* graduate of Harvard Law School and will be an Associate at Wilmer, Cutler and Pickering in Washington, D.C.

JOHN QUILTY is a Senior Vice President and General Manager within the MITRE Corporation's Command, Control and Communications Federally Funded Research and Development Center.

COLONEL BRUCE REMBER was a National Security Affairs Fellow at Stanford's Hoover Institution, and is now assigned to the Air Staff; a graduate of the U.S. Air Force Academy, he also holds graduate degrees from Boston University and the U.S. Army's School of Advanced Military Studies, and is an F-15 pilot.

SHANE SMITH is the Coordinator of the Preventive Defense Project, for which he also serves as Research Assistant; he was previously a Research Associate for National Security Studies at the Council on Foreign Relations.

Other publications of the Preventive Defense Project

Ashton B. Carter and William J. Perry. *Preventive Defense: A New Security Strategy for America.* Washington, D.C.: Brookings Institution Press, 1999.

Coit D. Blacker, Ashton B. Carter, Warren Christopher, David A. Hamburg, and William J. Perry. *NATO After Madrid: Looking to the Future.* Preventive Defense Project publications, vol. 1, no. 1, 1997.

Ashton B. Carter and William J. Perry. *The Content of U.S. Engagement with China.* Preventive Defense Project publications, vol. 1, no. 2, Center for International Security and Cooperation (CISAC), Stanford University, July 1998.

Ashton B. Carter, Steven E. Miller, and Elizabeth Sherwood-Randall. *Fulfilling the Promise: Building an Enduring Security Relationship Between Ukraine and NATO.* Preventive Defense Project publications, vol. 1, no. 3, Center for International Security and Cooperation (CISAC), Stanford University, January 1999.

John P. White, Steven J. Kelman, and Michael J. Lippitz. *Reforming the Department of Defense: The Revolution in Business Affairs.* Preventive Defense Project publications, vol. 1, no. 4, Center for International Security and Cooperation (CISAC), Stanford University, February 1999.

Ashton B. Carter, John M. Deutch, and Philip D. Zelikow. *Catastrophic Terrorism: Elements of a National Policy.* Preventive Defense Project publications, vol. 1, no. 6, Center for International Security and Cooperation (CISAC), Stanford University, October 1998.

Warren Christopher, David A. Hamburg, and William J. Perry. *Preventive Diplomacy and Preventive Defense in South Asia: The U.S. Role.* Preventive Defense Project publications, vol. 2, no. 1, Center for International Security and Cooperation (CISAC), Stanford University, August 1999.